The Scenographic Model, Third Edition

The Scenographic Model

Third Edition

Darwin Reid Payne, Ronald Naversen, and Brad M. Carlson

Southern Illinois University Press | Carbondale

Southern Illinois University Press
siupress.com

Printed in the United States of America

First published July 2025.

This publication was made possible in part by financial support from the School of Theater and Dance at Southern Illinois University Carbondale.

Cover illustrations: Presentation models made by Darwin Reid Payne. *Front*: *The Effect of Gamma Rays on Man-in-the-Moon Marigolds*, by Paul Zindel. *Back, left to right*: *As You Like It*, by William Shakespeare; *Pirates of Penzance*, by Gilbert and Sullivan; and *Dracula*, by Steven Dietz. *From the Darwin Reid Payne Collection in the Special Collections Research Center of Morris Library at Southern Illinois University Carbondale.*

ISBN 978-0-8093-3976-1 (paperback)
ISBN 978-0-8093-3977-8 (ebook)

Printed on recycled paper ♻

SIU
Southern Illinois University System

Contents

Illustrations and Tables

Figures

Gallery

Tables

Preface to the Third Edition

We began revising *Theory and Craft of the Scenographic Model* with its author, Darwin Reid Payne, in 2014. The first two editions of this book documented Darwin's very personal design theories and processes and were illustrated primarily with examples of his own models. With Darwin's passing, we chose to expand upon his methods by including the work of other scenographers to broaden the knowledge of theatrical modelmaking. As a course in scenography is often the springboard for designers pursuing careers in other entertainment venues, we also felt it essential to reach out to designers in television, film, and themed entertainment to provide a wider discussion of entertainment modeling. Because no book could cover all the traditional and new modelmaking techniques and materials, we started a Facebook group called Theatrical Modelmaking in which modelers could display their models, ask questions, offer guidance, and share a wealth of information learned through years of experience and happy accidents. We invite readers of this book to join our group and explore the world of scenographic modelmaking. We also created a website to continually augment the information and examples found in this book: www.thescenographicmodel.com/.

Since this book's last edition there have been stunning advances in materials and technology that influence contemporary modelmaking. Scenographers can now "print" dimensional objects using 3D printers; cut precise and repetitive components with automated die and laser cutters; digitally capture and manipulate imagery through image-editing software; program automated stage animation in models as a means to teach and facilitate full-size automated design; and create virtual models that can be electronically sent to directors, design teams, and production staff all across the globe. Some of these tasks can be accomplished using just a smartphone.

While this edition touches on scenographic theory and analysis, it primarily concerns itself with the practicalities, aesthetics, and history of scenographic model artistry and its use as a catalyst in the design process. Darwin wrote his modelmaking book as an adjunct to his *Design for the Stage: First Steps*, later revised as *The Scenographic Imagination*, and we recommend that readers refer to these works for further study. Darwin's final contribution to this new edition was to change the title to *The Scenographic Model* in reference to his design textbook *The Scenographic Imagination*, which itself had been named in homage to Robert Edmond Jones's seminal *The Dramatic Imagination*.

Many of Darwin's models, perspective renderings, and paint elevations are housed in the Darwin Reid Payne Theater Collection at Southern Illinois University Carbondale: https://collections.carli.illinois.edu/digital/collection/sic_payne

Ronald Naversen
Brad M. Carlson

Acknowledgments

There are always many people and organizations to thank when composing a book like this. First, we want to thank the College of Library Affairs at Southern Illinois University Carbondale, which houses the University Archives Special Collections Research Center; the University Museum; and Southern Illinois University Press. The University Archives were essential in creating the Darwin Reid Payne Design Collection and developing its website. Former director Pamela Hackbart-Dean, university archivist Matthew Gorzalski, and research specialist Aaron Lisec were instrumental in helping to catalog and preserve the many renderings and papers in the collection. The associate dean of library affairs, Jennifer Horton, aided Darwin in 3D printing items to refurbish his models, and John Pollitz, dean of library affairs, secured permission for us to use images of Darwin's scenography in this revised edition. The museum staff, including museum director Donna Bachman, curator of exhibits Wes Stoerger, and curator of Anthropology II Susannah Munson specifically dealt with preserving and restoring Darwin's models. Theater research assistants Ken Ellis and Aaron Barkley were responsible for reviewing the collection to create a design index and chronology. The library's Center for Teaching Excellence scanned the second edition of Darwin's *Theory and Craft of the Scenographic Model* into a usable text file of the book. The SIU Press staff was especially helpful in their encouragement of this project. Acquisitions editors Kristine Priddy and Jennifer Egan were generous in sharing their knowledge and enthusiasm with these novice authors.

Special thanks to the staff of the New York Public Library for the Performing Arts, including curator Doug Reside, assistant curator Annemarie van Roessel, and assistant curator and chief reference librarian John Calhoun, who gave a personal tour through their scenographic model collection and assisted in researching Boris Aronson's papers.

There are also many individuals who helped generate the illustrations for this third edition, including research assistant Dan Klenk, who photographed high-resolution color images of Darwin's models and entered the metadata into the collection's online database. Gennie Neuman Lambert, assistant professor of scenic design in the School of Theatre and Dance at Kent State University recreated and updated Darwin's potential design studio and workstations. Gennie also helped draft our white card model exercise and used it as an assignment for her design class to provide photographs of the finished models. Michael J. Griffith, emeritus professor of scene design at Miami University, allowed us to use his Composition Chess exercise as a method to strengthen creative play and collaboration skills in theatrical modelmaking. Thanks also to the Production Design Seminar class of the School for Theater and Dance at Southern Illinois University Carbondale for playing the Composition Chess game to create illustrations for this book. Thanks also goes to Dr. Wendy Waszut-Barrett, for her extensive study of historic American scene painters, and Dr. David Bisaha, for his illuminating research into the labor practices of early twentieth-century scene design, which complimented our own research into the history of theatrical modelmaking.

We also need to acknowledge the over fifteen thousand members of the Theatrical Modelmaking Facebook group that have generously shared their models and collective knowledge of modelmaking materials, techniques, and experiences. In particular, Lauren M. Nichols has provided numerous modelmaking tips and illustrations to our group that we have incorporated into this text. Many other scenographic modelmakers have gratuitously provided us with examples to illustrate the book. These contributions have allowed us to extend the scope and content of theatrical modelmaking to include examples of modelmaking for film, television, and themed entertainment design. Gratitude goes to Nathan Naversen for reviewing the section on studio lighting and providing theme park model examples. Thanks also to Jonathan E. Cagle of 3D Workshop Inc. for providing the architectural model examples. A special thank you to production designer John Chichester and his student Andrew Chung in the Dodge College of Film and Media Arts of Chapman University for providing the film and television interior and exterior production design models. All of these generous individuals have waived their permission fees so that we can keep the price of the book low for students.

We owe a special acknowledgment to Dr. Anne Fletcher, emeritus professor of theater history in the School of Theater and Dance at Southern Illinois University Carbondale for reviewing an untold number of drafts of this text as they were written.

Finally, we must thank the School of Theater and Dance in the College of Arts and Media at Southern Illinois University Carbondale and the Department of Communication and Theatre Arts at Truman State University for their support of this publication.

The Scenographic Model, Third Edition

Introduction: The Scenographic Model in History

> A model is a rehearsal for reality, a way of making a trial that minimizes the penalties for error.
>
> —Horace Freeland Judson, *The Search for Solutions*

Modelmaking is an ancient, uniquely human activity, and models have been vital to the development of creative ideas throughout history. Modeling is indispensable for architects; interior and landscape designers; production designers and art directors for television and film; themed entertainment designers; scenographers for theater, opera, and ballet; and practitioners of any discipline that previsualizes interactive environments. The materials, techniques, steps, and purposes of modeling for each discipline vary, but the models must meet a level of verisimilitude to communicate design ideas effectively.[1]

An important quality of verisimilitude is scale. Scale allows the viewer to understand the relationship between a drawing or model and reality. A scale model is a physical representation of an object, usually a reduction or an enlargement, that maintains a consistent dimensional ratio to that object. In one modeling process, a scale model is created to represent an existing object, such as a railroad hobbyist fashioning a smaller version of an existing locomotive. In the reverse of that modeling process, the model is created first to develop, study, test, and simulate what an object will be prior to constructing it in full scale. Using this process an architect constructs a model of a home to visualize and communicate what a house will look like for a client. This is the modeling process that most concerns the scenographer, as shown in Beowulf Borrit's model for *New York, New York* (figure I.1).

> The word *model* comes from the Latin *modulus,* meaning "a small measure," then from the old Italian *modello,* "a model" or "mold." The verb form *to model* or *modeling* is the act of molding, forming, or shaping.[2]

The two types of measurement systems used in scale modeling are the imperial system and International System (SI) or metric system. Scenographers

Figure I.1. *New York, New York* by John Kander, Fred Ebb and Lin Manuel Miranda. 1/2" model by Beowulf Boritt, 2023.

in the United States work in imperial scale, using inches and feet, for measurements represented as 1/2" = 1'-0" (pronounced "one-half inch equals one foot, zero inches"). Scenographers in countries that use the metric system dimension their drawings and models as a numerical ratio represented as 1:24 (pronounced "one to twenty-four"). This ratio explains that the realized set is twenty-four times the size of the model. The imperial 1/8" = 1'-0", 1/4" = 1'-0", 3/8" = 1'-0", and 1/2" = 1'-0" are equivalent to the metric 1:96, 1:48, 1:32, and 1:24 respectively.

> Scenographic models historically were constructed in 1/2" = 1'-0" scale, but the 1/4" = 1'-0" has now become professionally accepted for study, working, and even fully colored presentation models. This is due to the time and expense incurred building, transporting, and storing larger models. Some designers prefer 3/8" = 1'-0" (1:33) scale models because 1/4" is too small to allow sufficient detail and 1/2" is too cumbersome.

The Scenographic Model in History

Making a scenographic model is not a new practice in theater. In fact, models may have been in use for as long as there has been scenery itself. Vitruvius (c.70–15 BCE) discusses the use of scaled models in his *Ten Books on Architecture*, and from his writings one can conjecture that Greek and Roman architects used variously scaled models to design and construct the skene and scaena frons of the classic theaters.[3] Renaissance scenographer Sebastian Serlio, in his *The Five Books of Architecture*, describes how he used scale models of "wood and paper" to assure that his theatrical spectacles would fit within the grand halls of Italian palazzos (*teatro della sala*).[4] In fact, every period of theater history from the Renaissance on provides written accounts of models used in scenographic design, but relatively few historical models have survived in comparison with the large number of flat theatrical drawings and sketches that are preserved in museums and libraries around the world. Our oldest extant scenographic models were created for the Paris Opera between 1757 and 1761.[5] Built to approximately 1/2" = 1'-0", scale these gouache-painted paper and cardboard "maquettes,"[6] as they are known in France, clearly illustrate the flat wing, border, and shutter staging of the baroque and rococo periods (figure I.2). As the principle method of communicating the scenic design the scene painter-decorator created sketches that were then developed into models. The "stage manager"[7] used the model to plan blocking while the carpenters and scenic artists referenced it for building and painting the set. These maquettes then became a visual inventory of the opera's scenery stock when productions were remounted. It is conjectured that the painter-decorator would swap the various model wings, borders, and shutters as a means to reduce expenses when designing new productions.[8] Historical design sketches rarely show the positions and outlines of wings and shutters, so these rare maquettes furnish a more complete understanding of eighteenth-century staging practices.

Scenographic models have been preserved in various library and museum collections around the globe. The Netherlands Theatre Institute in Amsterdam has an excellent collection of historic scenographic models, including a candlelit miniature chamber theater with functioning angled wing and shutters commissioned by Baron van Slingelandt (1762–1829) (figure I.3). Noted scene painters Pieter Barbiers (1749–1842) and François Joseph Pfeiffer (1778–1835) designed twelve settings for this theater, providing another unique opportunity to view historic staging practices.[9]

In sixteenth-century England the royal court's Exchequer Treasury of the Receipt records frequent payments to the Revels Office for various "models."[10] In 1773 Paris-trained Philip James de Loutherbourg (1740–1812), became the supervisor of scenery and machinery for the Drury Lane Theatre

Figure I.2. *Proserpine* by Jean-Baptiste Lully and Philippe Quinault. Maquette attributed to Piero Bonifazio Algieri, c. 1764. Paris: Théâtre de l'Opéra-Le Peletier, 1727. *Photograph by Benjamin Gavaudo. CMN Dist. Art Resource, NY*

Figure I.3. Slingelandt Theater. Model for "Het Winterbos" (the winter forest) with "Stadspoort" (city gate) backdrop, 1824 by François Joseph Pfeiffer. *Courtesy of Allard Pierson Theatre Collection, University of Amsterdam*

in London. In his application letter to manager David Garrick he stated: "I must make a small model of the settings and everything which is required, to scale, painted and detailed so as to put the working painters and machinists and others on the right track by being able to faithfully copy my models."[11] Advertisements for provincial theaters were keen to publicize that their scenery was based upon models provided by Loutherbourg or "painted after the Models sent from the Theatre-Royal, Covent Garden."[12] Loutherbourg's 1785 models for *Omai; or a Trip around the World* (figure I.4), housed in the Victoria and Albert Museum Theatre Collection, are the oldest scenographic models in Britain and furnish evidence of his innovative use of asymmetrical angled scenery and cut drops.

Figure I.4. *Omai; or a Trip around the World* by John O'Keeffe. Model for act 2, scene 3, by Philip James de Loutherbourg. Pen, ink, watercolor, and oil on cutout cardboard, c. 1785. *Courtesy of the Victoria and Albert Museum*

Loutherbourg's practices set a precedent, and soon the head painter-decorators of large theaters were no longer expected to do much actual painting; instead, they directed their energies primarily to the tasks of painting sketches and building scenic maquettes. This practice was so successful that the playwright often conferred directly with the painter-decorator on the appropriateness of the scene during the design process.[13]

In the mid-nineteenth century, engraved illustrated newspapers, magazines, and books revealed the use of models in scene painting studios.

Loutherbourg also devised a miniature mechanical theater approximately 6 feet wide, 4 feet high, and 8 feet deep called the *Eidophusikon* (Greek for "image of nature"). The Eidophusikon delighted viewers with dramatically lit sunrises, sunsets, moonlit vistas, special effects presenting seasonal changes, thunder and lightning storms, shipwrecks, and erupting volcanos. Loutherbourg claimed the Eidophusikon was the product of twenty years of meditation and experimentation with models while devising his elaborate theatrical spectacles. The only existing image of the Eidophusikon is an ink and watercolor drawing by Edward Francis Burney depicting a scene from Milton's *Paradise Lost* in the Theatre Collection of the Victoria and Albert Museum.

Frederic Villiers reported how the painter-decorator "may be seen employed in designing the most important scenes and fitting them into the exact miniature of the stage (an indispensable article in good paint-rooms)."[14] The article included an illustration of the painting room of scenic artist William Roxby Beverly (1810–99) at the Drury Lane Theatre that included the "indispensable" scenographic model as shown in figure I.5.[15]

The librarian of the Paris Opera, Charles Nuitter (1828–99), began curating its historic scenography in 1864.[16] This extensive collection now housed in the National Library of France illustrates how both two-dimensional

Figure I.5. "Mr. Beverly's Painting Room at the Drury Lane Theatre," drawn by F. Wentworth. From Frederic Villiers's "The Property, Painting and Dressmakers' Rooms." In *The Illustrated Sporting and Dramatic News*, December 19, 1874. *Courtesy of the Mary Evans Picture Library*

graphics and three-dimensional models were integral to the opera workshop staff. Figure I.6 shows how Charles-Antoine Cambon's (1802–75) painting for the cathedral scene in *Faust* effectively conveys mood, atmospheric lighting, and color while his tonal model communicates spatial information, scenic units, entrances, and sightlines. Colored models like Marcel Jambon's (1884–1908) *Otello* shown in figure I.7 illustrate how models also functioned as painters' elevations.

Figure I.6. *Faust* by Charles Gounod, Jules Barbier, and Michel Carré. Compare the tempera painting with the maquette of act 3, scene 2, by Charles-Antoine Cambon for the National Opera Theater of Paris, Palais Garnier, 1875. *Courtesy of the National Library of France*

Figure I.7. *Otello* by Giuseppe Verdi and Arrigo Boito. Act 1: a square near the castle, a tavern. Maquette by Marcel Jambon. Paris: Théâtre de l'Opéra-Le Peletier, 1869. *Courtesy of the National Library of France*

In *L'Envers du Théâtre* (*Backstage in the Theatre, Scenes, and Machines*),[17] French lithographer and scene painter Jean-Pierre Moynet (1819–76) provides descriptions of the painter-decorator, director–stage manager, and carpenters using scenographic models to conceive, build, and paint their productions.[18] Moynet's son, Georges, provides an illustration of a model being consulted in the scene painter's atelier in his own backstage book, *Machinerie Théâtrale: Trucs et Décors*, as shown in figure I.8.[19]

Figure I.8. Atelier of the painter-decorator with model. *From Georges Moynet's* La Machinerie Théâtrale: Trucs et Décors *(Theatrical machinery: Tricks and scenery), 1893*

The first professional stage sets in the United States were imported from Europe, but as local painters and carpenters gained theater experience, it became more economical to ship models and sketches as production guides.[20] Later European painter-decorators including Charles Cicéri (1782–1868) of the Paris Opera and Charles Milbourne (fl.1777–1809) of Covent Garden Theatre were invited to design in America further disseminating European scenographic practices.[21] By the nineteenth century repertory theater companies in large urban centers could employ full-time scenic painter-decorators for their season. Companies in smaller towns found it economical to purchase stock scenery from scenic studios in major cities, who would send models for approval and then ship the finished scenery by rail. So widespread was the use of models that scenic studios called the scene painters who designed and built the models "model men" and the room where they worked the "model room."[22] It must be noted that there were women and minorities working as scenic artists in this period, but their work has until recently been undocumented. Wendy Waszut-Barrett in her blog *Tales from a Scenic Artist and Scholar* presents excellent research into underrepresented women working as scenic artists-designers in this period.[23]

The commercialization of theater in the United States upset designers like Richard Marsten (fl. 1866–91), who described how the profitmaking nature of theater conflicted with the time and expense of making scenographic models: "The scene, when modeled in true perspective proportion, shows the effect of full natural scale. However, the preparation of a model may take a full week of the artist's time to complete and only a few American managers like Augustin Daly and A. M. Palmer are willing to incur this extra expense."[24]

Another historically significant theatrical model still in use today is the *juvenile drama* or *toy theater* popularized in the nineteenth century. In his essay "Penny Plain, Twopence Coloured" Robert Louis Stevenson describes how publishers sent writers and artists to the openings of new plays to annotate the script and sketch the costumed actors and scenery. These scripts and drawings were printed either in full color on paper sheets or as lined cartoons to be painted by the patron at home. These prints included ornate prosceniums, act curtains, wings, backdrops, borders, properties, orchestras, and actors in dramatic poses. The printed sheets were cut out, pasted onto cardboard, and assembled into miniature stages, allowing the family to reenact the play for home entertainment. There is evidence that these toy theaters were even used as models for provincial theater company productions. Toy theaters continue to inspire scenographers today as evidenced by Heidi Ettinger's design for *The Secret Garden* and Alexander Dodge's design for *The Gentlemen's Guide to Love and Murder* shown in figure I.9.

By the end of the nineteenth century, scenographers embraced the innovation of electric lighting to explore and define their theatrical environments. In 1889 *The World* magazine visited Joseph A. Physioc (1865–1951) in his New York studio, reporting that the designer built 3/4" = 1'-0" scale models and illuminated them with multicolored lights controlled through an electrical switchboard to create "the effect of dawn, of early morning, of high noon, of dusk, of night, of storm and moonlight" (figure I.10).[25]

In 1912, *Scientific American* magazine published early photographic evidence of the use of scenographic models of various scales in the Paris atelier of Marcel Jambon (1884–1908) and Alexandre Bailly (1866–1947) (figure I.11).[26]

Figure I.9. *The Gentlemen's Guide to Love and Murder* by Robert L. Freedman and Steven Lutvak. 1/4" model by Alexander Dodge, 2013

Figure I.10. Joseph A. Physioc's miniature stage. *From "How the Theatrical Scenery is Made."* The World, *March 1898*

Figure I.11. Studying maquettes at the Jambon-Bailly studio. *From Dr. Alfred Gradenwitz's "A Glimpse of the Scene Painter's Studio," in* Scientific American *107, no. 17 (October 26, 1912)*

In the twentieth-century, European designers Adolphe Appia (1862–1928), and Edward Gordon Craig (1872–1966) led a movement away from the naturalistic nineteenth-century conventions of trompe l'oeil painted backdrops and box sets. Appia and Craig advocated for abstract, simplified scenic environments composed of architectural steps, levels, walls, and screens allowing the actor to move through dynamic spaces. Appia and Craig also believed that scenic design was not simply a decorative practice but an integral and active production element that allowed design, direction, and acting to create a unified approach to a production. The scenographic model was especially well-suited to explore the sculptural nature of this "New Stagecraft," as shown by Craig exploring space with his model screens in figure I.12.

Another influence on American stage design was the emergence of theater as an academic discipline. At the turn of the twentieth century, only a handful of American colleges offered play analysis, acting, or play production coursework. In 1914 the Carnegie Technical Institute created the first comprehensive undergraduate program in theater arts, and in 1925 Yale University established the first master's degree in drama. The purpose of these programs was to certify the applied arts of theater as professional disciplines. Both schools included traditional sketching, drawing, and modelmaking in their scene design curriculums.[27] Yale's new theater building even included a "model studio" for its design students.[28] The graduates of these design

Figure I.12. Edward Gordon Craig experimenting with his model stage screens, 1910. *Courtesy of the British National Trust*

programs would no longer be scene painter-decorators trained in the family business or through apprenticeship but university-trained scenic designers. With the New Stagecraft came a shift in the manner of presenting scenic designs. Robert Edmond Jones, the "father of American stage design," toured Europe in 1912 through 1914, meeting and studying with influential theater practitioners. Jones, like his colleagues, continued to use models to help develop his designs, especially when of a sculptural nature as shown in figure I.13.[29] But with the advent of new stage lighting technology, Jones preferred to communicate his ideas through storyboards and perspective sketches that allowed him to depict his characters within evocative atmospheric environments.[30] So effective were Jones's sketches that they set the standard for American scenographic practice for many years to come, and models were relegated to a more prosaic role in the American scenographic design process.[31]

Likewise, Jo Mielziner (1901–76) the most prolific designer of the mid-twentieth century, preferred to communicate his designs through his exquisite watercolor renderings. But like Physioc, he built an elaborate lighting system in his studio to view and assess his models and renderings under various lighting conditions.[32] Yet once the shows were completed, the models he considered "just a tool" were consigned to the dustbin, leaving only random photographs to document their use.[33]

Figure I.13. *Macbeth* by William Shakespeare. Model by Robert Edmond Jones. *From Walter Fuerst, René Fuerst, and Samuel J. Hume,* XXth Century Stage Decoration *(Alfred A. Knopf, 1921), plate # 201*

The New Stagecraft aesthetic influenced the new generation of American designers to use a "simplified," "suggested," or "poetic" realism that thrived throughout the twentieth century. This aesthetic and the commercial nature of American theater influenced theatrical modelmaking practice. In 1930 the scene painters, who held majority membership in the young United Scenic Artists union, voted to require designers to provide models to scenic studios. The older painters, who traditionally painted from models, complained that they could not work from the small design sketches submitted by the younger designers. Models, as previously noted, require more time, materials, and labor, which ultimately came out of the designers' fees, so they understandably preferred to submit less costly sketches. This "model rule" was later overturned in negotiations, but the cost-effectiveness of sketching over modelmaking still impacts scenography today.[34] Robert W. Bergman, owner of Bergman Studios, reflects upon the old guard scene painter-decorator tradition of using models for their designs: "All of these men [*sic*] made a thorough study of their craft. They made their own models and sketches. There was little need for blueprints, for the constructions were for the most part of such a simple nature that the carpenter could build from the model."[35]

Norman Bel Geddes (1893–1958) also worked extensively with sketches, renderings, and models to conceive his theatrical, architectural, and industrial designs. However, Bel Geddes uniquely showcased his models by hiring theater and fashion photographer Francis Bruguière (1879–1945) to document his models under special lighting to enhance the design presentations and create storyboards for each scene (figure I.14). Throughout the 1920s Bel Geddes offered an influential stage design class for promising young designers, including Mordecai Gorelik (1899–1990), Henry Dreyfuss (1904–72), Aline Bernstein (1880–1955), and others.[36] The in-class projects included assisting in building his monumental models.[37]

Figure I.14. *The Divine Comedy* by Dante Alighieri. Model by Norman Bel Geddes, Photograph by Francis Bruguière, 1927. *Norman Bel Geddes Theater and Industrial Design Papers, Job 69, Harry Ransom Center, The University of Texas at Austin. Copyright by The Edith Lutyens and Norman Bel Geddes Foundation, Inc.*

The latter half of the twentieth century saw a revolution in American theatrical design. Collage, assemblage, montage, and installation art techniques filtered in from art and design. Nontraditional materials became available, which allowed the introduction of innovative technologies and construction techniques. Off-Broadway and regional theaters began to explore thrust, arena, and found space stages, while scenographic influences from Europe infiltrated the American theater. These influences stimulated scenographers to reimagine their art as sculptural, textural, organic, and existing within the fourth dimension of time, all of which could be effectively explored through models.

Czech designer Josef Svoboda (1920–2002) experimented with new materials and technologies to create arresting nonrepresentational architectural spaces informed by Appia and Craig. In his research facility at the Czech National Theatre, Svoboda utilized scale models to experiment with plastics, mirrors, hydraulics, projections, low-voltage lighting, lasers, and electrostatically charged aerosols to create kinetic multimedia productions (figure I.15). Additionally, Svoboda advocated for the title "scenographer" to designate the role of the designer as a coauthor with the playwright and director in theatrical production.[38]

Figure I.15. Josef Svoboda with model. Photograph by Jaromír Svoboda. *Courtesy of the Czech National Theatre Archive, Prague*

Boris Aronson (1889–1980) was noteworthy for using collage and assemblage techniques in his models. Abstract constructivist training inspired Aronson to assemble rough, unscaled models to explore the inner workings of a play. From these rough models his assistants, often including his wife Lisa, constructed detailed models incorporating an assortment of collaged materials (figure I.16). Like Mielziner, Aronson used a lighted model stage to explore lighting and projection effects on his models.[39] Aronson also experimented with projecting images on his models, as well as drawing and

Figure I.16. *Follies* by Stephen Sondheim and James Goldman. 1/2" model by Boris Aronson, assisted by Lisa Aronson, 1971. *Courtesy of Marc Aronson*

painting on top of Polaroid photographs and photostats of models to experiment with light, color, and patterns.[40]

Ming Cho Lee (1930–2020), assistant to both Mielziner and Aronson, began his own successful career designing theater, opera, and dance (figure I.17). In 1969 Lee became head of the design program at the Yale University School of Drama, and through classes and frequent design workshops he mentored a generation of American scenographers, emphasizing models as an essential element of the design process. Lee's students first drew conceptual "what if" sketches and then moved to 1/8" and 1/4" models to develop their designs. Lee was known to say that "you can lie in a sketch but not in a model."[41] Lighting design students experimented with lighting and photographing the models to share as inspirational images and storyboards. Lee preferred smaller-scale models so his students would not get caught up in minute details and lose sight of the overall design.

In the 1990s personal computers became both affordable and powerful enough to enable computer-aided design (CAD) to create virtual models, thereby revolutionizing all visual design disciplines. But despite the use of "model" in its name, a virtual model is still a two-dimensional depiction of a three-dimensional environment. A physical model can be held and rotated by hand, allowing the viewer to fully understand its space and form while

Figure I.17. *Much Ado about Nothing* by William Shakespeare. 1/2" model by Ming Cho Lee. New York Shakespeare Festival, 1972. *Courtesy of Ming Cho Lee Archives*

also providing satisfying tactile evidence of its reality. Designers continue to use physical models and sketches to develop their designs, often translating these into virtual model presentations for further exploration and presentations. The physical model and the virtual model convey different information and together help to fully communicate the scenographic idea, as shown in figure I.18.

Models are increasingly preserved in museums, libraries, and personal theater collections, gaining appreciation as works of art in themselves and

Figure I.18. *Fabulation: Or the Re-Education of Undine* by Lynn Nottage. Vectorworks™ virtual model and 3D printed model by Dirk Durossette. *The Lantern Theatre Company, Philadelphia, 2022*

attaining value beyond the productions they were built to serve. Digital photography and the internet have vastly accelerated the dissemination of inspirational model images in theatrical periodicals, design textbooks, modelmaking tutorials, design websites, social media, and on image and video-sharing platforms.

Why the Scenographic Model?

This brief history of the scenographic model illustrates how modelmaking has adapted to changes in materials, technology, aesthetics, and commercial influences. Further, it explores how models have been viewed as either a stimulating tool in the design process or a functional but cumbersome expense of material, time, and labor. There are, however, very practical reasons why the student of scenography should master the necessary skills to make these miniatures. A scenographer's education remains incomplete without some model-based design projects. The model is frequently an easier design tool for the novice designer to create, whereas sketching and rendering require greater training and expertise. Models clearly illustrate entrances and exits, playing areas, blocking opportunities, and sightlines for the director, production team, and performers without the need of extra graphics of floorplans and sectional elevations. While sketches and renderings can capture mood and atmosphere more successfully, they can also exaggerate, suppress, and even conceal the dimensional aspects of a design. This is particularly true when working in a thrust or arena theater configuration. It would take dozens, if not hundreds, of sketches to show all the viewpoints for a design on an arena stage, like the one shown in figure I.19.

Models are interactive and invite the designer and director to "play" in their conception and use while sketches and renderings tend to be solely the designer's medium. Some designers encourage their directors to work with them on the model in its preliminary stages, thus improving the lines of communication by engaging and investing the director in the collaborative process by literally giving them "a hand in the design."[42] Models highlight texture, mass, and form, whereas sketches and renderings only suggest these elements. The model shows its scenery in scaled units, making it useful to the construction crew in understanding each individual component. These components can then be used to demonstrate scene changes. The downside to modelmaking is that it includes larger work and storage spaces along with greater time and expense in construction and transporting the model from design studio to rehearsal room to scene studio.

Virtual modeling blends the strengths of traditional modelmaking and painted perspective rendering. While still a two-dimensional medium, it can quickly show various perspectives of the setting, including ground plan

Figure I.19. Model by Todd Rosenthal and associate designer Alan E. Schwanke for *Watch on the Rhine* by Lillian Hellman. *The Lantern Theatre Company, Philadelphia, 2022*

and section views. Like sketching or rendering, it can show mood and atmosphere more easily than the physical model. A virtual model is easily imported into the technical director's construction software, reducing drawing time. Perhaps the most advantageous feature of virtual modeling is that making changes to a design is usually faster than traditional modelmaking or perspective rendering. However, the expertise needed for virtual modeling involves a great deal of training, and the time required to develop a virtual model can often take as long as that of a physical model. In addition, virtual modeling programs vary in cost and sophistication. Free or inexpensive modeling programs lack sophistication in rendering while subscription fees for more advanced software can be expensive. A major drawback in virtual modeling in the theater is that the director and other members of the production team rarely use the software, so the designer must share static images with their colleagues, diminishing the many benefits of virtual modeling.

Scenographers still rely on models, either real or virtual, because they recognize that theatrical art is not solely that of the painter or the architect but an art of space, form, light, color, movement, and time. The choice of model, rendering, or virtual model is up to the personal preferences of the scenographer and the needs of the director, as well as the requirements of the design assignment itself. We hope that this text will benefit those who choose the physical model as their means of developing and presenting their design.

1. Model Preparation

The Scenography Studio

Scenographers often locate their studios in small spaces or rooms within or adjacent to their living quarters or office. No two artists have identical workspaces or work patterns, which explains the wide variety of studio layouts. However, design workspaces do share a number of common features. The workspace profoundly affects the kind of work performed, the amount of work produced, and the quality of the work itself. The more deeply artists become invested in their profession, the more particular they become about their tools, materials, and the studio where these are employed. Few scenographers are fortunate enough to realize their perfect workspace, but any space and arrangement must be conducive to producing the best work possible. A potential studio layout is illustrated in figure 1.1. Artists should consider several essential criteria for a functional and effective studio.

Studio Needs:

1. A place to think and conference with other production members either in person or remotely.
2. A workstation to sketch and paint in pencil, pen and ink, pastel, and watercolor, either manually or digitally. This may require a nearby water source.
3. A workstation to draft technical plates, paint elevations and renderings. This will include a drafting table and/or a computer with a large monitor(s), and a printer, scanner, or plotter.
4. A workstation for experimenting with model mockups and scaled units.
5. A model stage or model box to position the scenographic model in its architectural setting.
6. Display areas or bulletin boards for ideas, images, schedules, and important notes.
7. Shelves for art supplies, reference books, catalogs, instruction manuals, and finished models. Shelves may need to be deep for larger models.
8. File cabinets to organize contracts, image morgues, and letter-sized drawing papers. Digital archiving reduces the need for cabinets.
9. Flat file cabinets for storing large technical drawings, sketches, renderings, drawing papers, and flat model materials.
10. Bins to save dimensional pieces, including model materials, scale furniture, accessories, and old model pieces.

11. A video projection unit (VPU) projector to convert small images into larger ones and for experimentation with projections on models.
12. Advanced studios may include a space for a 3D printer, laser or electronic cutter, or desktop vacuum-forming machine.
13. An entertainment center, to review music and videos pertinent to productions or for relaxation. Computers and smartphones often fulfill this requirement.
14. General illumination for the entire studio and individual lighting for each workstation.
15. Adequate ventilation to refresh the air and vent toxins.
16. An ergonomic chair to prevent back, neck, and shoulder fatigue caused by hours of bending over the various workstations.
17. Adequate electrical outlets and power strips with circuit breakers.
18. Waste disposal with separate recycling containers. Used knife blades should be stored in a metal can that, when full, can be put in a recycling bin for metal waste.

Scenographers spend a great deal of their time in their studios, so in addition to the above necessities, a comfortable and appealing workspace environment will benefit the designer and their assistants. This may include an area for refreshment, but only if care is taken to prevent food and drink from spilling onto workspaces and if food is kept away from art supplies and chemicals to prevent contamination. Frequent breaks are advisable to stretch the muscles, clear the mind, increase productivity, and maintain emotional health.

Studio Layout

Potential Studio Layout

A. Study and conference area with computer, camera, and monitor(s).
B. Storage for drafting materials and art supplies.
C. Drafting table with reference materials and supplies close at hand.
D. Bulletin or display boards.
E. Worktable for model building.
F. Deep shelving for models and storage bins.
G. File cabinets.
H. Flat file cabinets.
I. Bookshelves.
J. Printer-scanner, 3D printer, and laser cutter.
K. Video projection unit.

Modelmaking requires more work and storage space than that needed for rendering, sketching, drafting, or computer-aided design. While a single working area can be used for most projects, it is helpful to have separate

Figure 1.1. Potential studio layout. *Rendered by Gennie Neuman Lambert*

workstations for different tasks. For instance, when possible, the drafting workstation should not be used for cutting or painting as this can damage the surface of the table needed for clean drawings. The modelmaking table undergoes a great deal of wear and tear and should have a replaceable, resilient surface. A potential modelmaking workstation is shown in figure 1.2, and a potential graphics workstation in figure 1.3.

Potential Modelmaking Workstation

A. Worktable. It is helpful if this table has an overhang to allow the use of clamps and vises.

B. Replaceable working surface. Even if the worktable is constructed to withstand hard use, a durable but replaceable material should be used for cutting, pinning, gluing, and texturing model parts. A heavyweight illustration board, fiberboard like Homasote®, or a self-sealing cutting mat can be changed as needed.

C. Flat material storage (either horizontal or vertical) for papers, paperboards, foam board, plastic sheets, and other flat supplies.

D. Storage for basic supplies.

Figure 1.2. Potential modelmaking workstation. *Rendered by Gennie Neuman Lambert*

E. A model stage or model box located next to the working area so model pieces can be quickly assessed for size, scale, and placement.
F. Storage shelves for commonly used supplies including gesso, modeling paste, paint, pins, tapes, and adhesives.
G. Storage for long, thin materials like balsa and basswoods, styrene strips, and metal rods. Clear glass or plastic jars and tubes protect these fragile materials from damage and help the modelmaker easily see what is available or needs to be replenished.
H. Pegboards or similar storage systems to provide easy access to tools, and an organized storage location when not in use.
I. Bulletin or display boards for notes and images that inform and inspire current projects. Online bulletin boards allow sharing and remote collaboration.
J. A shelf above the working area to keep small items and materials out of the way and from being misplaced. Modelmaking frequently involves several projects in process at the same time, requiring numerous materials and tools. An orderly workspace helps prevent confusion.
K. The best place to keep completed models is on shelving out of the immediate work area but within reach for reference. Deep shelves help accommodate large models.
L. Light sources that do not cast harsh shadows located above and to the front of each workstation.

contrast and concentration. Scenographers, event designers, and architects envision work that will be viewed under a variety of lighting conditions, so the opportunity to view their models in the studio under approximate color temperatures can be advantageous.[1] There are smartphone applications that can perform a spectrum analysis of various lighting sources to measure their CRI, CCT, lumens, and more. See figure 1.4 for approximate color temperature measurement and color rendering index of common light sources.

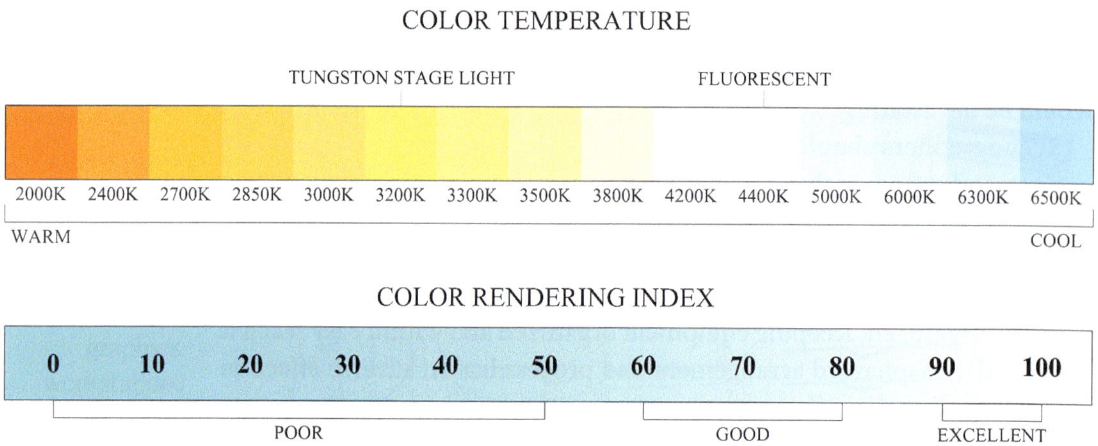

Figure 1.4. Approximate color temperature measurement and color rendering index of common light sources

Ventilation

Studio ventilation is an important consideration that is often overlooked or misunderstood by artists who assume that an open window, fan, or air conditioner will sufficiently clean the air in their workspaces.[2] The wide variety of natural and synthetic materials, paints, and adhesives in the studio today requires a proactive approach to protect the modelmaker from particulates, fumes, and vapors. The first preventive measure is to understand that vacuuming or damp or wet mopping surfaces is safer and more effective than dusting or sweeping. The second measure is to research materials using the safety data sheet (SDS) and substitute harmful products for less hazardous alternatives whenever possible.[3] The SDS specifies hazards and safety requirements, including appropriate ventilation. Third, the artist should keep an inventory of materials in their studio and have contact information for their local Poison Control Center easily accessible. The fourth measure is to review the workspace for appropriate ventilation systems. Fumes, vapors, and airborne particulates that are inhaled into the respiratory system can remain in the lungs or be absorbed into the bloodstream. Toxins may trigger immediate symptoms like sore throat, coughing, headaches, and dizziness, or they can accumulate in the body over months and years causing serious illness later in life.

Dilution ventilation and local exhaust ventilation are two basic systems that are used to properly ventilate the studio. Dilution ventilation, also called cross-ventilation, pushes clean air into the studio where it mixes with contaminants, thus "diluting" them before they are exhausted outside. This is accomplished by providing two openings on opposite sides of a room with a fan at each opening. The first fan pulls clean air into the room through a door or window while a second fan exhausts air out a vent or window. The fan blowing air into the studio should be behind the artist, pushing contaminants away from the face, while the second fan should draw the air away from the face to the outside. A constant flow of fresh air will help clear the studio of pollutants.

Dilution ventilation is ineffective when using aerosol paints and adhesives, so the modelmaker should employ local exhaust ventilation when using these products. Local exhaust ventilation draws contaminants away from the artist by placing a booth or hood around the object being sprayed and exhausting the contaminants directly outside. Small, inexpensive spray booths can be purchased or built. There are several online sources for building do-it-yourself (DIY) spray booths. See figure 1.5 for illustrations of dilution and local exhaust ventilation.

One final note on the workspace is that, while the studio should be comfortable and inviting, it should also reduce visual and aural distractions, allowing the scenographer to focus and concentrate on their work.

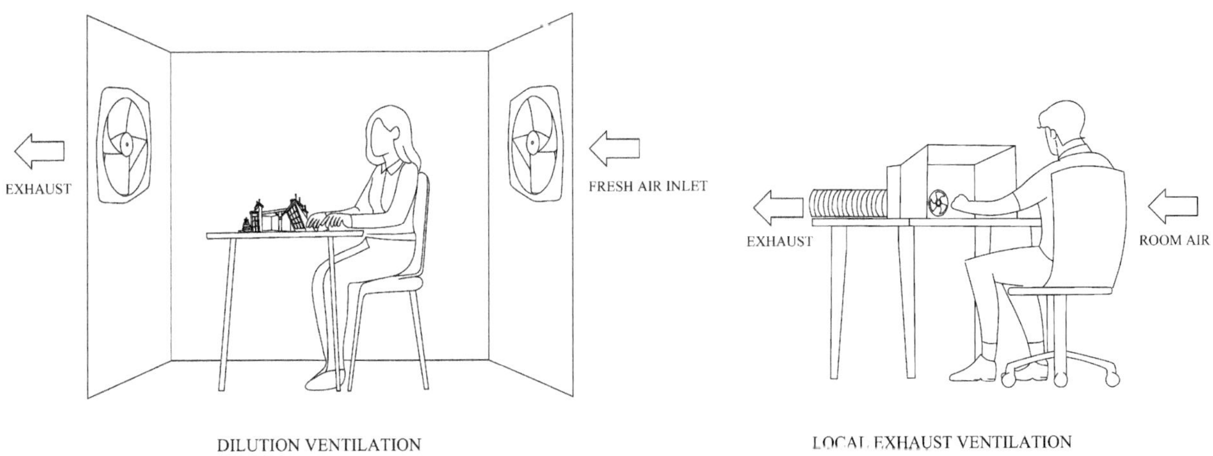

Figure 1.5. Dilution and local exhaust ventilation systems

Modelmaking Tools

This section introduces the modelmaker to the fundamental tools needed for drawing, cutting, assembling, texturing, and painting the scenographic model. Each modelmaker will develop preferences for specific types and brands of tools as their craft develops, so this inventory tends toward generic descriptions. Craft model catalogs are filled with hundreds of tools for every conceivable task, but the basic tools listed here, when kept clean and in good repair, will serve the modelmaker very well in transferring their vision into practical reality.

Drawing and Sketching Tools

While most present-day drafting is done by computer, traditional drafting equipment is still often necessary for modelmaking, and most scenographers have a set of these indispensable implements in their studio.

A. T square. At least 24 inches.
B. Triangles. 30°-60°-90°, 45°, and adjustable.
C. Architect scale with 1/8", 1/4", 3/8", 1/2", 3/4", and 1" scales.
D. Pencils. Hard "H" pencil leads are preferred for drafting while the softer "B" leads are better for sketching.
E. Mechanical pencils. There are a wide variety of mechanical pencils with standard leads of 0.3, 0.5, 0.7, and 0.9 mm diameters in both soft and hard lead types.
F. Ink pens. Pens use both water-soluble and permanent inks and come in a range colors and line widths, from 0.3 mm to 2.0 mm.
G. Felt-tip pens and markers. These popular pens are relatively inexpensive, come in a wide range of tip shapes and sizes, and use different colored inks or dyes, including water-soluble, permanent, oil, alcohol, and acid-neutral-based formulations, making them versatile sketching tools.
H. Erasers. White plastic or kneaded rubber erasers are soft and do not abrade paper surfaces as much as firm rubber erasers.
I. Compass and beam compass for drawing circles. Brands with cutting attachments are useful for model building.
J. French and flexible curves. These aid the artist in drawing clean and accurate curved lines.
K. Drafting cleaning brush. These help to keep the workspace clean of waste materials.

Although light boxes are more generally found in studios where traditional graphics are produced, scenographers will often find them useful when initial sketches need to be redrawn and refined. A magnifier lamp is another useful studio tool when drawing on a small scale or when small model parts are being constructed. It can also serve as a light source when photographing models.

Model-Cutting and Assembly Tools

The following list of cutting and assembly tools is illustrated in figures 1.6 and 1.7.

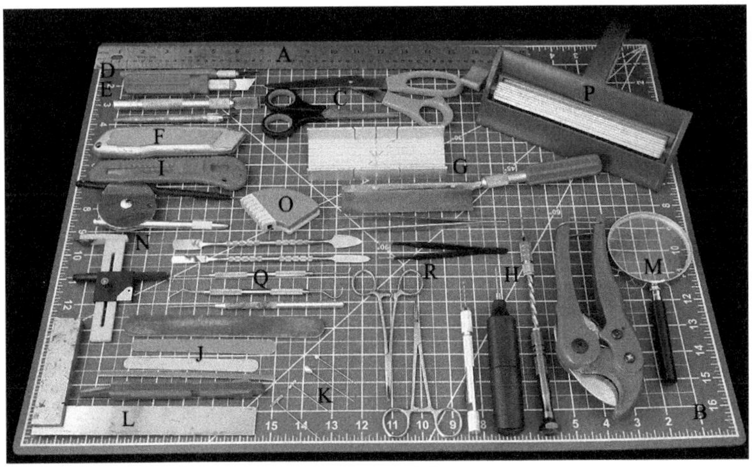

Figure 1.6. Model-cutting and assembly tools

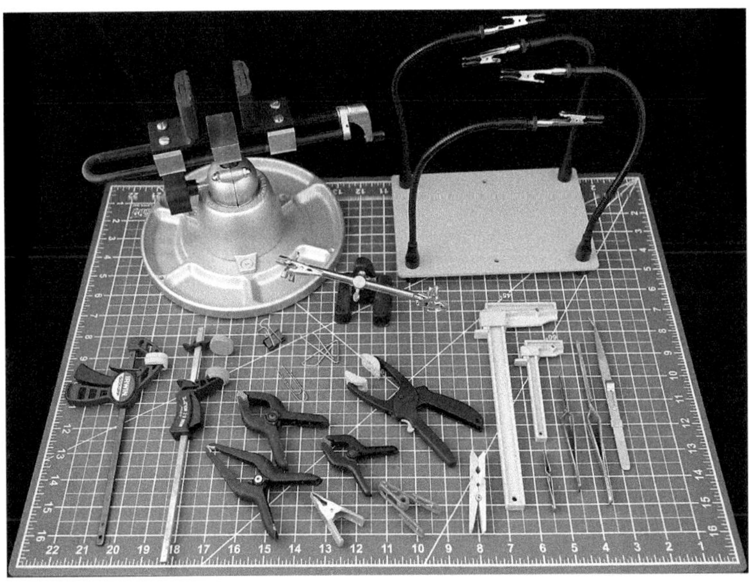

Figure 1.7. Bar and locking clamps, tweezers, hemostats, "helping hands," and miniature vice

A. Stainless steel rule/straight edge 18–24" with nonslip cork backing. The cork backing will get dirty over time and should be replaced periodically. Self-adhesive cork sheets are available in scrapbooking sections of hobby stores and online. Masking tape is an acceptable short-term substitute, although it will need to be removed, the gummy adhesive cleaned, and the tape replaced periodically.
B. Self-healing cutting mat at least 24" × 36". This mat will protect the worktable underneath and help keep knife blades from dulling too quickly. Smaller mats are useful for small side projects. Do not use paint or glue on cutting mats.
C. Scissors. One large pair and a smaller sewing-kit size are useful.
D. Slim barrel hobby craft knife. These knives come in various shapes and sizes to suit the diverse needs of model makers. Craft knives are sold in sets or individually with interchangeable blade systems and a variety of blade types (straight or curved edges, chiseled tips, etc.). The #11 blade is standard for modelmaking. British model makers use scalpels instead of craft knives due to their precision and sharpness. Common handle sizes are #3 and #4, and #11 blades are preferred for their pointed, triangular shape. Unlike the rounded barrels of American craft knives, the scalpels are flat, so there is less confusion of which direction the blade is facing. Toothbrush holders are useful when transporting craft knives and scalpels.
E. Thick-barrel hobby craft knife.
F. Utility or mat knife.
G. Hobby craft razor saw with miter box.
H. Hobby craft drill with interchangeable bits. Hand and powered versions are available.
I. Snap-off utility knife. These retractable knives with breakaway blades are safer to use and easily changed, but the long blade can wobble in its handle and affect the cut.
J. Nail files or emery boards to sand rough cuts and texture surfaces.
K. Dressmaker and T-pins. These pins do not bend as easily as straight pins, and the large heads are easier on the fingertips.
L. Tri or set square for cutting 90° angles and holding pieces at 90° while gluing.
M. Reducing glass. The opposite of the magnifying glass; this lens improves the field of vision by reducing the size of objects being viewed.
N. Circle cutters. The compass cutter blade angle increases as the radius increases, so it is best used for cutting small circles from 2 to 7 inches in thinner papers. The bar compass cutter is designed to cut larger circles in thick papers as the blade remains fixed at 90° to the surface.
O. Foam board rabbet cutter. These specialty cutters notch the edge of foam board leaving one side of the paper ply to overlap and cover the exposed foam edge of the adjoining board.

P. Paper corrugators. These are particularly useful for corrugating or pleating paper, card, and metal foils to replicate curtain fullness and corrugated surfaces.
Q. Dental probes for texturing, making small holes, and holding pieces together while applying glue.
R. Tweezers, angled forceps, and hemostats for handling small pieces.
S. Clamps. These are fundamental tools for joining and supporting model pieces that need to be glued, soldered, cut, filed, or drilled. Simple clamping can be accomplished with clothespins and paperclips, but more intricate work requires a hobby clamp.

As the modelmaker progresses from novice to professional, more sophisticated tools will become necessary. Useful tools that the professional modeler might acquire later include the following (see figures 1.8 through 1.11).

T. Manual or electric mini bench top cutoff saw for repetitive or angled cuts in balsa and basswoods.
U. Hobby scroll saw to save time and effort when making decorative cuts in thick pieces of balsa, bass, or plywood. The edges of cut materials will need to be sanded for cleaner-looking cuts.
V. Hobby table saws for ripping small strips, cutting wood boards and plastics, and for miter cuts on molding and frames.
W. Rotary tools (multipurpose devices with interchangeable bits) to cut, sand, grind, carve, engrave, and polish. Flexible shaft attachments make the tool easier to hold and offer more precise control. Add-on base attachments adapt these tools into drill press, router-shaper table, and circle cutters. Battery and corded models are available.

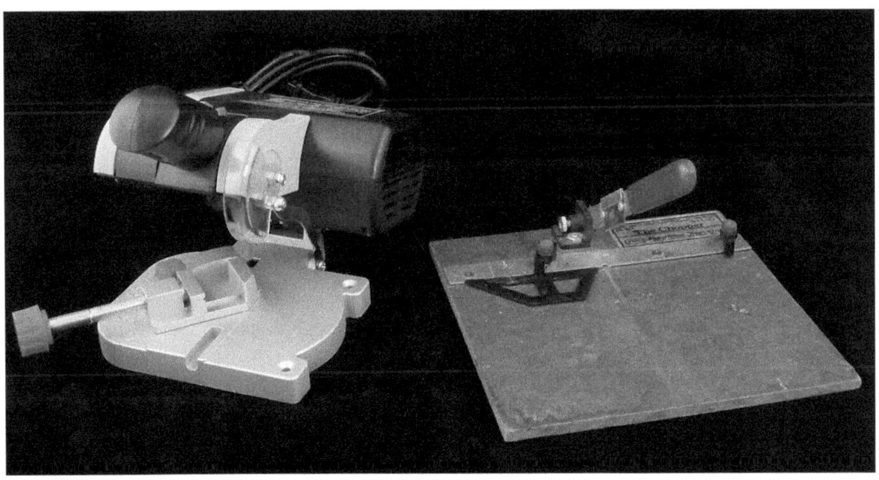

Figure 1.8. Power and manual mini tabletop cutoff saws

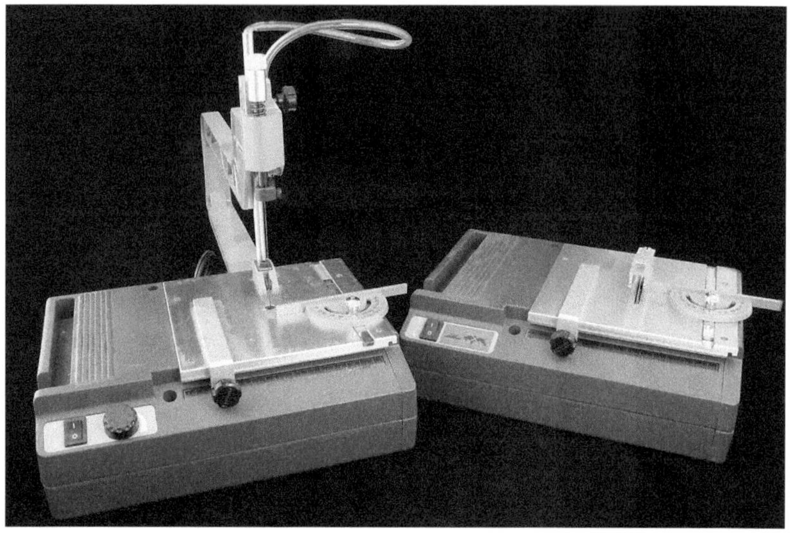

Figure 1.9. Hobby scroll and table saws

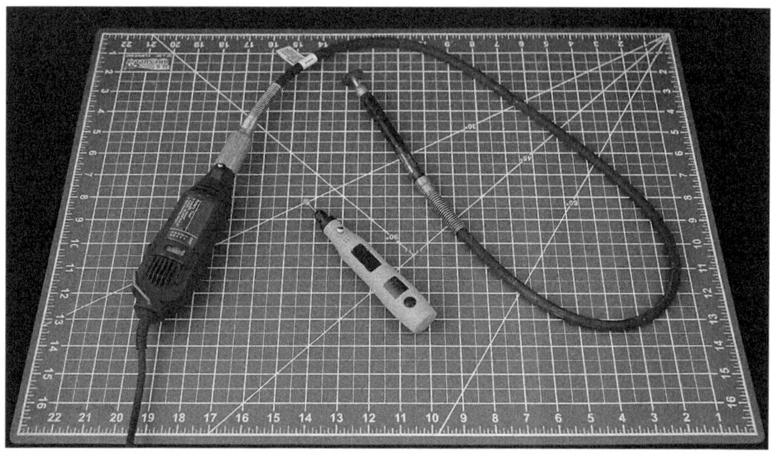

Figure 1.10. Rotary tool with flexible shaft and cordless miniature rotary pen

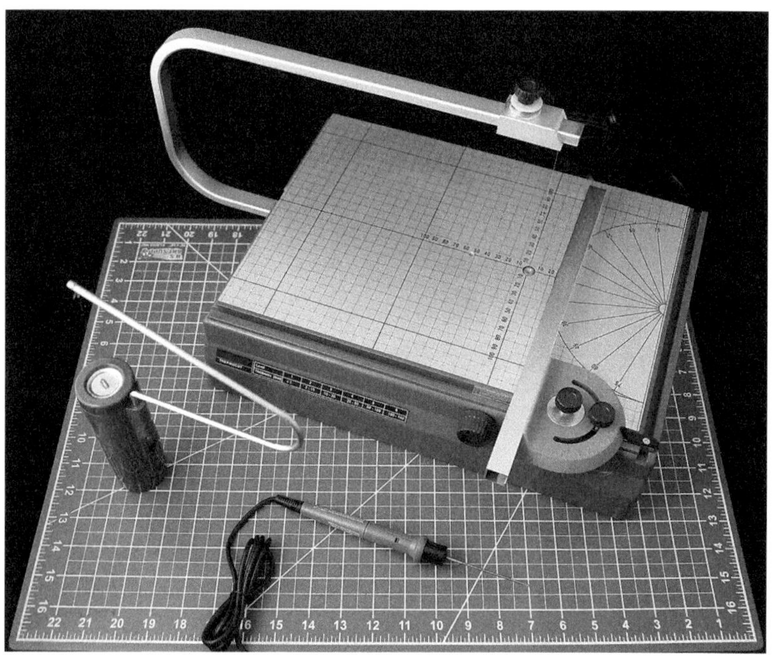

Figure 1.11. Polystyrene hot knife and wire-cutting tools

X. Hot wire cutters and knives for making intricate cuts to polystyrene foam without producing particulates. However, the resulting fumes require appropriate ventilation. Battery and corded models are available.
Y. Hobby wood-carving tool kits to aid in small intricate carving.
Z. Manual and electronic digital calipers. These can save the modelmaker a great deal of time when measuring and converting model material thicknesses.

Serious modelmakers will need to become proficient in working with metal and metal tools for models and accessories that are delicate but retain strength and rigidity. Figure 1.12 shows various metalworking tools that are useful for the modelmaker.

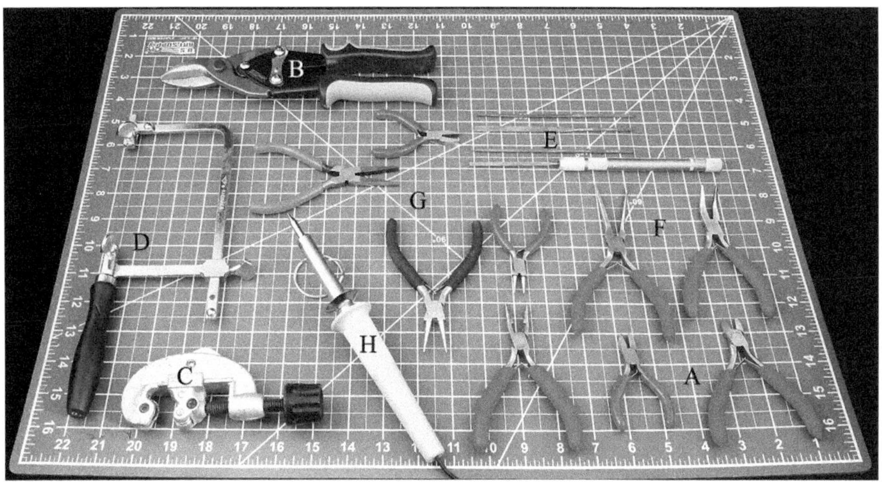

Figure 1.12. Metalworking tools

Metalworking Tools

A. Flush-cut wire cutters for cutting small gauge metal wires and rods.
B. Tin snips for wire mesh and thin sheeting.
C. Tube cutter.
D. Metal hacksaw or jeweler's saw.
E. Mini metal file set. Cutting metal creates sharp edges and burrs that must be cleaned with small metal files or sandpaper.
F. Needle-nose pliers. These are available with wire-cutting edges.
G. Jewelry pliers.
H. Soldering iron and solder.

Texturing and Painting Tools

Models are hard on paint brushes as they often have rough surfaces and frequently require unusual brush techniques. Reasonably priced brushes are available in sets of assorted sizes and shapes. Midsize round brushes are the most versatile, but smaller brushes are necessary for detailed work; at the opposite end, larger brushes are indispensable for broad coverage. It is also beneficial to purchase flat and wash brushes for painting large areas and creating lining textures. Brushes are available with natural or synthetic

Small brushes increase in size by increments of 1 (1, 2, 3, etc.). Brushes larger than 10 increase by increments of 2 (10, 12, 14, etc.).

A. Red sable or good-quality synthetic watercolor brushes.
B. Acrylic brushes (stiffer bristles) for applying thick paints.
C. Camel hair brushes (coarse bristles) for use with acrylics and gesso. These are made from various animal hair (except, oddly, camel hair).
D. Palette knives for the application of gesso, modeling paste, and spackling compound.
E. Toothbrush for texturing and paint spattering effects.
F. Small atomizer or spritzer bottle to wet surfaces, tone, and create spatter effects.
G. Gesso. White, black, and clear varieties are available. Gesso is also available in aerosol spray cans.
H. Modeling paste and spackling compound.
I. Acrylic matte, gloss, and extender mediums. Acrylic mediums allow different paint effects by thinning the paint, changing its opacity, and producing shiny or matte effects.
J. Watercolor paints for transparent effects.
K. Gouache paints for opaque matte effects.
L. Acrylic paints for both opaque and translucent water-resistant effects.
M. Inks. India and colored.
N. Colored pencils.
O. Watercolor pencils.
P. Watercolor markers in black, gray tones, and colors.
Q. Permanent markers in black, gray tones, and colors.
R. Paint pens in black, white, colored, and metallic colors.
S. Enamel paints for metalwork.
T. Paint palette for mixing paints.
U. Paint jars.
V. Airbrush for controlled shading, gradation, blending, and spattering effects.
W. Aerosol spray paints and sealers for large models to create a consistent color and texture. White flat primer is useful for white models.
X. Metallic paste. Water insoluble gold, silver, copper, and brass finishes can be used to enrich and add highlights to the textured surfaces on presentation models.

bristles, but either kind must hold their shape and spring back after each stroke to provide greater control. The quality and length of the bristles determine a brush's capacity to hold paint also known as its "charge." A greater charge allows for longer uninterrupted brushstrokes and more control in color blending. See figure 1.13 for a chart of useful brush sizes. Palette knives are a useful tool for applying paints and creating texture. Various shapes are available, as shown in figure 1.14.

Round Brushes

Brush Size No.	Imperical Measurement	Metric Measurement
0000	Less than 1/64"	0.3mm
000	1/64"	0.4mm
00	Less than 1/32"	0.6mm
0	1/32"	0.8mm
1	Less than 1/16"	1.2mm
2	1/16"	1.6mm
3	Less than 3/32"	2.0mm
4	3/32"	2.4mm
5	Less than 1/8"	3.0mm
6	1/8"	3.2mm
7	Less than 5/32"	3.6mm
8	5/32"	4.0mm
9	3/16"	4.8mm
10	7/32"	5.6mm
12	9/32"	7.2mm

Flat Brushes

Brush Size No.	Imperical Measurement	Metric Measurement
0	1/32"	0.8mm
1	Less than 1/16"	1.2mm
2	3/32"	2.4mm
3	1/8"	3.2mm
4	5/32"	4.0mm
5	Less than 3/16"	4.4mm
6	3/16"	4.8mm
7	7/32"	5.5mm
8	1/4"	6.4mm
9	9/32"	7.2mm
10	5/16"	8.0mm
12	3/8"	9.5mm

Figure 1.13. Brush sizes and shapes

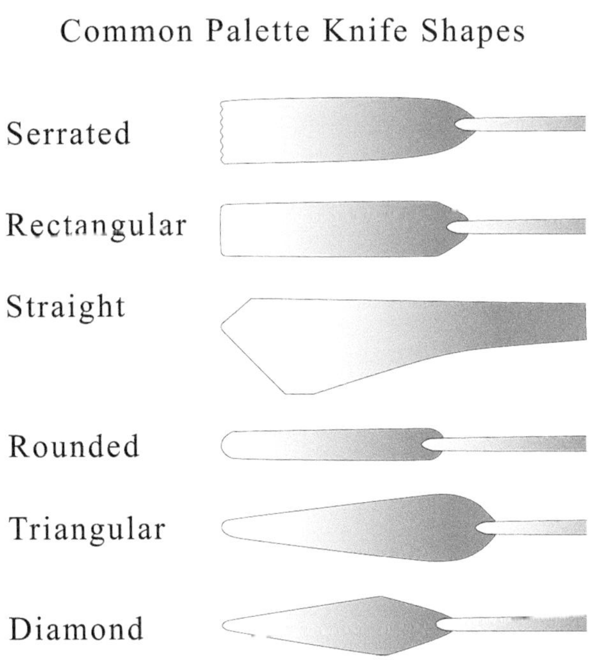

Figure 1.14. Palette knife shapes

Tip: Modelmakers often save old brushes to use for creating interesting textures. The old bristles can also be used for model grasses.

Modeling Materials

Because his laborers could not read drawings, Renaissance architect Filippo Brunelleschi (1377–1446) made models of paper, wood, wax, clay, and even carved "turnips."[4] Wood, wax, paper, and clay are still commonly used by modelmakers today, but new innovations have greatly increased the modelmaker's options. A list of common modelmaking materials includes the following.

A. Various papers, paperboards, and foam boards.
B. Balsa, basswood, and craft plywood.
C. Polystyrene and polyurethane foams.
D. Metal foil, wire, screen, and mesh.
E. Found images from magazines, catalogs, online sources, etc.
F. Found objects, including twigs, chain, beads, jewelry findings, bottle caps, toothpicks, packaging materials, doll furniture of various scales, holiday ornaments, recycled model pieces, etc.

Paper

Paper is composed of pulped cellulose plant fibers (wood, cotton, flax, linen, etc.) sized with natural or synthetic starches, and pressed into sheets. Paper is inexpensive, can be cut and folded, and readily accepts adhesives and paints. However, paper is easily crumpled, wrinkled, or torn, and water and humidity will expand and shrink the fibers, causing the paper to warp, lose adhesion, and mildew. Paper will also bleach and grow brittle under ultraviolet light. Therefore, any models made with paper should be kept in cool, dry spaces out of direct sunlight.

Paper mills produce a bewildering array of papers of varying size, color, fiber content, grain, absorbency, reflectivity, opacity, finish, weight, and thickness. For scenographic modeling purposes, paper weight, thickness, and surface finish are frequently the most relevant qualities. Text refers to thinner papers used for writing, printing, and sketching, while paperboard refers to heavier, thicker papers, including cover, cardstock, tag, cards, file folders, and report covers. In North America, paper is sold by basis weight in pounds (lbs.), calculated by weighing a ream of 500 sheets of an individual paper type. Internationally, paper is sold by metric weight measured in grams per square meter (GSM or g/m^2). Paper sold in the United States will often list one or both weight measurements on its packaging. Generally, the heavier the weight, the thicker and more rigid the paper, but paper weight does not specify the actual thickness of a paper. Paperboards are also sold by their actual thickness listed as caliper points (thousandths of an inch) or millimeters. One caliper point is equal to 1/1,000 of an inch (.001), so paperboard that is 20 points is equal to 20 thousandths of an inch or 0.020 decimal inches (this is the average thickness of cereal boxes). An inch equals 25.4 millimeters, so papers measured in millimeters can be converted to decimal inches by dividing by 25.4. For a comparative chart of paper thicknesses, see figure 1.15.

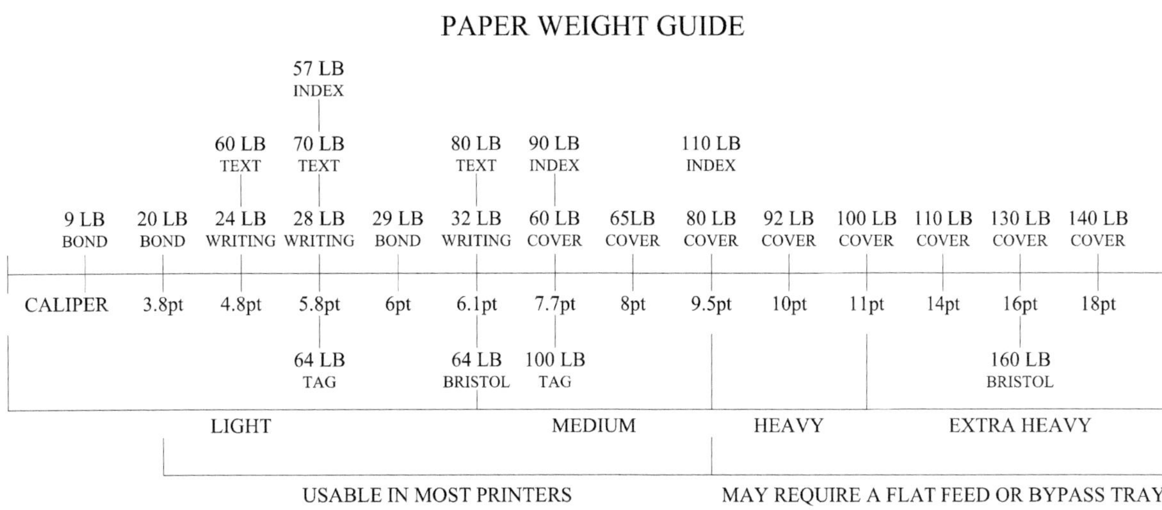

Figure 1.15. Chart of approximate paper weights and thicknesses

The second paper characteristic modelmakers should understand is that the surface finish determines its relative smoothness, capacity to absorb liquids, and ability to accept various media. A paper's finish is determined by fiber content, heat, pressure, coating, and sizing. Sizing is a starch that binds and strengthens fibers and controls the paper's porosity. Unsized paper will absorb moisture like a blotter, while sized papers allow wet media to dry on their surface. Paper is pressed using either hot or cool rollers. Hot press paper has a smoother surface suited for pencil, pen, ink, markers, and dry mounting. Cold press paper has a lightly textured surface suitable for blending pastels, watercolor, gouache, and acrylic paints. Tooth is often used to describe paper texture. The greater tooth a paper has, the rougher its texture. Textures can also be embossed onto the paper. Papers used for painting are typically composed of cotton fibers, which are effective at absorbing water.

Cotton refers to the use of virgin cotton fibers, while rag indicates papers made with cotton textile remnants. Rag and cotton are often used interchangeably, causing some confusion.

Paperboard

Paperboards are thicker and more durable than text, making them ideal for creating quick, inexpensive models. The terms *cover stock* and *cardstock* are frequently interchanged, but cover is often coated and textured while card is typically smoother. Card comes in a vast array of colors, printed patterns, textures, and surfaces, including flat, glossy, metallic, glittered, iridescent, and velour cloth. Designs can be drawn or printed onto paperboard and then enhanced with colored pencil, crayon, marker, and ink. Wetter media like watercolor can warp and buckle paperboards. Card is commonly used for 1/8" and 1/4" study models but is often not rigid enough for larger scales. Card models require simple tools, including craft knives, scissors, steel-edged rulers, a cutting surface, masking or transparent cellophane tape, and glue.

Bristol, a laminated paperboard made of plies of art paper, has been used for scenographic models since its development in the 1800s.[5] Bristol is typically white or buff in color with an uncoated finish ranging from smooth plate to lightly textured vellum. The smoother plate finish is suitable for pencil, pen, ink, marker, and airbrush, while vellum's coarser surface makes it appropriate for friction-based media, including pencil, colored pencil, charcoal, pastels, as well as light watercolor. Bristol finishes are durable, allowing erasures without damaging the surface. Two-, three-, and four-ply Bristol are approximately 67, 100, 120 lbs. in weight, making them extremely useful for modelmaking. Bristol is too thick to be used by most photocopy machines and printers, so graphics must be drawn by hand.

Poster board is a paperboard available in thicknesses between .024" and .058" (approximately 12 pt. and 24 pt.). Most poster boards have a chalk coating, giving it a smooth surface that accepts colored pencils, ink, markers, and simple poster paint, but will decompose when paints are blended on its surface. Poster boards come in a variety of sizes and colors, with specialty surfaces including fluorescent colors, glittered, metallic, and reflective mirrored faces.

Chipboard, variously called bookboard, binderboard, or backerboard, is a thick paperboard produced for cartons, book covers, notepad backings, or scrapbooking, rolled into cylinders for paper towels and packing tubes, and compressed into paper sticks. Test board uses unbleached recycled fibers that vary in size and color, creating a mottled appearance. Kraft board is a higher quality paperboard made from virgin wood fibers producing a uniform brown surface. Chipboard can be given a clay coating for a printing surface. It is easily reused from commercial cartons and boxes making it an excellent material for green modelmaking. Acid-neutral chipboard is available when preservation is an issue.

Fiberboard

Fiberboard is a broad term that refers to heavy paperboards made of plant and wood fibers or chips extending up to engineered wood products like particleboard, Homasote®, and Masonite®. Corrugated cardboard is a generic term for corrugated fiberboard or containerboard that consists of flat sheets of a liner or linerboard adhered to sheets of fluted fiberboard.

Fluting makes corrugated containerboard an interesting material for modelmakers. Walled containerboard is rigid, making it useful for flat surfaces, while single-faced containerboard is flexible and effective for curved surfaces. The variety of flute sizes and spacing allows containerboard to replicate surfaces like corrugated tin, terra cotta roof tiles, and fluted columns in various scales (see figure 1.16). The walled linerboard surface can also be stripped off to create interesting textures.

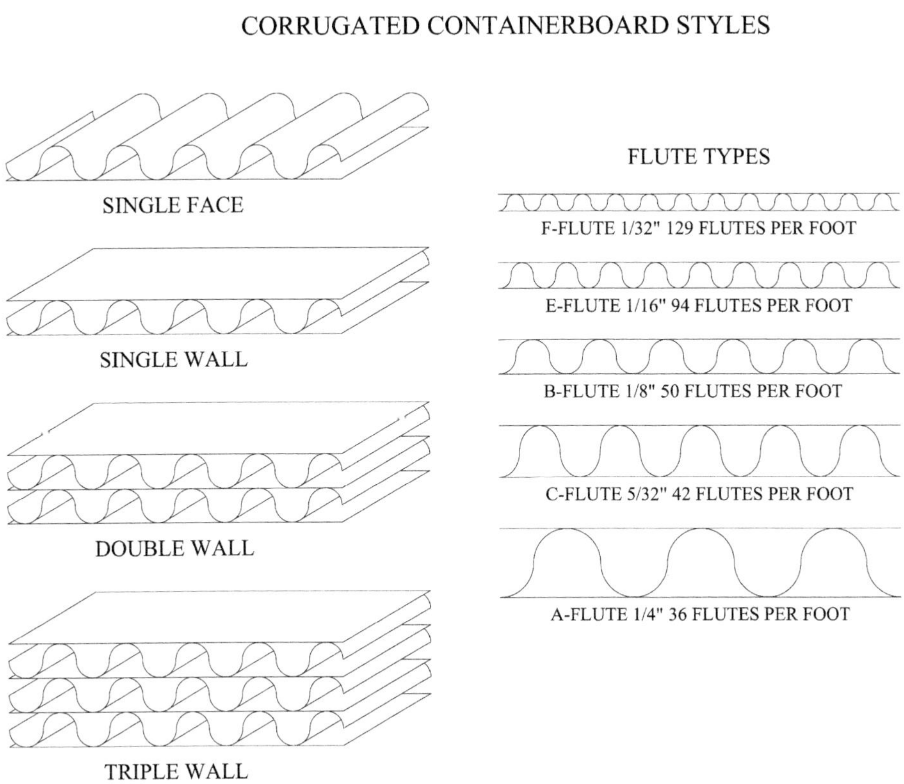

Figure 1.16. Corrugated containerboard styles

Corrugated containerboard is manufactured with kraft quality fibers, but white and colored containerboard is also available. Containerboard is easily dented or torn, and it can disintegrate when wet. Its porosity will also absorb and mute paint pigments. Therefore, containerboard is used primarily for rough modeling and packing, but it can be sheathed with paper or fabric for presentation purposes. Single-faced and walled corrugated containerboard sheets are sold at packing and shipping stores but can be recycled from old boxes. Acid-neutral containerboard is available if preservation is a concern. Embossed and perforated kraft boards used for packing offer interesting textures and patterns for models (see figure 1.17).

Figure 1.17. Examples of embossed, perforated, and pressed paper and paperboards

Pulp Board

Modeling pulp board and Finnboard were formulated specifically for sculpting and modelmaking. These fiberboards are cream colored, flexible, and acid neutral. They are easily cut with craft knives and can be sanded to create textures or clean up rough cuts. They become flexible when water is applied to their surface, but once dry they retain their new shape (see figure 1.18). These boards accept craft glues, dry media, and paints, although very wet paint treatments can re-soften the board. Both are available from art stores in sheets measuring 30" × 40" × 1/32" thick.

Figure 1.18. Modeling pulp board

Illustration Board

Illustration board is a laminated board with a rigid center ply of chipboard sandwiched between an art paper on the front and a service paper on the back. Hot press illustration board has a smooth surface suited for pencil, pen, ink, markers, and dry mounting. Cold press illustration board has a lightly textured surface appropriate for pencils, pastels, watercolor, gouache, and acrylic paints. Both are available in light, medium, and heavyweight thicknesses (1, 2, and 3 mm or 3/64", 5/64", and 1/8" respectively). The chipboard center helps prevent warping, making it useful for larger white and painted presentation models. Heavyweight illustration board makes a sturdy base, middle and lightweight boards are good for walls, and lightweight is thin enough for furniture and more delicate pieces. The thicker boards are more difficult to cut with craft knives, but laser cutters can cut clean, intricate designs. Illustration board will accept various adhesives, but the outer surface papers can be torn from the center core if too much stress is placed on the glued joint.

Matboard

Matboard is composed of three plies of paperboard. The chipboard core is made of cotton fiber and comes in white, buff, and black, while the front surface paper is available in dozens of colors, textures, and materials. The backing board is made of acid-reduced cotton fiber to prevent damage to the artwork it touches. Matboard is specifically manufactured to protect the artwork it frames and is available in acid-neutralized, archival, and museum board varieties. Since the modelmaker rarely knows the final destiny of a model, using archival-quality materials and glues is advisable for presentation models. The uniform fibers make matboard easy to cut with a craft knife or laser cutter. While the front surface paper is not specifically manufactured to be drawn on or painted, it will accept pencil, ink, markers, and even watercolor and acrylic paints if the water content is not too high. For unity when making white models, a white core mat should be used, and a black core mat should be used when making a black model box.

Tip: *If black core matboard is unavailable, the white edge can be blackened by running a broad-tipped black permanent marker along the edge.*

Foam Board

Foam core board or foam board is used extensively for architectural, scenographic, and display models, and for prototyping objects. Foam board consists of a sheet of polystyrene foam sandwiched between surface paperboards. White, black, and colored foam boards surfaces are available in matte finishes or coated with a smooth clay surface suitable for markers, pen, ink, and dry mounting. Black matte foam board is especially useful for model boxes. Foam board allows light sketching with pencil, but sharp points or too much pressure can make indentations, and erasures tend to smudge the clay surface. Foam boards are relatively sturdy, lightweight, and easy to cut with craft knives. Laser cutters can incise repetitive and complex shapes, but as this involves melting the polystyrene core, makers should follow safety procedures outlined in the operator's manual and provide adequate ventilation. Foam board is available in different grades or densities that refer to the foam's durability and resistance to crushing. Lower-quality foam boards use low-density polystyrene in their core and are easily damaged. Higher-quality foam boards use denser polystyrenes designed to resist compression and expand back into shape after cutting. Makers should experiment with available foam boards to see which are best suited to their tasks. Foam board is mildly acidic but is available in acid-neutral versions. Some glues will dissolve the styrene core, and water-based glues and paints can buckle the paper surface. Common foam board thicknesses are 1/8", 3/16", and 1/2". The 1/2"-thick foam board provides a solid base and walls for a large model box. The 3/16"-thick foam board is acceptable for smaller model box walls. The lighter 1/8"-thick board is often reserved for the scenographic model itself. The 1/8"-thick board equals a 6" stair rise in 1/4" scale and 3" rise in 1/2" scale. The 3/16" board approximates a 9" stair rise in 1/4" scale and a 4½" stair rise in 1/2" scale.

Gatorfoam®

Gatorfoam® is another laminated board composed of a polystyrene core sandwiched between plies of resin-permeated wood fiber and sold in sheets from 3/16" to 3" thick. The hard outer surface is smooth, water-resistant, and available in black and white, and it accepts most paints, stains, and adhesives. Gatorfoam® can be cut with a craft knife using multiple scorings, but power saws bladed for laminated countertops achieve better results. Gatorfoam® is expensive but strong in comparison to its light weight, making it an excellent material for models that undergo a great deal of wear.

Papier-mâché

Papier-mâché, literally "mashed paper," refers to pulped paper fibers mixed with water and adhesive, often wheat paste or polyvinyl acetate (PVA), to create a moldable paste that solidifies when dry. Once it has dried, papier-mâché can be sanded, cut, and drilled. It takes paint well but requires a sealer due to its porosity. Papier mâché products are also available in premixed pastes that dry when exposed to air, so they must be stored in airtight containers. These products often include strengthening agents like clay or plaster of Paris. Makers should look for nontoxic varieties and wear a particulate mask as the small fibers and particles easily become airborne. Papier-mâché adheres to porous surfaces, so individual pieces should be molded on a nonporous surface like plastic wrap, aluminum foil, or a silicone mat. Papier-mâché is useful for modeling organic shapes like landscaping or stonework and can be cast in flexible molds using a release agent.

Wood

Wood is valued in modelmaking for its workability, strength, and acceptance of adhesives and paints. Wood can be stained but requires a prime coat prior to painting. While it is tempting to stain wood to enhance its natural texture, the grain may be out of scale and may not match the other painted surfaces of the model. Hobby shops and specialty lumber stores carry wood products specifically for hobbyists working in small scales.

Balsawood is lightweight, buff in color, with a straight coarse grain that allows it to be bent, shaped, cut, and carved with craft knives. It is sold in sticks, planks, rods, and triangles, in lengths from 18" to 48" and thicknesses from 1/32" to 1". Balsa sticks and planks mirror common lumber sizes, making them useful when simulating construction materials. Sheets span from 2" to 6" wide and are typically used for platform tops, walls, doors, and flooring. Rods are available from 3/32" to 1¼" in diameter. Balsa triangles are cut in 45° × 45° × 90° angles and range from 1/8" to 1" thicknesses. Blocks are square or rectangular in shape, ranging from 1" to 6" in thickness and can be carved into shapes like rocks, furniture, statuary, and human figures.

Balsa's strength, weight, density, and grain direction can vary depending on how the original log was milled. Balsa is classified by grain. A-grain has long fibers that are flexible when bending across the grain, making it useful for curved pieces. C-grain balsa has mottled grain of shorter fibers, producing a more rigid, brittle wood and making it best suited for flat surfaces. B-grain combines characteristics of A and C, making it useful for various tasks (see figure 1.19). Balsa quality varies quite a bit, so makers should examine each piece before purchasing. Balsa of more precise density and strength can be purchased online from specialty dealers.[6]

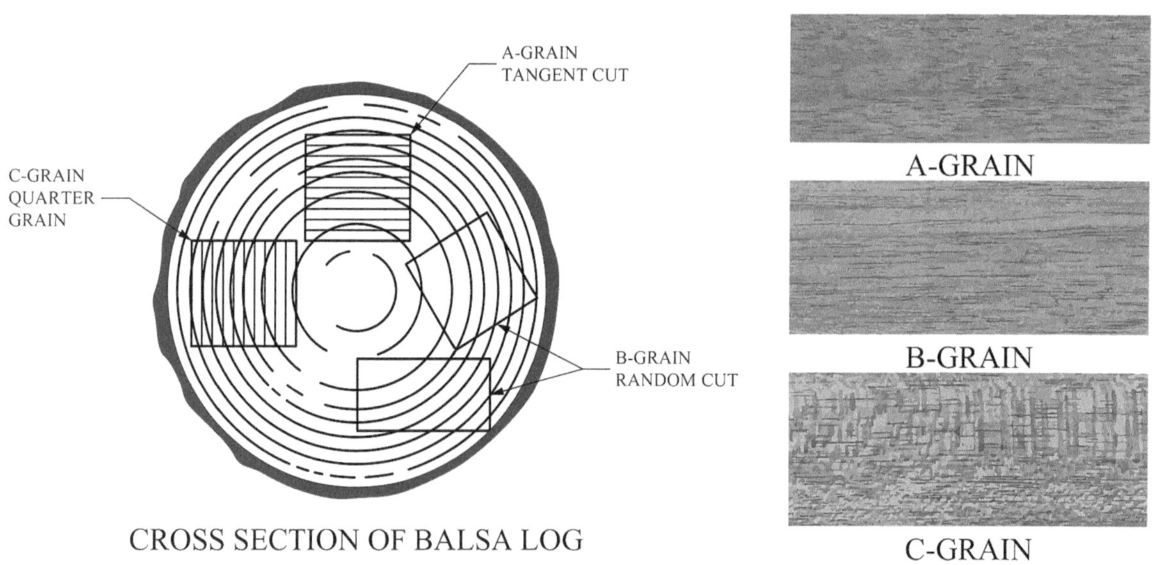

Figure 1.19. Balsa grain classification

Basswood has many of the same qualities of balsa but is stronger, more rigid, and heavier. Thin basswood may be cut with craft knives, but cutting pieces thicker than 3/16" requires a fine-toothed saw. Basswood is used extensively for commercial dollhouse furniture, doors, windows, railings, balusters, clapboard, and shingled sidings. Of particular use to the scenographic modeler are the moldings that correspond to baseboard, chair, picture railing, and cornice moldings.

> ***Tip:*** *Most dollhouse moldings are made in 1" scale, but the modelmaker should keep in mind that a chair rail molding in 1" scale might make an acceptable cornice molding in 1/2" or 1/4" scale.*

There are also useful plywood products made for crafts and modelmaking. Being composed of five to seven hardwood birch veneers, birch or "aircraft" plywood is strong and lightweight. "Lite ply" has a balsawood core sandwiched between exterior veneers of poplar, making it lighter in weight and more flexible. Craft plywood is available in 1/32" to 1/2" thicknesses, a variety of lengths and widths, and cuts easily with power saws and laser cutters. Lauan plywood is available in 1/8" and 1/4" thicknesses and is commonly used for inexpensive dollhouse kits. Lauan frequently has imperfections that are filled and sanded, so it should only be used where the surface will be hidden, covered, or painted.

Metal

Metals, including copper, brass, iron, and aluminum, have a long history in modelmaking. However, metals are heavy and challenging to work with, so contemporary modelmakers often substitute newer plastic materials that are available in similar forms. But metals are stronger and hold their shape after bending, making them a necessity when delicacy, strength, and flexibility are factors. Various metals come premade in wire, screen, mesh, sheets, foil, strips, channels, I-beams, and round and box tubing (see figure 1.20). Metal foil, wire, chain, screen, and mesh are especially useful to modelers and not available in comparably sized plastics. In terms of metal thickness, "gauge" refers to a standard measurement indicating the thickness of a sheet metal or wire. A higher gauge number corresponds to thinner metal, while a lower gauge number represents thicker metal.

Thin-gauge metal foils can be embossed with stencils to simulate antique tin ceilings, paneling, and wallpapers. Piano wire or music wire is made from tempered high-carbon steel, making it difficult to bend and cut, but

Figure 1.20. Metal materials

this rigidity makes it ideal for long straight runs when building model scaffolding or rigging line sets.

Flexible wire made of copper, iron, and aluminum make excellent tree trunks, branches, vines, and figures. Aluminum foil and pie plates can be used to replicate bed clothing, tents, tarps, banners, and flags; cut and shaped into large leaf shapes or molded around wire trees to build up trunks and branches; or formed into landscaping, rocks, and figures. Aluminum soda cans are thicker and can be used when foil is too thin. Screen wire mesh can simulate chain-link fencing, be draped and shaped to suggest fish nets, or be filled with modeling paste and spackling compound to create rolling landscapes. Heavier-gauge woven and welded wire mesh can simulate prison bars or reinforced iron rods in concrete. Electronic- and laser-cut perforated metal makes strong lightweight fences, gates, tracery, and foliage. Figure 1.21 showcases projects made from various metal materials.

Joining metal pieces requires soldering, which involves melting a filler metal or solder over the connecting joints (see figure 1.22). The solder melts at a lower temperature than the metal being joined, allowing it to flow around the joint and bond the pieces together. Metals oxidize at high temperatures, requiring a chemical cleaning agent called *flux*. Flux protects the metal from oxidation and reduces the surface tension of the metals, creating a stronger bond. The flux must chemically match the joining metals to ensure a secure bond, so the modeler must check the product information to match the metal

Figure 1.21. Metals used in various model projects

Figure 1.22.
Soldering brass

with the appropriate flux. Copper and brass oxidize more slowly than iron and aluminum, making them easier to join by soldering. These softer metals cut easily with metal snips, fine-toothed jewelers' saws, and even old craft knife blades by repeatedly scoring through the piece. Tubes can be cut with a jewelers' saw or by slowly rolling the tube on a flat surface while holding the blade on the cutting line.

Plastic

Plastics refer to natural or synthetic polymers that can be molded into shapes when soft and then solidified through heat or chemical reaction.[7] Plastics are composed of individual molecular units linked into chains, endowing them with such properties as density, strength, flexibility, compressibility, transparency, and resistance to heat, humidity, and electricity. A common weakness of plastics is that they can be damaged by ultraviolet light and should be painted with a protective coating if they will be exposed to prolonged sunlight. Softened plastics can be injection molded, cast, or shaped like clay, and when solidified be cut, carved, and sanded like wood. Plastics are more resistant to warping when painted, but each variety requires specialty priming coats prior to painting. Different plastics also require specific adhesives when joining, many of which are flammable and toxic.

The use of plastics should be weighed with the understanding that they may contain volatile organic compounds (VOCs) that are considered toxic. VOCs can irritate the skin, eyes, and respiratory passageways, and may cause coughing, nausea, headaches, and dizziness. Plasticizers, added to make plastics more pliable, can leach out (outgassing) over time rendering the plastic brittle. This affects the long-term life of models made with plastics while also creating potential health hazards. Small plastic particles (called nano plastics) can be inhaled and ingested, so particle masks should be worn when sanding or rough cutting. Finally, most plastics cannot be recycled and may take hundreds of years to biodegrade.

There are literally hundreds of plastics manufactured today, far too many to cover in any single text, but plastics commonly used by modelmakers should be discussed (see figures 1.23 and 1.24). Polystyrene (PS) is a thermoplastic, meaning it can be softened with heat, reworked into a new shape, and harden when cooled. Polystyrene can be cut with conventional craft knives and saws then carved and sanded. Styrene is available in sheets, strips, channels, I-beams, round and box tubing, figures, and furniture for architectural models, hobby railroading, doll house miniatures, and role play gaming. Thin styrene sheets, strips, and rods are flexible and useful for making curved shapes. Sheets are available in vacuum-formed textures, including clapboard, shingle, corrugated siding; brick and stone walls; tile and stone flooring; and embossed wallpaper and tin ceilings through model railroading and dollhouse manufacturers.

Expanded polystyrene (EPS), best known by the brand name Styrofoam®, is a white foam composed of small hollow beads. EPS beads expand to form sheets for packaging and insulation, beverage cups, and objects like blocks, balls, eggs, and cones. EPS foam is easy to work, but the beads flake off, preventing fine detail in small carving. A static charge resulting from friction attracts the beads to skin, clothing, and tools, requiring a vacuum cleaner to collect the beads. A particulate mask should be used whenever one is working with EPS foam to prevent inhaling or ingesting beads and residue.

Extruded polystyrene foam (XPS) is commonly called "blue" or "pink" foam, referencing the colors their manufactures use to brand their products. XPS is a closed-cell foam without beads and therefore cuts and carves more cleanly, giving finer detail. XPS residue is also easily statically charged so the same precautions listed above should be followed when working with this foam. EPS and XPS are lightweight with up to 95–98 percent of their

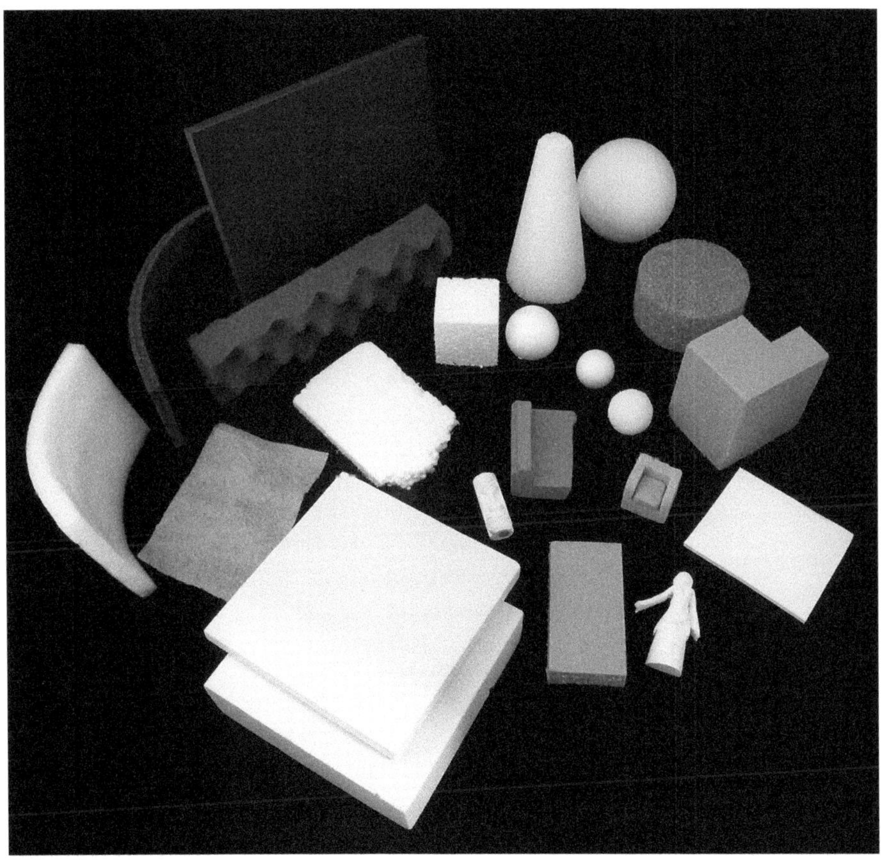

Figure 1.23. Foam materials

structure being gas. As a result, styrene foams are easily damaged and require coatings of gesso, modeling paste, spackling compound, or a foam coating product to protect them and provide a priming surface for painting. Both EPS and XPS are sold in sheets of assorted sizes, thicknesses, and densities at hobby and home improvement stores.

Another useful styrene is acrylonitrile butadiene styrene (ABS) best known for making LEGO® blocks. ABS is used in injection molding for kit models, railroading accessories, architectural and engineering elements, as well as 3D printing. ABS is particularly useful in architectural modeling due to its strength and solubility in acetone, allowing modelmakers to "cold-weld" pieces together into larger models. ABS is not porous, so its surface should be primed by cleaning with soap and water followed by a light sanding with 120-grit sandpaper or higher. A prime coat of latex, acrylic paint, or gesso will provide a surface for further detail painting.

Figure 1.24. Plastic products, including bottle caps, packaging materials, dollhouse, architectural, engineering, and model railroad elements

Polyurethane (PUR) is a thermoset plastic, which means it can be softened with heat only once and permanently sets into a solid form after it cools. PUR is available in flexible and ridged foams used for insulation, sound dampening, and fine carving. High-density PURs are used by modelmakers, artists, and product designers to create intricately detailed sculptures using modeling tools, rasps, rotary tools, and CNC routers. Finishing is completed with files and sandpaper.

Transparency and translucency are often essential elements in modelmaking, particularly for window treatments and scrim effects. Transparent sheets for laser and inkjet printers are made of acetate or polyester and sold in office supply stores. Makers should consult their printer specifications before purchasing these sheets.

Acrylics refer to synthetic thermoplastic resins derived from acrylic acid and used to manufacture a variety of materials, including plastics, coatings, adhesives, and paints. Acrylics offer a number of desirable properties, including strength, durability, toughness, abrasion resistance, and resilience. Acrylic sheets are favored in theatrical modelmaking as they are easy to cut, shape, and mold, and they exhibit a desirable transparency and durability. They can be painted, glued, and combined with other materials to simulate glass, ice, and water effects (ponds, rivers, or lakes), and can be used to build model display cases.

Clay

Clay is probably the first material humans used to model objects. Clays are made of fine-grained soil and minerals that become pliable when wet and harden when dry. Early humans learned how to fire clays into ceramics to make durable pottery and statuary. Modeling clays are still used as a quick and expressive means of creating mass and form in architectural study models, but their weight often limits their use in scenographic models, except when used for casting objects.

Paper clay is a mixture of clay and paper cellulose fibers. The fibers function as a filler and help bind the clay, making it lighter in weight while maintaining strength. Like ceramics, some paper clays require heat to harden while others solidify when exposed to air for approximately 24 hours. The drying time is dependent on room temperature, humidity, and the size of the molded object. Some air-dried clays harden enough to be sanded, whereas others remain pliable. Paper clays may shrink from 5 percent to 15 percent while drying and form cracks that will need to be filled with the same material. Other paper clays increase their fiber content to reduce shrinking while drying. Air-dried paper clay is similar to the papier-mâché products mentioned above but has a finer texture, allowing greater detail. Paper clays come in a variety of colors, but the dyes used to color the clays will run when wet, so it is best to purchase white clays. Paper clay is usually porous and accepts many adhesives and paints.

Polymer clays refer to synthetic modeling materials composed of polyvinyl chloride (PVC) resin, pigment, plasticizers, and fillers. Polymer clay is used in crafting jewelry, pottery, sculpture, and modelmaking. It is malleable and cured by heating it in a toaster or kitchen oven. Oven temperatures vary, so a baking thermometer should be used for accuracy. The curing temperature and time is different for each brand of clay, so product instructions must be followed. Some brands of polymer clay will shrink slightly in the firing process. Polymer clay can be sanded and polished after firing but often requires special adhesives and paints.

Fabric

Fabrics can be problematic in scenographic modeling. The size of the threads, weave, weight, and pattern are difficult to replicate realistically in scale so the use of most common fabrics for bedding, table linen, or drapery will create an inappropriate dollhouse-like impression. There are exceptions like the open weave of cheesecloth or plastic produce bag netting that can simulate burlap, erosion cloth, and fishnets, or sheer gauzes that can mimic voile curtains and scrims (see figure 1.25). Finely woven fabrics can suggest drapery, but their light weight will not allow them to hang and drape realistically. Fabrics can be coated with fabric stiffener made with PVA or by thinning PVA glues to soften the fabric; this adds weight and allows the fabric to be draped as it dries. Alternative materials and techniques to simulate fabric are covered in chapter 2, "The Scenographic Modeling Process."

Figure 1.25. Draped burlap, fruit netting, and cheesecloth stiffened with PVA and shaped while drying

2. The Scenographic Modeling Process

Scenographers rarely envision an idea whole and complete within their mind's eye. Every artistic endeavor is a multistep process involving research, analysis, incubation, inspiration, experimentation, assessment, and reassessment. The scenographic process varies from designer to designer, but there are common phases inherent in all creative activities, and the making of a scenographic model does, out of necessity, progress through similar stages of development. But scenographic modelmaking is not a strict linear progression with a definite beginning and ending for each stage. Scenographers continually revise, revisit, and reevaluate their designs, occasionally skipping or leaping over some steps entirely.[1]

The early design phase typically involves conceptualizing through sketching or experimental modeling. Once a formative design direction is identified, it is developed, discussed, tested, revised, and refined through study models. Study models help advance and improve the design, leading to an expanded and detailed working model. The working model is shared with the production team for discussions on blocking and staging, budgeting and construction, costume and scenery interaction, properties and set dressings, lighting, and sound issues. When complete, the working model is used to familiarize the actors with their scenic environment and serves as the benchmark for the construction staff in building the actual set. A working model in conjunction with a perspective rendering, paint elevations, and properties drawings provides the production staff with all the practical and aesthetic aspects of construction, texture, color, properties, and set dressing. But a scenographer may choose to paint and fully accessorize the working model into a finished presentation model to execute the design. Once the design is completed on stage, working or presentation models may take on a final role as an exhibition model in the theater lobby, art gallery, museum exhibition, or personal collection.

Model Stages

Constructing a model stage (also called a model theater) or model box is often the first step in the design process, especially if the designer is working in a new and unfamiliar theater. Like a painting in its frame, the scenographic design is contextualized within a miniature three-dimensional architectural environment. Constructing these small stages helps the scenographer become familiar with stage subtleties, wing and fly space limitations, architectural idiosyncrasies, and audience dynamics. The model theater will elicit questions that might go unasked if the design is developed only from floor plans and elevations. Many times, these model stages reveal insights and solutions to best communicate each play's unique story. Additionally, the time spent constructing the model theater offers the scenographer a welcome "incubation" period to contemplate the final design.

The model stage has been used by scenographers for centuries and is still employed by resident designers who consistently work for the same theater. A model stage tends to be large, often built in 1/2" = 1'-0" scale and is employed primarily in the scenography studio. Model stages include the proscenium opening, usually with a removable archway, and are open on the back, sides, and top to allow the designer to easily arrange scenic units. The stage floor is frequently drawn with a scaled grid to assist the designer in accurately positioning set pieces (see figure 2.1).

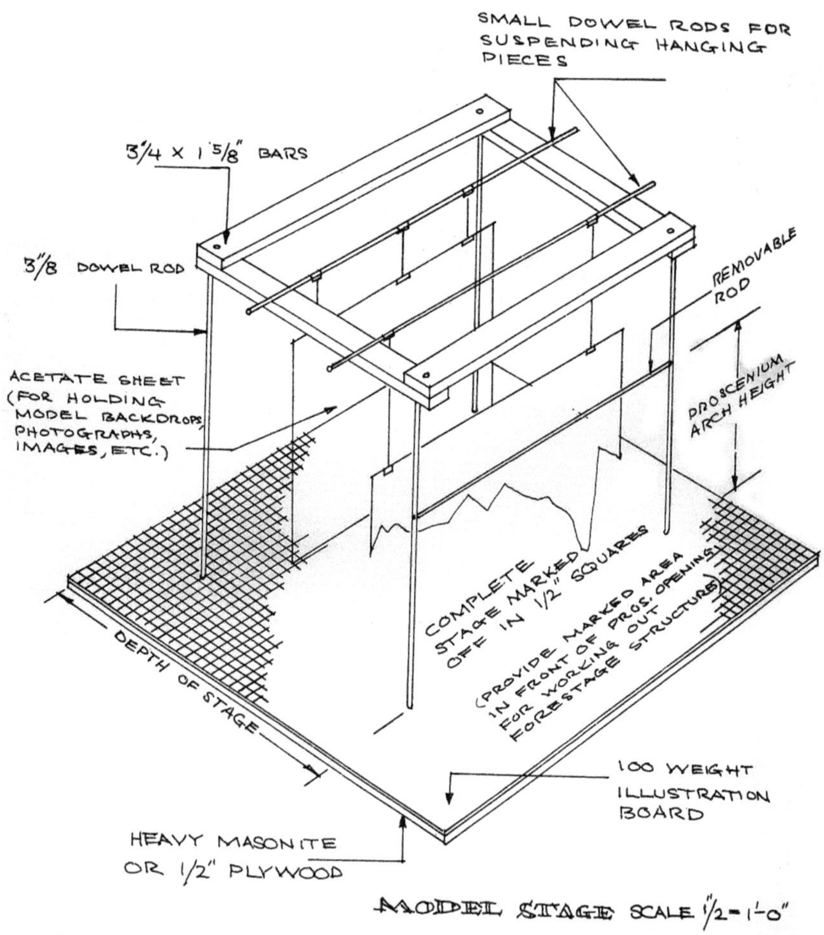

Figure 2.1. Diagram of model stage by Darwin Payne

The model stage can be a simple structure as shown above but may include trapdoors, turntables, masking, audience seating, rigging, architectural features, and miniature lighting systems.[2]

The model box is a more recent innovation evolving in response to the nomadic careers of contemporary scenographers who design for a variety of theaters located in distant cities, states, and countries (see figure 2.2). Usually made of foam and matboard, the model box must be lightweight and portable yet sturdy enough to protect the more delicate scenographic model.

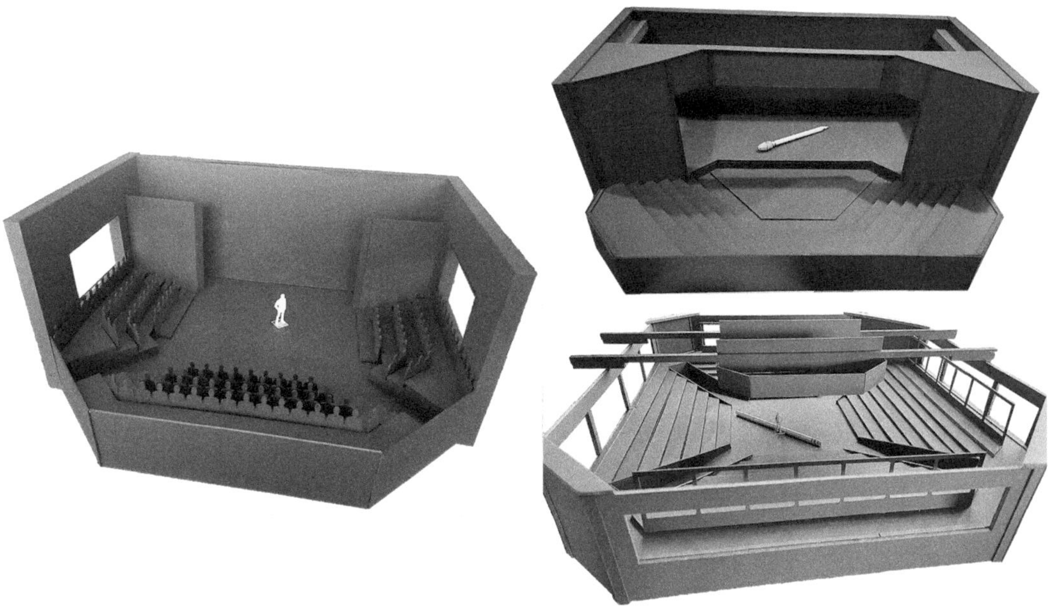

Figure 2.2. Model boxes for proscenium, thrust, and arena stages. *Courtesy of Lauren M. Nichols*

The model box, like the model stage, should be an accurate, scaled representation of the stage space, and it should include such architectural features that affect the design like the proscenium height, width, and depth; apron; stage; wings; and backstage spaces. The full fly tower, trap doors, freight doors, and orchestra pit may be necessary if these are integral to the design. In a proscenium model the first few rows of audience seating are often included to designate sightlines. In a thrust, arena, or alley format the seating risers and audience should be included as the spectators are often an essential element in these theaters (plus, it is always reassuring to the director to depict the theater with a full house). Model boxes are often constructed with panels that open on the sides to allow access to the scenographic model, and to position small lighting fixtures to simulate lighting effects.

Model boxes should be built in neutral tones using black or white materials so they do not draw attention away from the model itself. To simulate a darkened theater, it is widespread practice to build model boxes out of black foam board. Black materials help hide imperfections, dirt, and wear, and convey professional expertise. A black foam board model box can be sheathed in black matboard for greater strength and professionalism. A durable model box can be used for several shows if the designer works consistently with the same theater company, but many designers build a new model box for each design as these miniature stages are easily damaged during transportation. Designers may also need to build a special container or carrying box made of white foam board to transport and protect the model box (figure 2.3). The carrying box should be lightweight and sturdy, and it should include interior padding to hold the model box securely. If the model must be sent via a shipping company, it is helpful to construct the carrying box to fit within a standard-size shipping box. The modeler must also keep in mind the size limitations of cars, taxis, and rideshares when constructing these boxes. In one notable instance a designer and his assistant reportedly carried their large model over twenty New York City blocks to the scenic studio when it was discovered that their model would not fit into the newer streamlined taxi cabs.

Figure 2.3. Model box and carrying box. *Courtesy of Lauren M. Nichols*

Scenographers often begin to conceptualize their designs first through sketches or experimental modeling. Using models early in the design process allows the designer to explore abstract three-dimensional themes, masses, and spatial relationships in an experientially direct way to discover design possibilities by simply juxtaposing shapes and forms. Experimental modeling is, in effect, a form of creative play, but with the serious purpose of achieving a finished design.[3] Experimental modeling helps spark the design via accidental and unplanned compositions that may fortuitously lead to practical solutions. As experimental modeling is such a rich and multifaceted subject it will be explored more fully in chapter 4, "Experimental Modelmaking."

Study Models

Once a formative design is glimpsed through sketching and experimental modeling, the scenographer moves into a second, more methodical phase of the design. *Study models* help designers revise and refine initial design impressions into practical solutions. They are called study models because they are open to examination, discussion, adjustment, and improvement. Modelmakers use several types of study models often named for their construction materials and techniques. Study models are often called *rough models* because the scenographer "roughly" works out spatial relationships without concern for exact replication while also using "rough" unprepared or painted materials and objects. *Sketch models* are so named because they are quickly drawn on paper, then cut and assembled into simple models as if it were a "three-dimensional sketch." Sketch modeling is a quick and dirty process where models are revised, rebuilt, discarded, and begun again with little loss of time, effort, or expense, allowing the designer and director to quickly investigate relationships between scenic forms. Complete accuracy is not essential, but the scenographer should keep scenic units in correct proportion to one another and provide appropriately scaled human figures for reference. Sketch models are frequently built in 1/8" or 1/4" scale with advantages and disadvantages for each scale. Models in 1/8" scale save time, effort, and materials, and their small size prevents the designer from getting bogged down in details. However, some designers find 1/8" scale too small to accurately explore dimensional relationships, and directors may find it difficult to project themselves into such tiny environments. Sketch models in 1/4" scale can include crucial details and allow greater identification with the setting. As this is still a formative stage, the designer and director will play with multiple ideas and sketch models before determining the final direction. Frequently, entire ideas and models are thrown away.

If the scenographer has been concurrently drafting the design either by hand or in CAD as it progresses, it is quite simple to copy or print these plans onto white cardstock, then cut and assemble the units into what is variously called a *white model, card model*, or *white card model*. The printed floor plan can be transferred onto the model box floor using transfer paper. Transfer paper is a thin paper with one side coated with wax and graphite pigment. Black transfer paper has a dark pigment suited to transferring designs onto white or light-colored boards. White transfer paper is available for transferring designs onto dark surfaces. The waxy side is positioned on top of the surface where the image is to be transferred. The image to be transferred is then laid on top of the transfer paper and traced with a pencil or stylus so the pigment is impressed onto the bottom paper. The image being transferred should be taped or pinned down to the surface, so it does not shift during the transfer process.

A *white model* can refer to any model constructed out of white or off-white materials, including study, thumbnail, paste-up, card, and working models.

The design may also be transferred by laying out the floor plan on the model box floor and making pinpricks at each intersecting corner. Connecting lines can then be drawn between each point (see figure 2.4). A printed floor plan can also be adhered directly to the floor of the model box using spray adhesive or double-sided adhesive paper.

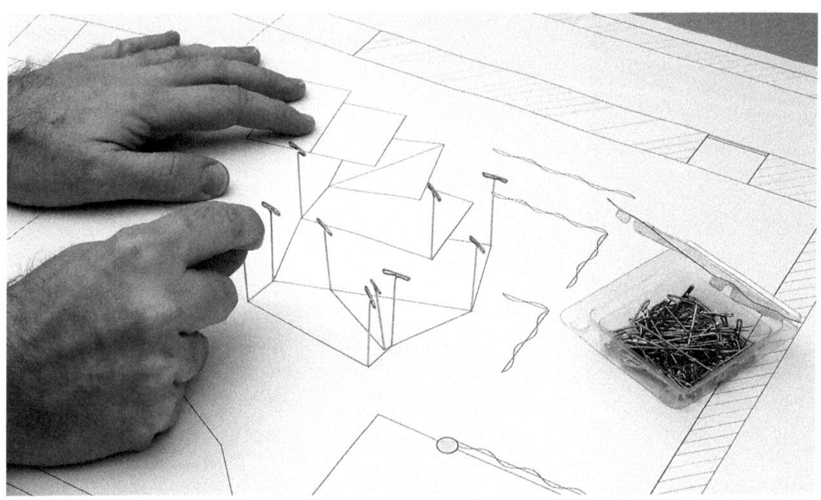

Figure 2.4. Transfer using pins in corners

Scenic elevations can be transferred or printed onto cardstock and then folded to create shapes and forms. Cardstock is a flexible material, but when folded it gains rigidity along the line of the fold. Drawing tabs on the tops, bottoms, and sides of the walls and folding these back will create surprisingly rigid theatrical flat-like structures. The bottom tabs are glued to the model floor using tape or pins to hold while the glue dries. Side tabs help to join walls and other units. Lightly scoring the fold line on the side opposite of the direction of the fold with a craft knife will create a clean sharp crease. If the knife accidentally cuts through the cardstock, the seam can be repaired with a strip of tape on the backside of the paper.

A *paste-up model* is created by "pasting" thin paper plans and elevations to sturdy illustration bord or foam board that is then cut out and assembled into a model (see figure 2.5).

Figure 2.5. *Guys & Dolls* by Abe Burrows and Jo Swerling. 1/4" paste-up model by Kent Homchick, Rocky Mountain Repertory Theater, 2011

Thumbnail model is a fluid term used to describe any small model typically built in 1/8" or 1/4" scales. Like the small thumbnail sketch, these models can be rapidly produced to explore design ideas while not requiring much time, labor, materials, or money. A thumbnail model may refer to a small study, rough, white card, working, or even a fully colored and accessorized presentation model (see figure 2.6).

A design with complete elevations can be quickly printed, cut, and assembled into a thumbnail model for the director to use as a guide in rehearsals. Fully colored plans can be assembled in the same way to make a thumbnail presentation model. If a design involves multiple settings, thumbnail models are an efficient and informative means to show each scene. Consecutive photographs of thumbnail models can be assembled into a storyboard to illustrate the scenic progression.

Figure 2.6. *Disney's Beauty and the Beast* by Alan Menken and Howard Ashman. 1/8" thumbnail models by Czerton Lim, Syracuse Stage 2019

Working Models

Once the study model has helped clarify the design idea for the designer and director, it can be further refined with greater information, detail, and accuracy into a *working model*. The working model should show all exits and entrances, door swing direction, masking, individual scenic units, how and where units move during scene shifts, wall treatments, furniture, and decoration. Anything with significant dimensions that affects blocking, lighting, and costumes, including walls, doorways, windows, shelves, cabinets, moldings, stairs, ramps, railings, balustrades, furniture, and hanging light fixtures, should be fully dimensional. Confusion regarding any of these units can create expensive delays in budget, construction, installation, and rehearsals.

The working model is shared with the entire production team and serves as a major communication tool. The stage manager, production manager, and technical director use it to address issues concerning exits, blocking, building material choice, and budgeting. Costume, lighting, and sound designers will examine matters such as door width and height, masking, and microphone and speaker placement. Two- or three-dimensional character figures should be included to provide human scale reference and to allow the director to consider staging options.

Placed within the model stage or box, the working model can be viewed from multiple angles and perspectives, allowing for the consideration of extreme audience sightlines from sides of the house and any balconies. When sent to the scenic studio, the working model facilitates the technical director and carpentry staff in determining construction requirements of individual units, and how components need to be assembled, joined, transported, shifted, and stored during performance. Due to the immense amount of physical and sequential information it conveys, a working model can be considered a "four-dimensional blueprint."

A working model may be assembled and glued into one piece, but if there are scene changes, it is helpful to keep units free so scene shifts can be demonstrated to the director, cast, and crew. If the scenographer intends to paint this model to use as paint elevations, then each unit should be made to come apart to facilitate texturing and painting.

The modelmaker should use sturdy materials when constructing the working model and building in a large scale to allow it to support heavy textures and dimensional elements and to protect it during transportation. Any non-white materials included in the model are usually painted white with gesso or sprayed with a flat white aerosol primer paint to unify all scenic elements, so no individual piece pulls focus. This model may be called a working white model. Low relief items such as brickwork, paneling, molding, rugs, and flooring may still be represented in two dimensions. Drapery, framed paintings, lighting fixtures, and other wall hangings may also be drawn or attached as cut-out appliques (see figure 2.7). When printing or reproducing any ornamental accessories like paintings or patterned rugs it is helpful to render these in lighter grayscale tones so that bold black outlines and shading do not draw undue focus. Designers may also add shading to two-dimensional elements to give a sense of three-dimensionality.

Designers may build fully dimensional model components to create greater verisimilitude. This can be highly effective especially if the scenographer intends to light the model. Textured surfaces can be created using gesso, modeling paste, and spackling compound to add a sense of weight and dimension to walls, brick, stonework, folds in drapery, and upholstery (see figure 2.8). There are commercially available scaled dimensional scenic elements and materials for the modelmaker to show brick, stonework, and other textures that are described more fully later in this chapter.

Grayscale or Tonal Models

Occasionally a scenographer may consider a white model too bright, pristine, or stark to represent a particular scenic environment. They may feel a specific color of paper will better convey the design idea and mood. In this case, they

Figure 2.7. *The Imaginary Invalid* by Molière. 1/4" Model by Richard Finkelstein. Example of working white model with two-dimensional details

Figure 2.8. Example of a white model construction using layered board to create dimensional molding details

may choose to use off-white, beige, gray, or neutral-colored materials to construct their "white" model. Another option scenographers may choose is to create what are called *grayscale* or *tonal models* (see figure 2.10). These models are like value study drawings used to explore shadow and depth by sketching and painting in shades of gray ranging from black to white. A tonal value chart is included in figure 2.9. Using yet another technique, the atmosphere can be explored by pasting various neutral-colored papers over the white model surfaces to create a gray model. These intermediary steps are like the painter's process of creating a grisaille sketch as a value study before adding color. While white models use cartooned lines to indicate changes in surface plane, textures, and individual items on the white surface, grayscale models add various levels of shading to suggest greater depth, mass, and dimension, and to simulate light and shadow. A gray model provides a greater sense of mood and atmosphere than a white model and is easier to see and comprehend than a white model when it is shown in photographs or when viewing it on a computer monitor. A lightly shaded model is conducive to capturing a comedic tonality, whereas a darker more somber shading is appropriate for

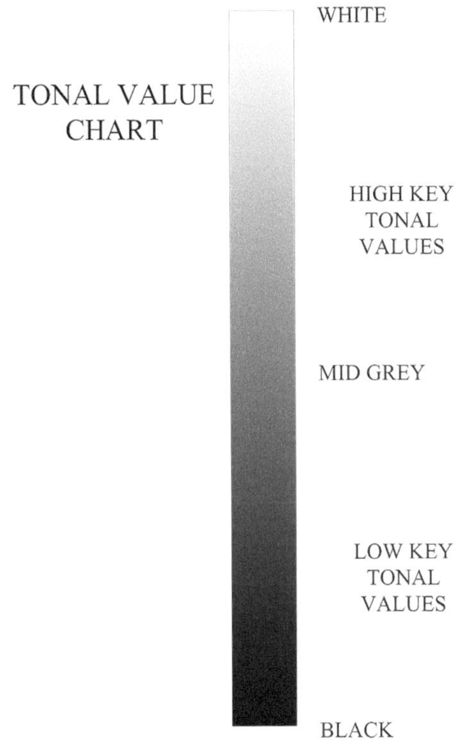

Figure 2.9. Tonal value chart

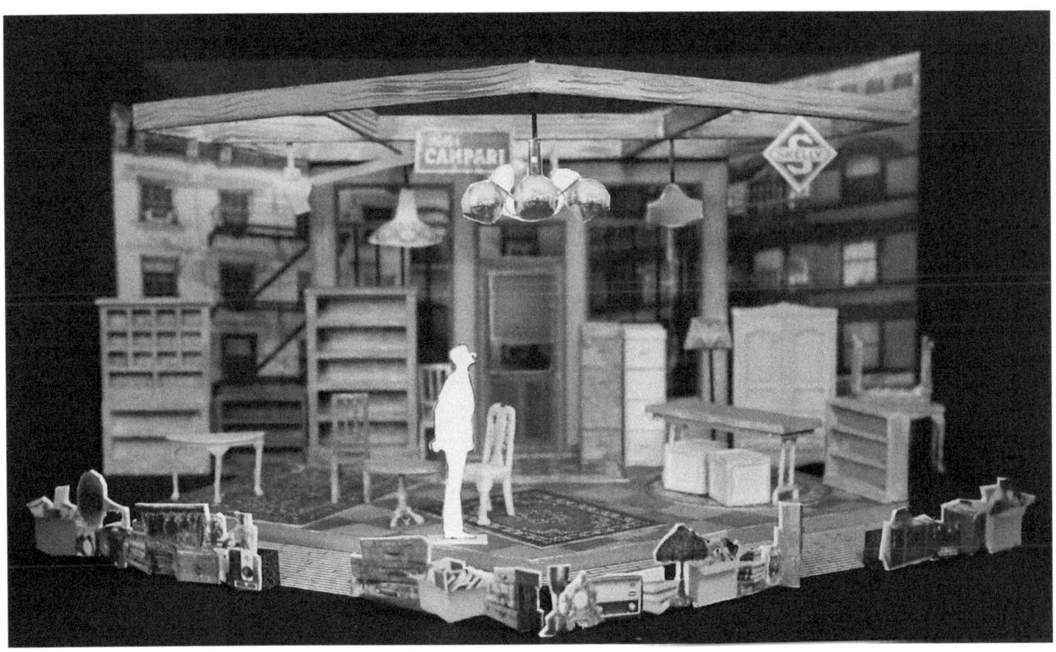

Figure 2.10. *American Buffalo* by David Mamet. 1/2" Grayscale project model by Andrew Robinson. Rowan University 2022

more serious plays. The gray model can also function as an intermediate step before committing the design to color in a presentation model. One problem that can arise when showing a gray model is that a director might fall in love with the idea of a monochromatic setting much as someone might prefer a captivating black-and-white photograph.

Presentation Models

The *presentation model* represents the final phase of modelmaking and provides the production team with the aesthetic features of texture, color, properties, and set dressing. A presentation model should not be started until the designer and director have agreed on all parts of the working model. A fully realized presentation model too early in the design process can stifle the creative impulse and limit options for the director and production team.

As noted above, the scenographer may choose to do a painted rendering and paint elevations rather than build a presentation model, as this maquette adds considerable time and expense while contributing little more practical information than that given by the working model. Some designers will take a shortcut by photographing their white working model and uploading this image into image-editing software to render it with color, texture, and light rather than drawing and painting a perspective rendering. But a fully textured, painted, and accessorized presentation model is frequently the most effective means to realize a design, particularly if the design is sculptural or organic in nature. On occasion, the producing organization can be convinced to pay for the added expense of materials and labor to build a presentation model, especially if it can be used for promotional purposes.

The potential danger of this final phase of modelmaking is the temptation to continue accessorizing the model with gratuitous and distracting details. It is not necessary to craft every leaf on a model tree or bush. Likewise, it is not productive to fill every shelf with detailed knickknacks and books when simple shapes can provide a sense of decoration. The scenographer should remember that the model is not "an end in itself" but serves as a roadmap to the finished setting on stage. When a scenographic model is overaccessorized, viewers become distracted from its purpose, no longer seeing it as a representation of the scenery to come. Instead, they become enthralled with the minute details, admiring the model as they would a diorama or dollhouse.

The presentation model can be an effective means of storytelling, especially if the designer selects a specific moment in the play and "stages" the figures in a dramatic configuration. A good presentation model creates enthusiasm among the director and performers, artisans, crew, as well as potential investors at an "angels party."

If the presentation model is intended to be used for the painter elevations, it should be constructed to come apart easily. Because scenic units are often scattered about the scenic studio, the model may need to be disassembled so various parts can be used in separate locations at the same time. The modelmakers themselves should plan how to break down the model into separate components rather than having the carpenters and scenic artists attempt to dismantle it. Presentation models are also fully accessorized with furniture and figures, so it may be necessary to glue these pieces to their units to prevent them from being lost during transportation between studios and rehearsal spaces. Before the model leaves the scenographer's studio it should be lit appropriately to enhance dimension and atmosphere and photographed from multiple angles as a record of the design. These photographs can be digitally edited to add lighting specials and highlights (see figures 2.11 and 2.12 for an example of image editing). The section on Texturing and Painting the Scenographic Model, later in this chapter discusses additional techniques and materials for the presentation model.

Exhibition Models

In specific cases, models may find a life beyond their intended purpose by being included as an *exhibition model* in a lobby display, art gallery, or museum, or photographed for catalogs, design magazines, and books. This is when the scenographic model comes into its own, ceasing to be a component of the production process to stand alone as its own autonomous work of art. The designer will need to work with the exhibiting organization on shipping the model to and from the exhibit venue, and the carrying box may need to be rethought and installed in a shipping crate. Everything in the model should be firmly secured inside the model box. As the model box will be a prominent frame for the scenographic model, it must be finished to a professional standard. In this case a foam board model box might be clad in matboard (typically black) for greater durability and attractiveness. Foam board model boxes dent easily, and the surface may not be uniformly black if it is made from whatever board is available in the model studio stock. The black matboard cladding adds a more durable surface and cleaner edges. The model box should also have a protective layer of paperboard or felt adhered to the bottom to prevent it from scratching the surfaces of tables or pedestals. The designer will often not be present to set up the model, so reference photographs should be included to assist in any reassembly and lighting of the model, or in case anything needs to be repaired. Additional insurance is advised to compensate for materials and labor to fix any damage during shipping. Exhibits often require an entry fee to be included in the exhibition,

Figure 2.11. *The Threepenny Opera* by Bertolt Brecht. 1/2" Presentation model by Darwin Payne. Wake Forest University, 1991

Figure 2.12. *The Threepenny Opera* by Bertolt Brecht. Computer Rendering by Darwin Payne. Wake Forest University, 1991. Example of model enhanced with additional lighting and scenery using image-editing software

and there may be additional fees if the scenographer wants to include photographs in the exhibition catalog or website.

LED Exhibit Lighting

Decorative LEDs (light-emitting diodes) are ideal for lighting stage models. An LED is a tiny semiconductor chip that emits light when an electric current is passed through it. LEDs are small and environmentally friendly due to their energy efficiency, long lifespan, and use of fewer and less hazardous materials. LEDs produce less infrared radiation than traditional incandescent lights, thus reducing heat output, which is crucial when lighting small models. LEDs also produce minimal ultraviolet radiation, reducing the risk of damaging sensitive materials and colors or causing them to fade. LED bulbs can be purchased individually or grouped within the same housing and are available in both battery-powered and plug-in options. LEDs project light in various distribution patterns (spotlight, floodlight, wash, globe, etc.), enabling the modelmaker to focus the attention of the viewer on specific areas of the model.

LEDs produce colors in two ways. Filter-based color generation involves applying a transparent filter or coating on the LED to modify the light emitted by the semiconductor material. It is commonly used in applications where specific colors are desired, such as decorative lighting for holidays or indicator lights. With this LED, the filter color is visible when the LED is turned off. LEDs that produce cool or warm white light can be modified using theatrical filters to color and diffuse the light. Emissive color generation relies on the intrinsic properties of the LED's semiconductor material to generate light of a specific color wavelength. In this process, the LED itself generates the desired color, with no need for external filters or coatings. These LEDs are white or clear when turned off, but colored when switched on. Emissive color LEDs in the primary colors of light (red, green, blue) enable the designer to have more sophisticated control when color mixing.

Mixing LED colors requires dimming control circuitry, which varies in complexity depending on the specific lighting product. LED lighting systems are controlled through wire, radio frequency, infrared sensors, Bluetooth, and Wi-Fi to adjust intensity and color, which can create the sense of movement in the lighting. LED lights can be dimmed smoothly, without color shifts, allowing for seamless changes during a presentation. This flexibility allows lighting to set a specific mood and create dramatic effects that enhance the visual appeal of a model and design.

LEDs are also used to light practical fixtures within a model, including floor and table lamps, sconces and chandeliers, streetlights, and electric signage. The physical size and design of the LED lights should match the scale and style of the light fixtures. There are many LED lighting packages offered by dollhouse and railroad hobby companies, or the modeler can source the materials needed to build their own systems.

As mentioned, most LEDs produce minimal amounts of ultraviolet radiation. However, there are LEDs specifically designed to produce UV light (black light) that are useful when building a model for a show that incorporates fluorescent or phosphorescent paints. Fluorescent paints contain special pigments that absorb UV light and re-emit it as visible light in vibrant colors. Phosphorescent paint, also known as glow-in-the-dark paint, contains pigments that absorb light (including UV light) that is slowly released as visible light over a period of time.

When choosing to use LEDs in a stage model, it is helpful to consider the sources of the light (sun, moon, lightning, windows, skylights, practical fixtures, etc.) that help create the appropriate mood and ambience for the design. A quick "light plot" can be sketched out showing the light placement to illuminate various parts of the model. It is helpful to consider the lighting as an integral part of the model construction by designing openings and channels to hide the wiring and lights. Tape and glue dots are helpful in securing LEDs and wiring in place.

Model Storage

Models are often the worse for wear after shuttling back and forth from design studio to rehearsal studio to scene studio. Of the fortunate ones that survive intact, only a select few can be kept by the scenographer due to the limitations of storage space. An extraordinarily designed and crafted model may be appreciated for its own merit and preserved in a private collection or donated to a library or museum. Bits and pieces of a model are often saved and reused in future models, particularly when these pieces take time and effort to build and can be reused in other designs. Some models can be flattened into renderings and shadow boxes. These "portmanteau models" can then be hung on a wall like a three-dimensional rendering requiring less space.

Models are often given to directors, producers, or other production team members. Models might also be given to teachers or students as examples of professional model construction and design. If the model is built of nonarchival materials, it will slowly decay on its own before finding its way to the landfill. This makes it all the more important for the designer to digitally document the conceptual, working, and presentation models at each stage of the design process. Otherwise, the legacy of the individual designer and the history of scenographic modeling will be lost.

Bauprobe

An interesting scenographic model that should also be discussed is the bauprobe, which means "work study" in German. The bauprobe functions as a full-scale mock-up of the set design on the stage or in a large rehearsal studio. Using stock flats, platforms, and furniture, the production team arranges these units to simulate the stage setting. Robert Wilson and Robert Brustein introduced the bauprobe to the United States with their American Repertory Theater production of Ibsen's *When We Dead Awaken*. John Conklin, the associate designer for Wilson's production, continued using bauprobe sessions at the Glimmerglass Opera, calling them "set looks." A bauprobe allows the director, designers, and actors to visualize the set in the actual space, make adjustments, discuss props, and play with lighting and cueing prior to the start of rehearsals. The bauprobe is, in effect, a full-scale model used to experiment with staging a production before committing to a final design.

Kit Bashing and Scratch Modeling

The scenographic modelmaker may run into two other terms used in other modelmaking venues. *Kit bashing or bash modeling* describes the process of mixing parts from various commercial model kits to create an innovative design (see figure 2.13). This process was popularized when production designers for science fiction films began combining parts from various airplane and ship models to create new spaceship and architectural designs. Kit bashing is now used for all types of modelmaking. The opposite of a kit bash model is a *scratch built model*, where a model is built completely by hand or "from scratch," not using pieces from a premade kit. Scenographic modeling tends to be a combination of both processes as the modelmaker creates parts of the design by hand but enhances and accessorizes it with pieces from various other model sources.

White Card Model Exercise

The following card model exercise is provided to help the novice modelmaker learn card model techniques (figure 2.14). This drawing can be downloaded as a PDF file in 1/8" or 1/4" scale from https://www.thescenographicmodel.com website. Once the model is printed, each piece can be cut out, and lines can be lightly scored on the side opposite to the direction of the fold. Note that the windows may be too small to cut out individually in 1/8" scale and should be left solid. One option is to cut the entire window out and on the back side attach a window printed on transparency film.

Figure 2.13. *God of Carnage* by Yasmina Reza. 1/4" kit bash model by David Court. University Players, School of Dramatic Art. University of Windsor, 2019

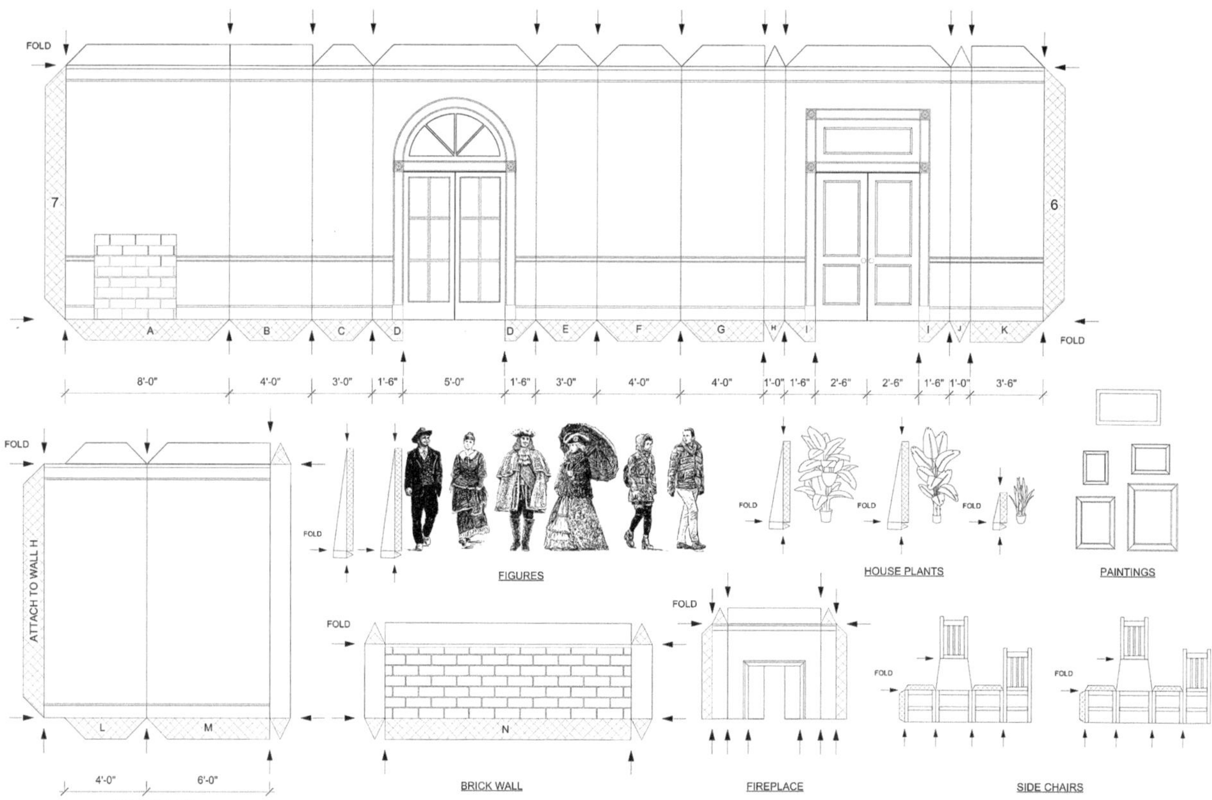

Figure 2.14. Card model exercise. Rendered by Gennie Neuman Lambert and Brad M. Carlson. *Printable version available at www.thescenographicmodel.com*

Using a tacky PVA glue, attach each lettered tab to the letter on the floor plan. Furniture, drapery, and wall hangings have been provided for the maker to explore different furniture arrangements and wall compositions. In this way the maker will see how each new arrangement tells a different story. The figures can also be cut out and placed about the room to illustrate how changes in position create new relationships and narratives. Before printing, the maker might wish to experiment by drawing or using image-editing software to add wallpaper, molding, and paneling on the walls as well as flooring and rugs on the floor plan. If printed in black and white, the walls, floor, and furnishings can be colored using dry media-like colored pencils and markers.

The assembled model can also be photographed, and the image transferred to watercolor paper or imported into image-editing software where the scenographer can add color, texture, and lighting effects to generate a perspective rendering (see figure 2.15). The model can be further enlarged to 3/8" or 1/2" scale if the cardstock is reinforced by pasting it to illustration board or foam board.

Figure 2.15. Assembled card model in 1/8" and 1/4" scales with sketch created by tracing a printed photograph of the model

Cutting Techniques

Model components discussed in this section could efficiently be created using a laser cutter or 3D printer. But as not all modelmakers have access to these technologies, each example in this section will be described in more traditional modelmaking techniques. Of course, for any technique and material shown here, countless variations can be found in books, online craft blogs, and video tutorials. Modelmakers should continuously explore sources outside this book to expand their knowledge of methods and materials.

Basic Cutting Tips

1. Place a self-healing cutting mat under the material to be cut to protect the table surface underneath. Some mats feature measurements and grid markings helpful to the modelmaker. If no cutting mat is available, a piece of illustration or matboard can be substituted. These boards will need to be replaced periodically.
2. Use a steel-edge ruler to guide the blade. Drafting tools like a T square or triangle with plastic edges will dull the blade and damage the tools.
3. When cutting flat materials, multiple passes with a sharp blade are preferred. A light first pass allows greater control over the knife, scores the material, and creates a track for later deeper cuts.
4. When cutting balsa or basswood, the blade must be securely held against the straight edge to prevent the blade from following the woodgrain.
5. Change blades often. While new blades are sharp and potentially dangerous, a dull one can be equally hazardous.
6. Hold the blade perpendicular to the material being cut. For initial scoring cuts, keep the blade handle as close to vertical as possible. As the blade cuts deeper, a shallower angle may be used.

Cutting Materials

In general, when cutting materials, modelers should use a sharp craft knife rather than scissors as the shearing action of scissor blades will curl thinner papers and compress the cut edges of thicker materials. Sharp craft scissors are useful for making small, short cuts in paper and thinner paperboards, but for longer cuts, a craft knife and steel-edged ruler will cut straighter lines.

When cutting thicker materials, the modelmaker should consider the connection method to be used when joining pieces. Joining methods used for woodworking are often applicable in modelmaking. A butt joint is the simplest joint that works for most model applications (figure 2.16). Butt joints usually involve materials joined together at 90° to each other, but greater or lesser angles may also be used.

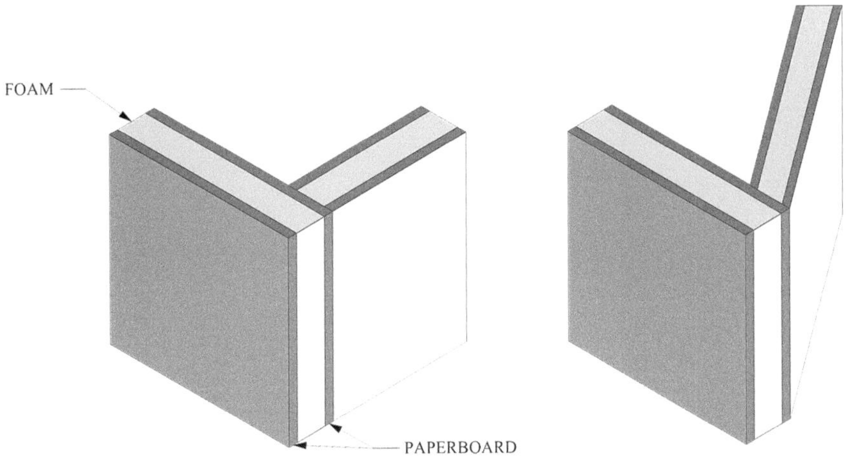

Figure 2.16. 90° and 45° butt joints

When working with materials like foam board, Gatorfoam®, or corrugated cardboard, the modelmaker may wish to hide or cover the interior of the material. Miter and rabbet joints hide the inner structure, creating clean joints. A miter joint forms a corner by cutting the materials to be joined at bevels of equal angles (figure 2.17). Most miter joint angles are cut at 45° to form 90° corners, but the bevel angles can be adjusted to create corners of various degrees.

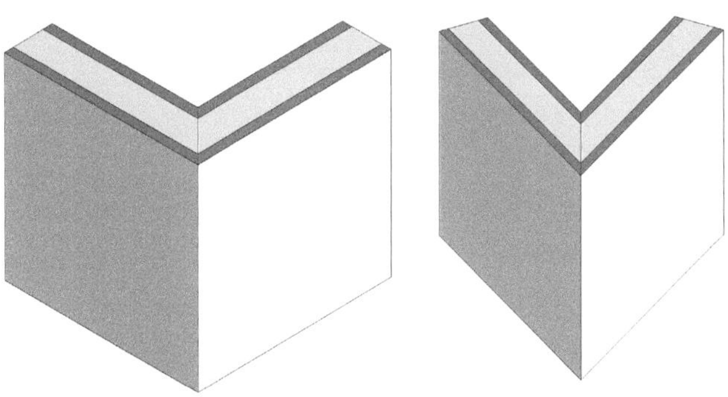

Figure 2.17. 90° and 45° miter joints

A rabbet is a notch or dado cut into the edge of a board (figure 2.18). When cutting a rabbet in a piece of foam board, measure and mark a line the thickness of the material along its back edge. Holding the knife perpendicular to the surface, score through the top layer of paper and into the foam board, being careful not to cut through the layer of paper on the front face. Next, cut between the front paper face and the foam removing this material to reveal the rabbet. A second piece of the same foam board will fit within this notch and hide the interior foam. Foam board rabbet cutters simplify the measuring and cutting process (see figure 1.6. in chapter 1, "Model Preparation").

Circular cuts can be made freehand or by using blade attachments on a compass (figure 2.19). When making a freehand cut, a clear circular line

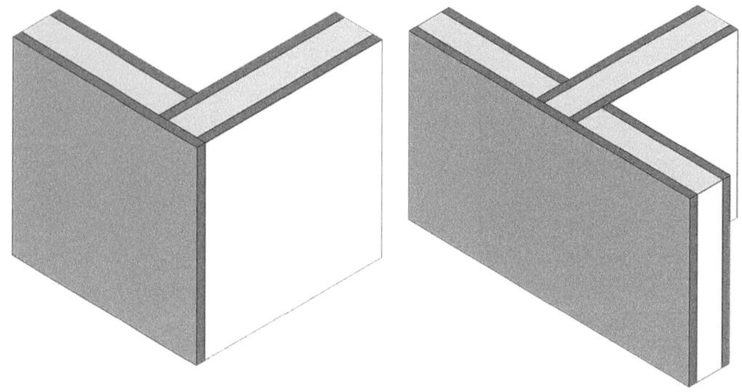

Figure 2.18. Rabbet joint at corner and rabbet (dado) joint in center

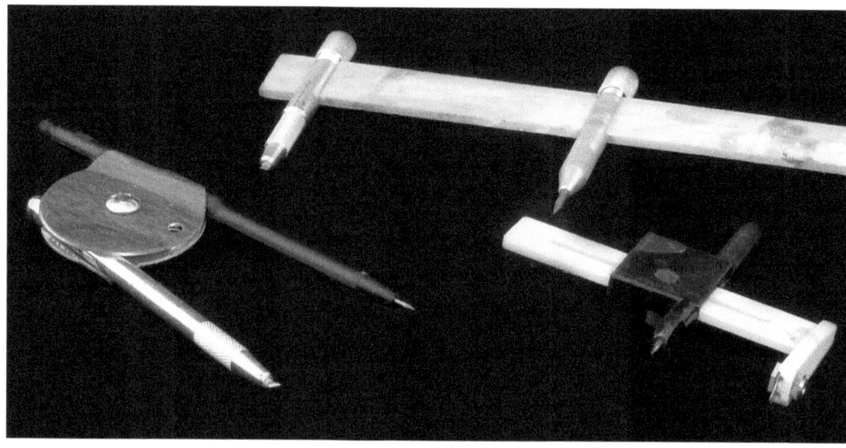

Figure 2.19. Compass with cutting attachment and beam compass cutters

should be drawn, and the blade should be held as close to 90° as possible, using only the tip or point of the blade to cut the material. The first cut should be a controlled light scoring on the surface of the board. Using this initial cut as a track, gradually cut through the material. Depending on the size of the circle, it may be easier to revolve the hand holding the material, so the cutting hand and blade point stay in the same position. Complex organic cuts can also be made using a similar freehand technique.

Flooring

To simulate planking, parquet, tile, and brickwork, it is cleaner to cut the desired pattern into illustration board rather than cutting each individual piece and gluing them to a backing board. The lines can be incised by scoring a channel with two parallel cuts or by cutting the edges in a V-shaped groove meeting in the center. The slice of material between the lines is then removed and the groove sanded clean with the edge of fine sandpaper (figure 2.20). Generally, these cuts should go no deeper than halfway through the material.

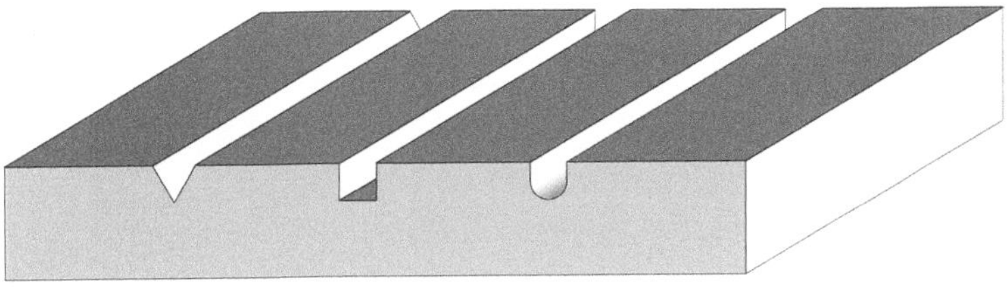

Figure 2.20. Channel and groove cuts

Platforms

Depending on scale, short platforms from 6" to 12" high can be made using different thicknesses of illustration, foam board, or thick sheets of balsa. Tall platform structures are built like a box using thicker illustration board for the top and thinner illustration board for the side facings (figure 2.21). When calculating height, it is necessary to subtract the thickness of the board that forms the platform lid to ensure the platform is the correct height. It is advisable to leave the upstage side of platforms open to allow access to the interior in case extra support or additional gluing is required.

When constructing curvilinear or unusually shaped platforms, the footprint can be traced and cut twice out of illustration board to make the top and bottom. Cardstock or a thin flexible board can be glued to the edges for the platform facing. Temporary holding pins, tape, or clamps will help secure curved materials until the glue sets.

Large platforms may need braces of balsa, basswood, or strips of illustration board to prevent warping, especially if the unit is to be textured and painted.

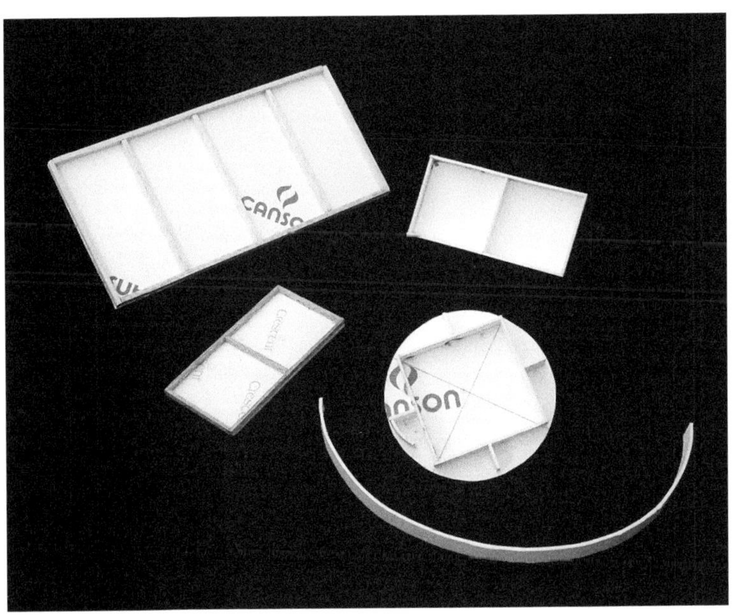

Figure 2.21. Platforming

Platforms with exposed legs and support structures often appear onstage. In this instance the modelmaker can replicate the platform construction methods in miniature by building the frame of balsa or basswood and covering the top with a balsa sheet or illustration board. The support legs and braces are attached with glue to mimic its full-size counterpart.

Walls

Small walls for 1/8" and 1/4" models can be cut from thinner illustration board, but like platforming, larger walls may need bracing to keep them from warping during texturing and painting. These walls can be assembled much like Hollywood flats, with rails and stiles cut from illustration board, balsa, or basswood for framing. This framing can be built around door and window openings to serve as reveals and provide the illusion of wall thickness (figure 2.22).

Figure 2.22. Framing walls for reinforcement

Curved Walls

Curved walls require framing supports at the top, the bottom, and possibly the center to retain their shape (figure 2.23). Illustration board, balsa, or basswood can be used for the framing, but it must be measured and cut to accommodate the thickness of the selected wall material. Flexible cardstock, paperboard, or single-faced containerboard can be used for untreated walls, but thicker materials are necessary if the wall is to be textured and painted.

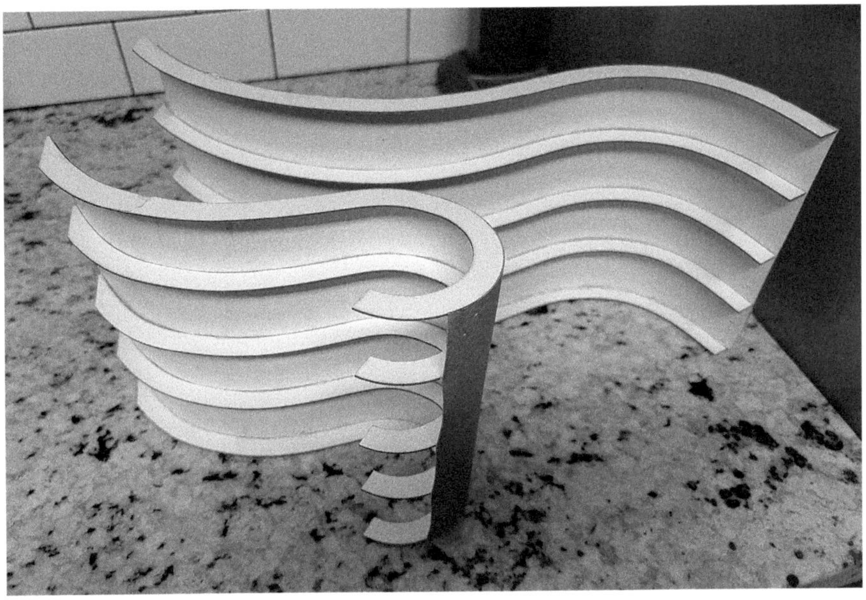

Figure 2.23. Concave and convex wall framing. *Courtesy of Lauren M. Nichols*

Lightweight illustration boards can be curved by dampening the convex side with a sponge and using clamps or weights to hold the board until dry. It may also be bent by gently running the concave side over the smooth edge of a table or other surface. Thicker illustration boards must be scored or grooved on the back side to bend them into the proper shapes. For concave walls, scoring the backside at regular intervals allows the board to flex. For convex walls, grooves must be cut at regular intervals to allow the board to fold back on itself. If either the scoring or grooves show on the front of the wall, they can be hidden by covering the front with cardstock or a thin paperboard.

Stairs

Model stairs are built in a similar fashion to their real-world counterparts, using either open or closed carriage construction (figure 2.24). The carriage (also called a stringer), treads, risers, newel post, balusters, and railings can be drawn on illustration board (see figure 2.25). A thinner board can be used for small scales and thicker board for larger scales. These components are then cut out and glued together to create the stair unit. A closed carriage staircase can be glued to a base to make it sturdier. Closed risers can be faced with cardstock, or illustration board can be cut to fit under each tread and between the carriages. Railings and balusters can be drawn and cut out as part of the stair carriage for greater strength or added to the staircase later. Newel posts, balusters, and railings can be constructed individually using dowel rods, tape, toothpicks, dressmaker pins, wire, and found objects like beads and jewelry (see figure 2.25).

Figure 2.24. 3D-printed, closed, open, and curved carriage constructed stairs

Figure 2.25. Railings and balusters made from beads, taped and cut from paperboard

Curved stairs are constructed using a similar process. Draw the stair tread pattern on two pieces of illustration board. One will be cut into individual treads while the other will be left whole to serve as a base for the staircase. For shallow curves, closed carriages can be inset in the staircase to help keep the treads and risers square. Glue the carriages to the base, and then glue the treads to the carriages. The side facings of cardstock or scored illustration board are placed against the staircase and traced. Once drawn and cut out, the facings are adhered to the treads and base. Temporary holding pins, tape, or clamps can stabilize the unit until the glue sets.

Spiral staircases pose a unique challenge for the modelmaker as they often have no carriage and are supported by the center post. Draw the floor plan of the stair treads on pieces of illustration board and cut out a complete set of treads. Draw the footprint on another board to serve as the base. For a strong connection, the inside edge of each tread can be cut to fit the shape of a center support, usually a wooden dowel or metal rod. A hole can be drilled in the tread if the center support has a small diameter. Mark the height of each stair tread on the support post and secure it to the base. Glue each tread to the center support, beginning at the bottom progressing to the top in a spiral pattern, matching the tread layout on the base. A piece of illustration board cut to the height of each stair can be taped to the outside edge of each tread to keep it properly aligned until the glue sets. For the handrail, a small hole can be drilled in the outer front corner of each tread to receive the balusters. The balusters can also be glued to the back edge of a tread and the front edge of the next higher tread. Pieces of piano wire or thin basswood can serve as balusters and 16- to 20-gauge floral wire can be bent into a spiral-shaped handrail and glued to the top of each baluster (see figure 2.26).

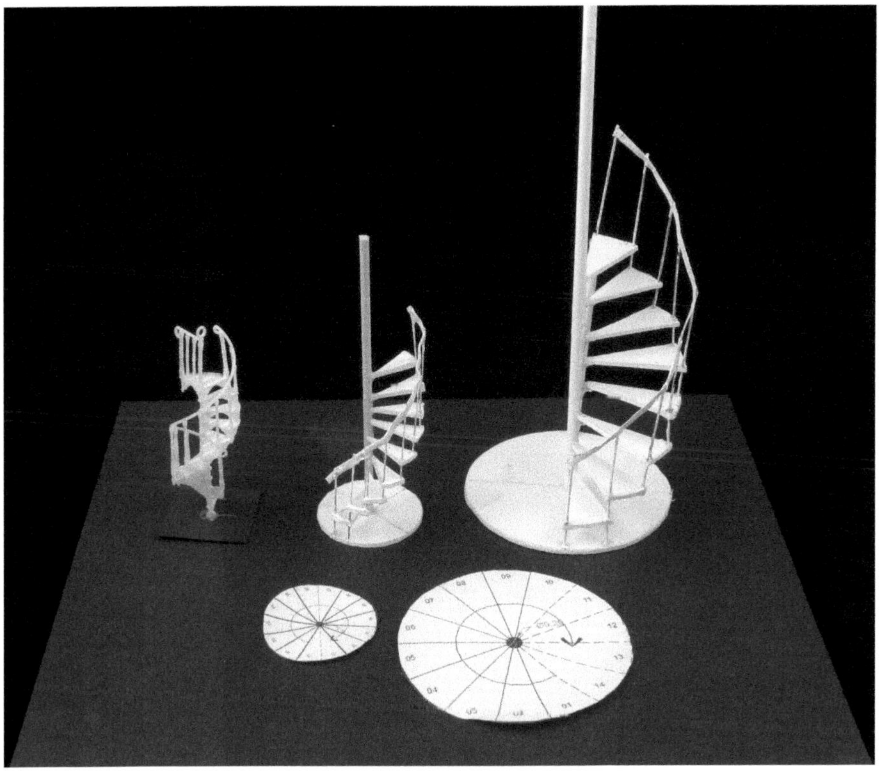

Figure 2.26. Spiral staircase, 3D printed, 1/4" scale, 1/2" scale

Windows and Doors

Paneling in walls, doors, and windows can be built up using several layers of cut-out papers and boards to build up a suggestion of molding and depth in the panels. Windows and doors with mullions or tracery are built up in a similarly layered fashion. An acetate sheet as the first layer will support the entire window. This piece should be cut slightly wider and taller than the opening so it can be attached to the back of the window opening. Window mullions can be printed directly on the acetate or on a second layer of cardstock or paperboard. Strips of balsa can be cut and glued to acetate or paperboard. Additional papers and boards can then be built up to correspond to the window molding.

> When cutting the door panels and window openings by hand, it is helpful to stick a pinhole in the corner to serve as a stopgap for the knife blade. Alternatively, a flat chisel blade can be used to punch through the two edges of each corner.

Moldings

Miniature moldings of the exact size, shape, and style are rarely available commercially for the modelmaker's purpose, requiring most moldings to be constructed. But scenographic moldings rarely need to be exact and are best suggested by layering pieces of paper, board, and balsa sticks. These moldings can be embellished with jewelry findings, holiday ornaments, decorative ribbon trim, and decorating supplies. Specific ornamentation can be molded and cast using materials and techniques discussed in chapter 5, "Emergent Technology."

Balusters, Railings, Spindles, and Posts

Decorative spindles and posts can be replicated simply by using a dowel, toothpick, or wire wrapped in layers of masking tape of varying lengths and widths. Cutting the tape in a triangular shape helps create a smooth transition into a bulb (see figure 2.27). Dowels can also be turned by inserting them in a small lathe or electric drill and shaped with files and sandpaper. Balusters and spindles can also be made by assembling decorative beads onto a wire or dressmaker pin. Cast-iron railings, grills and spindles can be suggested by printing the design on transparent film (figure 2.28).

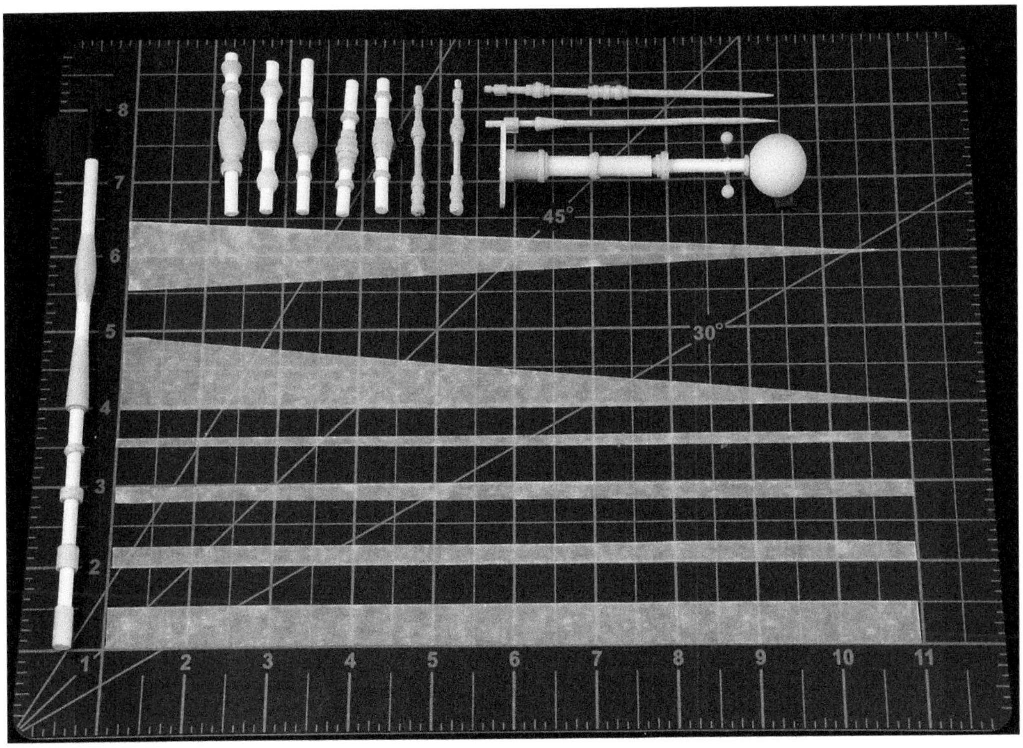

Figure 2.27. Spindles and posts wrapped with masking tape

Template Work

When identical units, such as a series of windows, are needed, it is helpful to make a template or jig using the following method.

1. Create the template by drafting the unit onto cardstock and covering it with a sheet of acetate or transparent film.
2. Cut, pin, or tape the materials to the film.
3. Apply glue to each joint piece by piece. Allow the unit to dry and then remove the pins and tape. Glue may drip onto the film and must be carefully cut away with a sharp craft knife.
4. Glue the back side of each joint.
5. Coat the unit with a thin layer of gesso to add strength.

Figure 2.28. Balusters, mullions, and tracery printed on transparent film

Columns and Capitals

Simple columns can be created by rolling cardstock into tube shapes and capping these either with paper capitals sized and printed from architectural drawings or with 3D-printed capitals (see figure 2.29). A sample of a cardstock column and capital are located on www.thescenographicmodel.com.

Organic Shapes

When creating organic shapes, metal foil or screen can be formed to resemble rocks, terrain, trees, and other irregular surfaces. Large units will require a support structure of paperboard, foam, or balsa. Once coated with spackling compound, modeling paste, and gesso, these foil shapes can be painted to add color. If smooth organic surfaces are desired, they can be carved out of foam, coated with gesso, and sanded to a smooth surface (see figure 2.30).

Foliage

Tree trunks and branches can be simulated by selecting small twigs and branches from actual trees and bushes or by twisting wire together and coating them with aluminum foil, spackling compound, modeling paste, and gesso to simulate tree bark. For trees with a shallow footprint, cardstock

Figure 2.29. Columns made with cardboard tubes sheathed with corrugated paperboard, or with balsa fluting, and 3D-printed capitals. Columns made from rolled cardstock with cardstock capitals. Molding made with illustration board, balsa, and fabric trim

can be cut to form masses of leaves (see figure 2.31). Individual leaves can be simulated by painting the branches with glue and sprinkling sawdust or commercial foliage flocking from railroad hobby suppliers. In addition, model-scale-size paper leaf punches are available from military diorama suppliers allowing the maker to paint their own paper and punch out leaves in colors.

Figure 2.30. Rock structures carved from balsawood and polystyrene foam with statue made with aluminum foil by Darwin Payne. Surfaces textured with modeling paste and gesso and then painted

Figure 2.31. Trees, bushes, and foliage made of twigs, wire, aluminum foil, and paperboard

Assembling and Joining Materials

A great deal of thought and care must be exercised in assembling and bonding the various parts of the model. Yet there is no one bonding agent suitable for all operations. Some common bonding agents are adhesives and tapes.

Adhesives

Adhesives and tapes may affect materials, so the modelmaker should evaluate adhesives and tapes on the respective materials prior to using them on the actual model. A list of common adhesives is available in table 2.1.

Tape

Tape is extremely useful to the modelmaker. Tapes are made of thin, easily torn paper, plastic, or cloth, with a pressure-sensitive adhesive on one or both sides. Hundreds of varieties of tapes are available in various backings, widths, lengths, and colors, and they are rated based upon the strength of the adhesive (see table 2.2). Household masking tape, named because it was originally designed to mask areas in painting, has a relatively low adhesion or *tack*, allowing it to be removed easily without leaving a residue or damaging most surfaces. This also makes it useful for temporarily holding model pieces in place while glue sets. Masking tapes include painting, drafting, and decorator's tapes.

Bonding Paper to Paper and Paperboard

For small glue jobs, general-purpose glue sticks provide an adequate bond; however, they can be messy. For large gluing operations, spray adhesives offer a smooth permanent bond. Care should be taken to use spray adhesives in well-ventilated areas. Water-based glues (Elmer's® Glue-All®, Tacky Glue®, craft and PVA glues) should be used sparingly to avoid water absorption and warpage of porous materials. Glues designed for scrapbooking, such as Tombow® Mono Aqua, offer a good option for bonding paper and paperboards but should still be used sparingly.

Bonding Paper and Paperboard to Wood

Polyvinyl Acetate (PVA) glues such as Elmer's® Glue-All® and Tacky Glue® work well for this type of bonding. Hot-melt glues are an effective adhesive for bonding paperboard to balsa or bass wood, and their fast-setting time makes them a good option for quick assembly. It must be noted that hot glue is thick and therefore can displace parts of a model. Its surface also does not accept paint or gesso easily, and the glue can be weakened with the introduction of heat, such as when parts are left in a hot car. A hot-melt glue pot can eliminate the awkward repetition of picking up the gun.

Table 2.1 Adhesives

Spray Adhesives A variety of spray adhesives are available including formulas for bonding paper and foam. There are also formulas that allow repositioning	
Pros	*Cons*
Good for large glue jobs Works particularly well when bonding paper to paper and other thin material Tends not to warp or deform paper and paper board	Toxic Flammable Messy Must be used in a well-ventilated area. Bonds virtually instantly, and work may not be repositioned if not aligned properly unless using a repositionable formula. The spray nozzle often clogs between uses. Holding the can upside down and spraying until just air comes out after each use helps to expel excess glue. If the nozzle is clogged, pull the tip off the can and soak it in a solution of adhesive cleaner.
Glue Stick	
Pros	*Cons*
Nontoxic[4] Bonds flat materials like paper to paper and paper to paperboard Permanent and repositionable varieties are available Useful for quick assembly of sketch and white study models	Does not bond well to nonpaper materials Not strong enough for structural purposes Dries out between uses
Polyvinyl acetate (PVA) PVA is often called "white," "hobby," or "craft" glue Brands include Elmer's Glue-All, Sobo Tacky Glue, Craft Glue Thinned solutions of PVA are used in fabric stiffeners like Spray Bond & Stiffen Quick	
Pros	*Cons*
Nontoxic Effectively bonds paper to balsa and bass wood Dries clear	May warp thin paper materials Does not work well on materials other than paper or wood Does not take to paint well and must be coated with gesso prior to painting

Table 2.1 Adhesives *(continued)*

Aliphatic Resin (Wood Glue) Also known as "carpenter's glue" or "yellow glue"	
Pros	*Cons*
Nontoxic Bonds well to wood and paper materials Heavy consistency dries faster than PVA glues Glued joins can be cleaned up with water before setting Can be sanded when dry	Remains yellow when dry Does not work well on materials other than wood or paper Does not take paint well and must be coated with gesso prior to painting
Epoxy Refers to a variety of strong types of adhesives	
Pros	*Cons*
Strong bond on many dissimilar materials, including wood, plastic, and metal	Toxic Two-part epoxies must be mixed precisely A relatively short working time when mixed Extended curing time May melt certain types of foam Does not take paint or gesso well
Cyanoacrylate (CA or "Super Glue") Commonly sold as "super" or "crazy" glue as it bonds dissimilar materials securely	
Pros	*Cons*
Strong bond on many dissimilar materials including wood, plastic, and metal Dries quickly Available in thin, gel, and thick consistencies Some CA glues have an accelerative activating compound that sets the glue almost instantly Used extensively for styrene railroad modeling and balsa airplanes	Toxic Chemical fumes require adequate ventilation Flammable Short shelf life (purchase small quantities and store in sealed containers) Crystals may form on surfaces exposed to cyanoacrylate vapors May melt specific foams and plastics Bonds to skin and can glue fingers together or to model parts Requires toxic solvents (acetone) for release

Table 2.1 Adhesives *(continued)*

Pros	Cons
Contact Cement Adhesives that are applied separately to the surfaces to be joined and allowed to dry; when the adhesive surfaces are brought into contact, they form a strong bond	
Pros	*Cons*
Strong permanent bond between a variety of materials, including some plastics Many varieties available, including water-based, and foam friendly	Some varieties are toxic Some varieties are flammable Some varieties may melt certain types of foam Difficult to work with
General Purpose Glues Nitrocellulose, and styrene-based glues Brands include Duco Cement™, E6000™, Oasis Floral Glue™	
Pros	*Cons*
Bonds to many dissimilar materials Many brands dry clear Flexible and hard varieties are available	Toxic Extended setting time May melt specific types of foams and plastics Does not take to paint well Dried glue should be coated with gesso prior to painting
Airplane Glues Styrene suspended in a solvent of methyl ethyl ketone (MEK); when the solvent evaporates, styrene parts are cold-welded together	
Pros	*Cons*
Dries quickly	Toxic Flammable Only works with styrene-based plastics
Hot Melt Glue Thermoplastics that become liquid when heated and return to a solid state when cool	
Pros	*Cons*
Nontoxic Quick setting time Various melting temperatures available Colored and glitter sticks available Available in craft sections of most stores	Can burn skin Relatively weak bond Does not stick to metals well May melt other thermoplastics Produces thin strings of glue that must be cleaned up once they cool Does not take paint or gesso Cannot be sanded May melt and loose cohesion if left in a hot location

Table 2.2 Tape

Masking Tape	
Pros	*Cons*
Ease of use Stronger bond than painter, drafting, or artist tapes Readily available in many stores	Nonpermanent. May damage paper surfaces when removed
Drafting or Artist Tape	
Useful for temporarily holding lightweight materials in place Ease of use Low tack will not damage paper materials when removed Offers some water resistance Available in small circles called "drafting dots"	Nonpermanent Only available from art or office supply stores
Photo (Masking) Tape	
Pros	*Cons*
Acid free Available in black and white Matte finish Useful for cleaning up edges of materials	May damage paper materials when removed Low tack may not adhere well to plastic or metal materials Does not accept paint well
Invisible Tape *Scotch™ and cellophane tapes.*	
Pros	*Cons*
Useful for quick assembly of sketch and white study models Relatively strong bond with paper materials Readily available at most stores Matte finishes disappear more easily While not truly invisible, can be hidden easily when used on the back of model pieces	Will damage paper materials when removed Tends to yellow and becomes brittle over time May not work well on plastic or metal materials
Packing Tape *Not used in scenographic model assembly except for carrying and container boxes for shipping and transportation*	
Pros	*Cons*
Strong bond with paper materials Readily available at many stores	Will damage paper materials when removed Tends to yellow and becomes brittle over time Does not accept paints

Table 2.2 Tape *(continued)*

Double-Sided Tape and Double Tack Sheets Useful for quick assembly of sketch and white models	
Pros	*Cons*
Relatively strong bond when used with paper materials Creates a secure bond allowing some painting without warping	Will damage paper materials when removed Tends to yellow and become brittle over time
Mounting Tape Similar to double sided tape, but with a thick foam substrate	
Pros	*Cons*
Strong bond when used with paper materials Sticks to some plastic and metal materials	Permanent bond will damage materials when removed May not remove completely
Gaffer's Tape A heavy cotton cloth-backed pressure-sensitive tape with strong adhesive; not useful for scenographic model assembly but effective in assembling carrying and container boxes for transportation	
Pros	*Cons*
Sticks well to a variety of materials, including plastics and some metals Available in a variety of colors	Will damage most materials when removed Tends to leave residue on materials Adhesive tends to yellow and become brittle over time

Bonding Balsawood to Other Materials

For a strong bond between balsawood and heavy material such as illustration board, a general-purpose nitrocellulose glue, such as Duco® Cement, is a good option. Nitrocellulose glues can melt foam products, so foam should first be coated with gesso, allowed to dry, and then bonded with nitrocellulose glue. Cyanoacrylate glues, also known as super glues, will also produce a strong bond between balsa and other materials. Super glues are particularly useful when assembling small model pieces. Clamps, holding pins, or tape will be necessary to secure the joints while the glue sets.

Bonding to Metal

Permanent spray adhesives like 3M® and Super 77® work well for bonding paper and fabrics to flat metal surfaces or for applying metal foil to wood or paperboard surfaces. When bonding wood to metal or working with wire or small metal pieces, nitrocellulose glues or epoxy-based glues like E6000® are recommended. These glues have a long setting time, so it may be necessary to temporarily support glue joints with pins, clamps, or tape until the glue has set. Be sure to follow all directions and safety precautions when using aerosol glues as they require adequate ventilation. Care should also be taken to avoid too much overspray in the model studio. A separate spray booth or ventilated spray area is recommended.

Adhesive Papers

Adhesive paper can be used to secure various scenic elements to the stage or model. This is especially useful for temporary attachments that need to be easily removed or repositioned. Double-sided adhesive paper is very useful when attaching dissimilar materials like wood, plastic, and metal. The thin consistent thickness of the adhesive allows for precise alignment of parts. Adhesive papers can also be used to create masking templates for painting. The adhesive paper is applied to areas that need to be protected and then painted. When the paint is dry, the paper can be peeled off, leaving clean edges. Adhesive paper can be used to adhere fabrics or curtains in place on models. This is especially useful for temporary or lightweight applications. When incorporating lighting or electrical components into a theatrical model, double-sided adhesive paper can help conceal wires by attaching them discreetly along the model surface.

With the wide variety of adhesives and materials available, it can be difficult to determine which adhesives will be effective for a given application. A chart of recommended adhesives for bonding diverse materials is provided in figure 2.32.

Texturing and Painting the Scenographic Model

While designers often use assistants to build their scenographic models, many prefer to paint their models themselves. The styles and techniques of painting are very personal, making it difficult to relegate this task to any but the most trusted of assistants. Also, the techniques used to paint the model often replicate those used by the scenic artist painting the full-scale scenery, with the key difference being the size of the brushes and sprayers being used and the size of the surfaces being painted. When painting the model, the designer can inform the scenic artist of the techniques by which they want the setting painted.

Painting the presentation model follows similar processes used in painting the scenographic rendering. At its simplest, painting the rendering can be outlined in the following manner as illustrated in figure 2.33.

	Metal	Fabric	Foam	Plastic	Balsa/Bass Wood	Foam Core	Illustration/ Paper Board	Paper
Paper	GP, SA	PVA, SA	CC*, SA*,	CC, SA	CC, PVA, SA	CC, GS, PVA, SA	CC, GS, PVA, SA	GS, PVA, SA
Illustration/ Paper Board	CA, E, GP	PVA, SA	CC*, SA*	CA, GP	CA, GP, HM, PVA, WG	CC, HM, PVA, SA	CC, HM, PVA, SA	
Foam Core	CA, E, GP	PVA, SA	CC*, SA*	CA, GP	CA, GP, HM, PVA, WG	HM, PVA, SA		
Balsa/Bass Wood	CA, E, GP	HG, PVA	CC*, GP*, SA*	CA, GP	CA, GP, HM, PVA, WG			
Plastic	CA, E, GP	GP	CC*, GP*, SA*	CA, GP				
Foam	GP*, SA*	GP*, SA*	GP*, SA*					
Fabric	GP, SA	PVA						
Metal	E, GP							

Cyanoacrylate (Super Glue) [CA]
Contact Cement [CC]
Epoxy [E]
General Purpose Glue [GP]
Glue Stick [GS]
Hot-Melt [HM]
Polyvinyl Acetate [PVA]
Spray Adhesive [SA]
Aliphatic Resin (Wood Glue) [WG]

*Some adhesives may soften or dissolve foam materials. The modelmaker should check container labels to ensure that the selected adhesive will work with the material they are using. It may also be advisable to test the adhesive on scrap material before using on model pieces.

Figure 2.32. Adhesives chart

1. Draw the outline in pencil or waterproof ink on the prepared material to define planes and objects.
2. Lay a basic tone using colored washes, allowing the outline to show through the various layers. The outline continues to define planes and objects while the tonal layer begins to establish form, mass, and texture.
3. Lay in deeper shadow colors on the background to further define mass and form. Add texturing details to further delineate mass and begin to add highlights at points where light would catch the forms.
4. Add final shading and highlights to finalize form while adding mood and atmosphere to the setting.
5. Spray several light coats of workable fixative or a matte sealant to glaze and protect the surface. This glaze will deepen and enrich the colors.

Figure 2.33. Steps in painting the scenographic rendering by Darwin Payne

Painting the scenographic model follows remarkably similar steps, except that models usually consist of a variety of materials requiring each piece to be primed with gesso or primer paint to provide a consistent painting surface. Figure 2.34 illustrates a similar painting process on the model.

Figure 2.34. Steps in painting the scenographic model by Darwin Payne

A. Apply a light coat of gesso to the entire surface. (Figure 2.35 shows various techniques for creating textures with gesso, modeling paste and spackling compound.)
B. Build up the basic tones with a brush, airbrush, or aerosol spray paint. In this model a transparent burnt umber was used to produce darker areas, allowing the paint to pool in the cracks and depressions of the textured surface.
C. Add layers of darker paints by brush or spray to produce deeper, more varied tones. The objective, as with the scenic rendering, is not to completely cover the surface with one coat but to build up layers of depth and luminosity. Aerosols, stains, and airbrush paints often have a slight gloss finish that catches the light, imparting a livelier surface to the model.
D. Add deeper shading and definition with inks and brushwork. Washes of sepia-toned ink create the effect of age as surfaces tend to turn brown over time. If dirt is the desired effect, shade with washes of black watercolor or India ink.
E. Found images such as wallpaper and signage can be incorporated into the model. These images often supply the scenographer with the basic desired tone. These appliqués can also be toned with ink and watercolor to blend them with the

model's existing tonality. Such embellishments must be securely glued to a sturdy backing material to prevent buckling and warping.

F. Metallic model parts may require a protective clear coating prior to any painting or distressing application to prevent future rust and tarnish.

G. Final accents on highly textured surfaces can be achieved using water-soluble, acrylic metallic paints, pastes, and paint pens.

H. Like the rendering, it is advisable to finish the model with light coats of workable fixative or a matte sealant to coat and protect the surface. This glazing will enrich and deepen the colors and make it easier to dust and clean the model in the future.

Tip: *As noted in the earlier model-building sections, it is best not to permanently assemble the model prior to painting as this can make it difficult to reach corners and crevices. If individual units are painted separately, these units can be blended, if necessary, after assembly.*

Priming Coats and Textures

Gesso is best applied with flat camel hair or stiff synthetic brushes used only for this purpose. Old brushes no longer suitable for watercolor are still useful for texturing and applying gesso. Gesso dries quickly, so brushes should be washed out immediately. All brushes should be cleaned in cold to lukewarm water as hot water will soften the glues that secure the bristles. A little liquid dish soap or shampoo will help rinse the bristles clean. When applying the gesso coat to model parts, it is helpful to create a light texture as these surfaces catch the light and give the model a greater illusion of solidity, while also presenting a more finished approximation of the full-scale setting. This is the same principle as applying painted textures and patterns, such as spattering, to flat surfaces to give a stronger impression of depth and solidity. Textures, such as wood grain, can be created by dragging a stiff brush or toothbrush through gesso that has been allowed to dry slightly.

If heavier textures are desired, other materials can be applied to the surface of the model at the same time as the gesso. For instance, sand can be evenly sprinkled over a surface coated with gesso and blended in with a brush. Other materials, such as cloth, tissue paper, string, wire, beads of polystyrene foam, and other materials, can also be applied to model surfaces and affixed in the same manner. Gesso will function as both a binder and coating for light materials, whereas heavier materials will need to be glued to the surface first and coated with gesso after the glue has set.

For heavier textures, gesso can be mixed with acrylic modeling paste and spackling compound in various proportions to create a variety of textures also shown in figure 2.35. If the paste and compound is too thick, it may crack as it dries. While cracks are occasionally desirable, best practices reduce cracking by building up thin layers, allowing each to dry before applying the next. If cracks still occur, they can be filled with more paste after the surface has dried. Very thick layers of paste are often too heavy to be applied with a brush. Painting and palette knives come in a variety of sizes and shapes and are good applicators for heavy pastes. It is advisable to have a well-defined understructure before applying the paste so that it will be thinner and lighter. Gesso provides a more consistent painting surface than modeling paste or spackling compound, so a light coating of gesso over the modeling paste surface is recommended before painting. Spray gesso is especially useful for creating a thin light coat over existing textures.

In most cases, light materials like sand, string, wire mesh, and small twigs can be adhered without gluing by embedding them in gesso, modeling paste, or spackling compound. After they are attached, the entire surface can be painted with another coat of gesso. The model for *Elektra* in figure 2.36 shows a variety of these different texturing techniques.

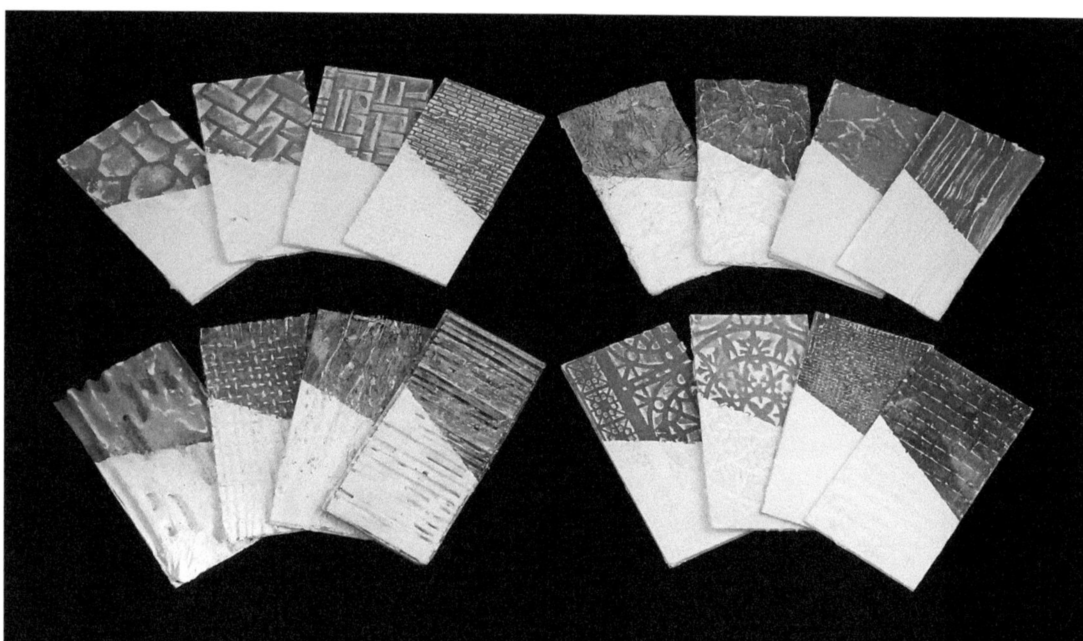

Figure 2.35. Scenographic model textures. *Top left*: Brick and stone stenciled with modeling paste. *Top right*: Textures created by scumbling and scraping gesso, modeling paste, and spackling compound over paperboard covered with tissue paper and aluminum foil. *Bottom left*: Gesso, modeling paste, or spackling compound coating various objects, fabrics, and textures. *Bottom right*: Textures created through painting stencils or by pressing objects and stamps into gesso, modeling paste, and spackling compound

Figure 2.36. *Elektra* by Euripides. 3/4" project model by Darwin Payne. Southern Illinois University Carbondale, 2013

***Tip**: Dollhouse, scrap boarding, and model railroading paint stencils, texture sheets, and rollers are convenient methods to add intricate and repetitive patterns, textures, or designs to surfaces in a consistent manner. Raised brick and stonework can be made by brushing or stippling gesso and modeling paste. Texture sheets and rollers can be pressed into malleable surfaces like papier-mâché, clay, and paper clay surfaces. These products are available in specialty stores, but if the desired pattern is not available, then stencils can be laser cut to scale and 3D printers can generate specific texture sheets and rollers (see figure 2.37).*

Textured surfaces will air-dry within a reasonable amount of time, but the drying process can be sped up by using a hair styling blow dryer, placing the model pieces underneath an incandescent lamp, or placing them in a very low-temperature oven and leaving the door open. If the force-drying is too quick, surfaces coated with gesso, modeling paste, and spackling compound may warp and crack. Modeling paste and spackling compounds are heavy, so the model floor and support materials need to be appropriately sturdy.

Textured walls of plaster, brick, and stone can be painted, carved in foam, sculpted using gesso, modeling paste, and spackling compound, 3D printed, or purchased from commercial modeling vendors. Commercial brick and

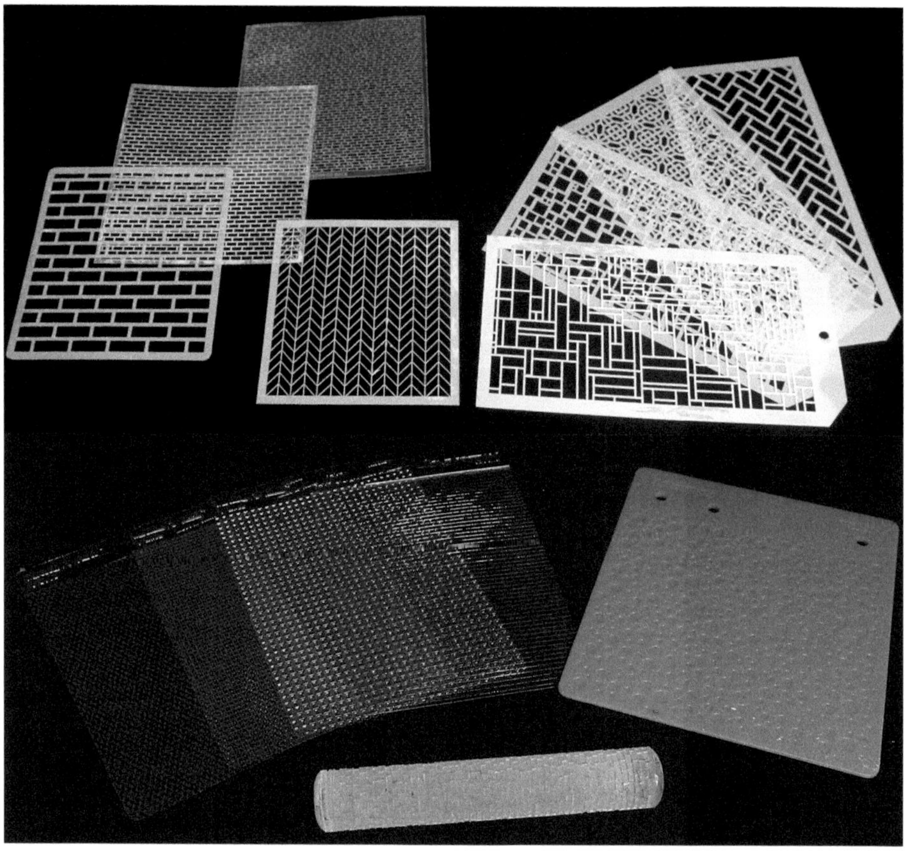

Figure 2.37. Commercial and laser cut stencils, texture sheets, and roller

stone panels may come already painted but should be primed and repainted to match the overall tone of the model.

Flooring

Stage floors are usually not heavily textured, as this would create a hazardous walking surface for the actors and technicians. Stage floors are typically painted to resemble stone, cobblestone, and any textured surface. Wood planking is acceptable, as it is smooth and provides an appropriate acoustic sound when walked upon. If wood planking is anticipated for the stage floor, it is appropriate for the model to simulate these boards by using balsa or basswood stained with thinned paints or wood stain (figure 2.38). Additional graining and weathering can be added with fine-tipped brushes, pens, and markers. If the stage floor will be Masonite® or plywood painted to simulate a specific surface, then it is advisable to paint on illustration board the desired color, texture, and technique (figure 2.39). Flooring can also be digitally assembled, printed, and glued to the model floor with spray adhesives.

Figure 2.38. Balsawood parquet and planking stained with watercolor and marker to show woodgrain

Figure 2.39. Steps for painting wood, marble, brick, and stone with watercolor on illustration board

Wallpaper

Scaled wallpapers are most easily reproduced by scanning a wallpaper sample from interior design books, sample books, or by downloading images from online sources. As wallpaper rarely comes in the desired color, size, and scale, the modelmaker will need to modify it using image-editing software. For white models, the wallpaper should be printed in a light grayscale, so it does not dominate the composition. Once the wallpaper is created and printed on paper, it can be adhered to the wall surface of the model with spray adhesive, double-sided adhesive paper, or printed on a paper with an adhesive backing. Spraying the wallpaper with light coats of workable fixative will help keep the printer ink from running and allow the modelmaker to tone the wallpaper to match the overall feeling of the model.

Molding or trim work should be painted separately and then glued to the walls and wallpaper to prevent dribbling paint on the wall surface. Likewise, if transparent plastic is used for window treatments, it is easier to paint the casement and any dimensional mullions and tracery before attaching the plastic to prevent paint from marring the clear surface.

***Tip:** Damian Gardner creates translucent stained glass windows by first designing and coloring the front and back elevations of the window. This can be done manually or by using a CAD software program. The front elevation shows the tracery, mullions, and stone framing. The tracery is rendered appropriately, but the glass is painted in a light gray or neutral tone. The back elevation is painted in the full colors of the stained glass. An inkjet printer is used to copy the front and back elevations onto inkjet-compatible transparencies. These transparencies have a slight tooth to them, which gives them a matte finish. Next Damian sandwiches a piece of drafting vellum (without gridding) between the transparencies using spray adhesive. He then cuts out the translucent window and attaches these to the tracery and wall frame. If the window needs additional structural support, he cuts out basswood and attaches it to the rear using super glue. Highlights and touchups can be added to the window before setting it into the model. When the window is frontlit, it is somber and unassuming, but when backlit it gains the full glory and radiance of stained glass. This same process can be used to create translucent drops (figure 2.40).*

Backgrounds

The background for the model can serve several functions. It will be part of the model, it may serve as a paint elevation, and it can also be photographed for use as a projection. The background can be developed in several ways. Watercolors and pastels are excellent for obtaining atmospheric effects and can be duplicated on stage with paint, lighting, and projections.

Found images, as shown in figure 2.41 can be collaged into a background image and adhered to a backing. The disparate images can be blended with inks and paints to match the model. Like flooring and wallpaper, backgrounds may also be created using image-editing software. Drawing or printing these images on translucent papers will allow the designer to create dramatic silhouettes by placing lights behind the model. AI technology is very useful in creating two-dimensional backgrounds and will be discussed further in chapter 5, "Emergent Technology."

Figure 2.40. Stained glass window by Damian Gardner for *Spring Awakening* by Duncan Sheik and Steven Sater. Pennsylvania State University, 2014

Figure 2.41. Background assembled from found images

Spattering the Model

Spattering is a useful technique used to blend and tone scenery that is replicated in paint elevations and the model by using a toothbrush, a small stiff bristled brush, a spritzer bottle, or an airbrush. Dip the brush into thinned paint, point the brush down toward the surface, place thumb along bristles, and pull backward. The painter should practice these techniques on another surface before attempting to spatter the painted model. Areas that do not need a spatter texture should be masked.

Airbrushing

Airbrushes use compressed air to atomize paint, propelling it onto the paint surface in much the same way as an aerosol spray (see figure 2.42).[5] Airbrushes are particularly useful for creating gradient color changes, painted shadows, spattering, and stenciling patterns (figure 2.43). Airbrushes come in two basic categories: single-action, and dual-action. Single-action airbrushes offer an on/off trigger mechanism, with the paint flow rate adjustment at the spray tip. The spray pattern size is set with replaceable spray tips of differing sizes. Small tips (listed as "Fine" on some models or by numbers 1–3) are useful for producing fine lines and shading on models. Larger spray tips ("Medium," or 5) are useful for stenciling and creating translucent or opaque washes over larger areas. Single-action airbrushes are easy to use and generally inexpensive. A dual-action airbrush allows the operator to adjust

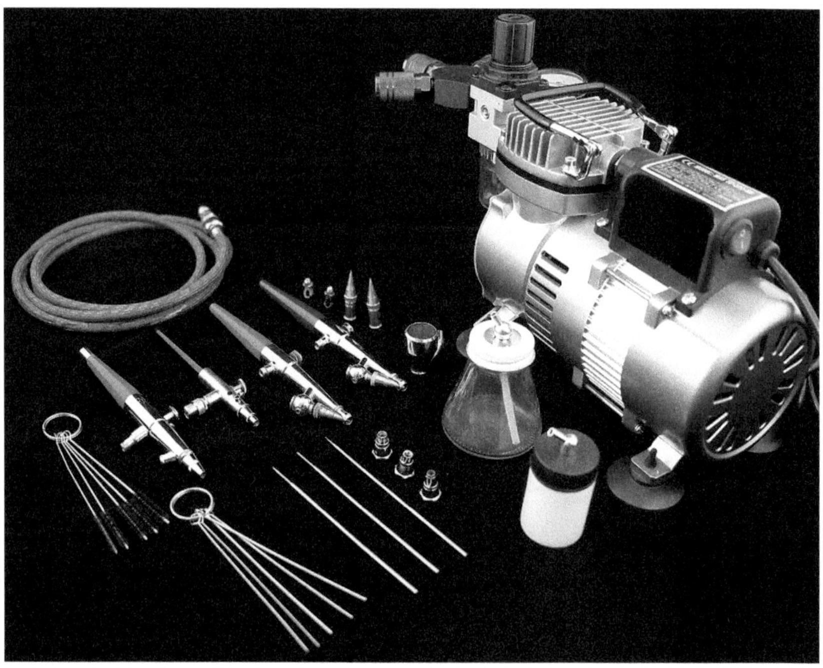

Figure 2.42. Single-action and double-action airbrushes

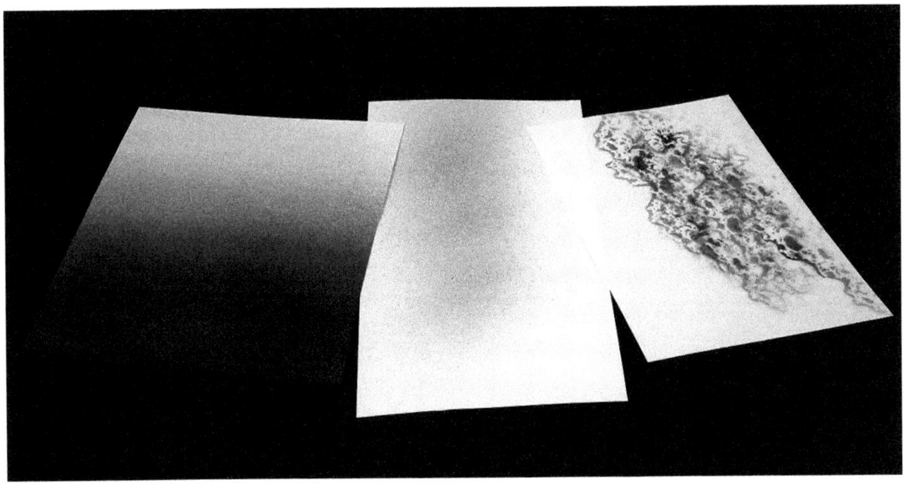

Figure 2.43. Airbrushing techniques. Gradation, stenciling, shadowing, and spattering

the paint flow rate at the trigger. When the trigger is depressed, the operator slides it back to release more paint or forward to reduce the flow. Dual-action airbrushes allow more creativity but require more practice to achieve proficiency. Airbrushes are either gravity or siphon fed, which determines how paint enters the airbrush. Gravity-fed airbrushes have an open hopper or reservoir on the top. Siphon-fed units have a reservoir underneath the airbrush and use air pressure running across the tip to create the vacuum to pull paint up from the reservoir. Regardless of the type of airbrush used, the modelmaker will need a source of compressed air. Airbrushes can be used with tool air compressors provided there is a method to regulate air pressure. Air compressors designed for use with airbrushes are preferable due to their small footprint, quiet motor, and built-in moisture filters to keep compressed air dry. Refer to the airbrush user manual when selecting an appropriate air compressor.

Accessorizing the Scenographic Model

Accessorizing is often the most painstaking and challenging aspect of the scenographic model. Scenic accessories, including human figures, furniture, set dressing, scenery elements and other décor, are small yet require meticulous attention to detail to produce the desired effect. Internet shopping, hobby stores, and 3D printing have aided the scenographer in acquiring furniture and set dressings in the appropriate period, style, and scale. However, purchasing these accessories can be extremely expensive, and the modelmaker must consider the added shipping costs and have the necessary foresight to order accessories to complete the model on schedule. For these reasons, scenographic modelmakers must be adept at constructing their own accessories and develop a miniature stock of prop furniture and dressing in various scales and styles. This section will concern itself with techniques and materials modelers can use to construct their own accessories. The unit "Related Modelmaking Disciplines" provides sources of premanufactured accessories useful for scenographic modeling.

Furniture

There are various methods to use in constructing model furniture. For white cardstock models it is customary to draft an orthographic projection of the furniture, print it onto cardstock, cut, fold, and assemble it as shown in figure 2.44. The orthographic drawings can be sketched in 1/2" scale or larger and printed in a smaller scale for greater accuracy and detail.

For sturdier furniture, an orthographic drawing can be transferred to a paperboard, waxed stencil paper, or lightweight illustration board, cut out, and glued as also shown in figure 2.44. The thickness of the board needs to be factored into the orthographic drawing, or the edges of the illustration board can be bevel cut at 45° angles. The finished furniture piece can then be primed with gesso and painted to match the model.

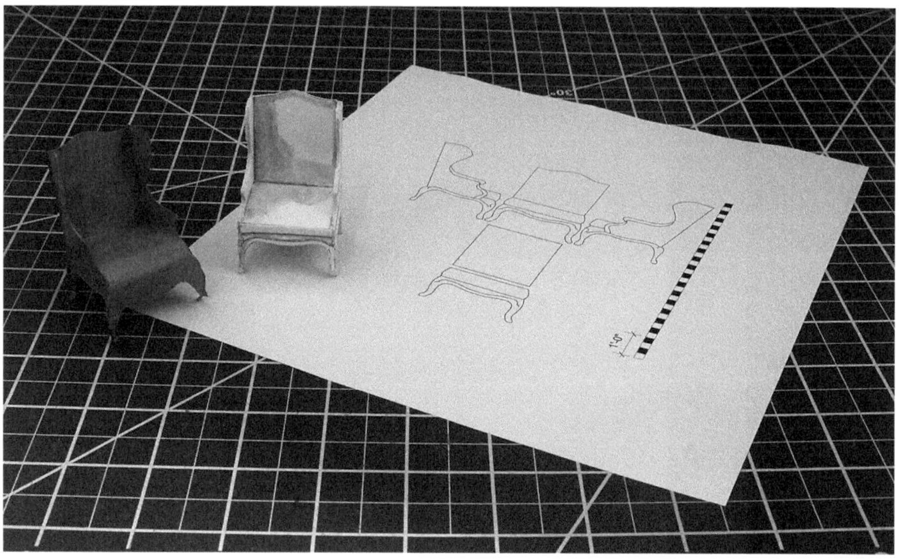

Figure 2.44. Chair construction using stencil paper and illustration board

Solid pieces of furniture like armchairs, sofas, and beds can be carved out of polystyrene foam, balsa, or basswood, with decorative beads and pins used for legs and finials (see figure 2.45). Absorbent papers and sheer fabrics can be draped over these forms, coated with gesso, and shaped while drying to replicate the texture of wrinkled, folded, and draped fabric. These pieces can then be coated with gesso and painted to match the model. If the color and texture of a sheer fabric needs to be preserved, a thin coating of clear gesso, acrylic matte medium, PVA sizing, or a fabric stiffener can be used to saturate the material, which can then be shaped as it dries.

Figure 2.45. Constructed, carved, and molded furniture

Brass rod is necessary when accessories need to be light and strong or when replicating actual metal items such as a brass bed or curved staircase railing. Gluing metal does not produce a strong bond, so soldering is the best, if not more difficult, method. The plans can be drawn onto cardstock and used as a template for cutting out all the pieces. The pieces are then secured to the cardstock using tape set away from the joints to be soldered. Making a small nick with a dull craft knife blade at the junction of the joint will make a notch to help hold the brass rod in place during soldering (see figure 1.22).

Drapery and Fabric

Real fabric, no matter how sheer, does not have the weight to drape realistically in scale models. Folds and textures are easily indicated graphically by drawing or painting on paper and paperboard using light-colored paint, pencils and pastels for highlights and darker paint, pencils, pastels, and markers for shadows.

Cardstock can be run through a paper corrugator to create dimensional pleating. Velour-surfaced cardstock is excellent for flat masking and can also be run through a paper corrugator to create drapery fullness. Thicker drapery can be simulated by carving or building up layers of paper, gesso, modeling paste, and spackling compound. Lightweight fabrics can be adhered to a backing of metal foil that is then shaped and pleated to suggest the desired draping. Very sheer fabrics and lightweight absorbent papers can be saturated with various PVA mediums and shaped and draped while drying (see figure 2.46).

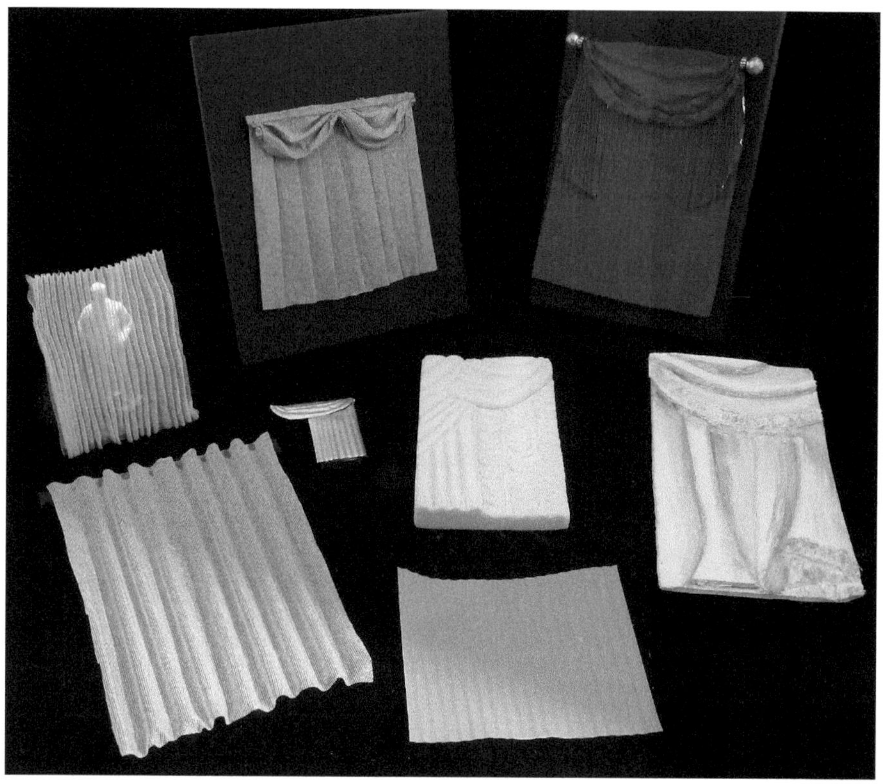

Figure 2.46. *From top left*: Draperies created using sheer fabric sprayed with fabric stiffener or PVA glue and draped and pleated while drying; adhering lightweight fabric to aluminum foil and pleated using a paper corrugator; carved from PUR foam; layered and sanded foam board; and transparent vellum pleated using a paper corrugator

Scrims

Transparent scrims can be replicated in scale by stretching gauze on a frame. If the scrim is to be painted, the gauze can be sized with starch or a workable fixative spray, then cartooned and painted with transparent watercolors and markers (figure 2.47).

Figure 2.47. Scrim simulated with watercolor painting on sheer semitransparent fabric

***Tip**: Designer/modelmaker Lauren M. Nichols creates model scrims by using spray adhesive to lightly adhere a piece of silk organza to a sheet of cardstock. This sheet is run through an inkjet printer to add the image, using a feed tray that doesn't require the sheet to flip on rollers. A rear feed slot is normally the best choice. For a darker image, the gauze can be run through the printer several times as needed. The paper is then gently peeled away, and the gauze is attached to a soldered brass frame or a lightweight plastic film. The sheer gauze with the printed design works like a painted scrim on stage (figure 2.48).*

Figure 2.48. Model scrim printed on silk organza. *Courtesy of Lauren M. Nichols*

Set Dressing

Pictures, murals, rugs, and other flat decorative items can be copied from magazines and catalogs or downloaded from online sources (figure 2.49). These images can then be modified with image-editing software to the correct size and color before printing. As mentioned previously, images should be rendered in grayscale for white models so they do not draw too much attention in the overall composition.

Figure 2.49. Rugs, tapestries, paintings, and wall hangings

The modelmaker must begin to visualize how small objects like beads, toys, dressmaker pins, fishing hooks, bottle caps, jewelry findings, and holiday ornaments can be repurposed to fabricate furniture, chandeliers, lamps, plants, and other set decoration for the scenographic model (see figure 2.50).

Foliage

Foliage dressing can also be made from a variety of materials such as cut paper, natural or wool sponges, sawdust, foam shavings, commercially available flocking, and small plastic plants. Natural rope fibers like sisal, jute, or manila can simulate grasses. Vines can be created with string or wire coated with gesso, leaves, or flocking. Houseplants are easily created by cutting the leaves out of paper or aluminum foil and gluing them to a thin wire stem and "planted" in a bottle cap or decorative bead (figure 2.51).

Figure 2.50. Lighting accessories made with beads, bottle caps, and pins

Figure 2.51. Plastic, metal, and dried foliage in beads and bottle caps

__Tip__: The previous section showed construction using heavier paperboards, but many of these same shapes can be created using cardstock. Printamodel offers the Build a Set series of cut-and-assemble furniture, flats, doors, windows, columns, platforms, stairs, ramps, railings, trusses, and many other useful shapes in downloadable PDF files (see figure 2.52).

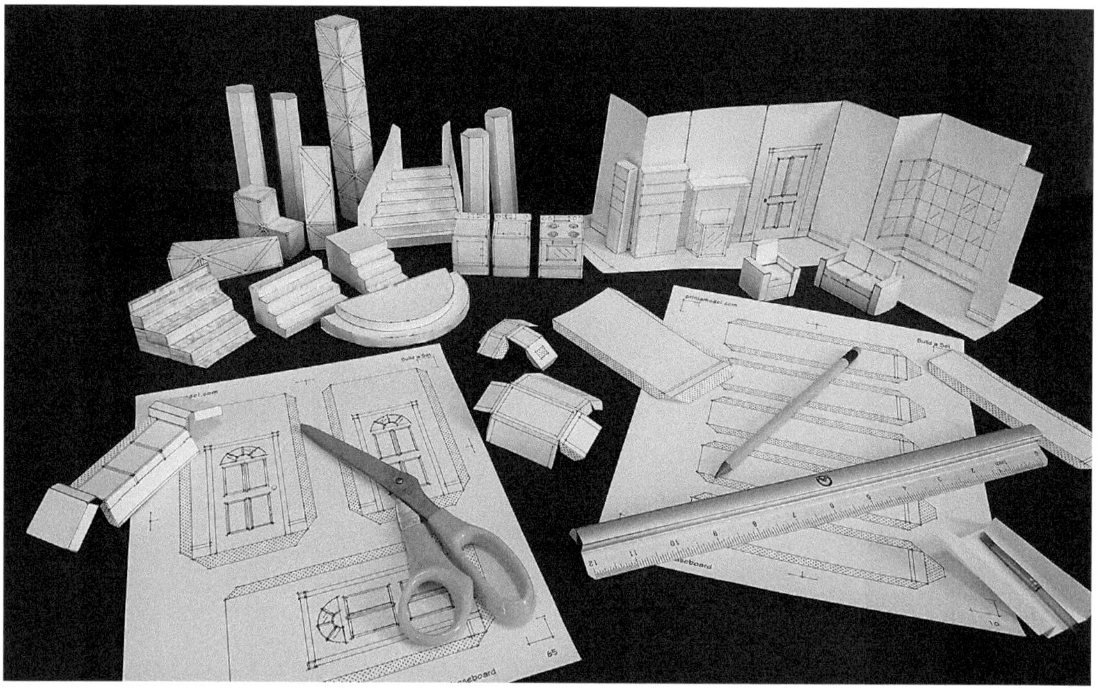

Figure 2.52. Printamodel Build a Set scenery. *Courtesy of Eric Glynwilliams*

Figures

A scaled human figure is an essential element for any model, as this miniature "performer" provides the necessary proportional information to the scenographic model. Note in figure 2.53 how the same model takes on entirely different proportion and therefore meaning when changing the scale of the human figures inhabiting the space.

On study models a simple, scaled two-dimensional or three-dimensional figure is sufficient to examine actor-environment relationships. But as the model evolves and begins to take on atmospheric and psychological tones, it is helpful to give more thought to these figures who, much like the human actors they represent, inject life into the model, making it truly a miniature stage. The style, history, mood, and genre of the entertainment is enhanced by the appropriate shape, form, color, and attitude of this figure and helps to shape the viewer's perception of how its character relates to its environment

Figure 2.53. Same setting with different sense of scale

and completes the dramatic action of the play. Figure 2.54 shows the same model photographed with generic figures and with expressive characters. The modelmaker should consider what kind of figure best complements their model and design. The quickest way to make figures is to draw them on cardstock or lightweight paperboard, cut them out, and attach them either to a pin or a small round disk or square of the same material. Another quick method is to import a suitable character from an illustration, painting, or photograph, print it, and cut it out. Photographing the costume designer's renderings (with their permission) and printing these in grayscale for white models and in color for presentation models will create a strong unity of design and greater identification for the director and performers.

Wire figures resemble dimensional gesture drawings and add a great deal of energy, expression, and movement to the model. Wire figures are particularly appropriate choices in models for dance and ballet design. Once a wire figure is made, it can quickly be reshaped into multiple poses. Wire figures can also serve as armatures for figures built up with paper clay and aluminum foil.

Figure 2.54. Generic figures vs. expressive figures

Figures can also be quickly modeled using only aluminum foil. These bodies are especially appropriate for organic designs, period costumed plays, and operas and provide dimensionally rich characters. 3D-printed figures also provide dimensionality and can be rendered in generic, realistic, and stylized versions. Commercial model figures for architectural and model railways work well for scenes ranging from the mid-twentieth century to our current day. Figure 2.55 shows examples of various human figures.

***Tip**: Online marketplaces like Etsy and eBay are excellent sources for modelmaking materials and supplies. Etsy is known for handmade and vintage items with a focus on individual creators, whereas eBay is a more general platform encompassing a wide range of new and used commercial products.*

Figure 2.55. Two-dimensional figures from illustrations, paintings, photographs, and costume sketches. Three-dimensional model figures sculpted from modeling clays, aluminum foil, wire, and 3D prints

***Tip**: Figure 2.56 shows a simple step-by-step method to make a wire figure.*

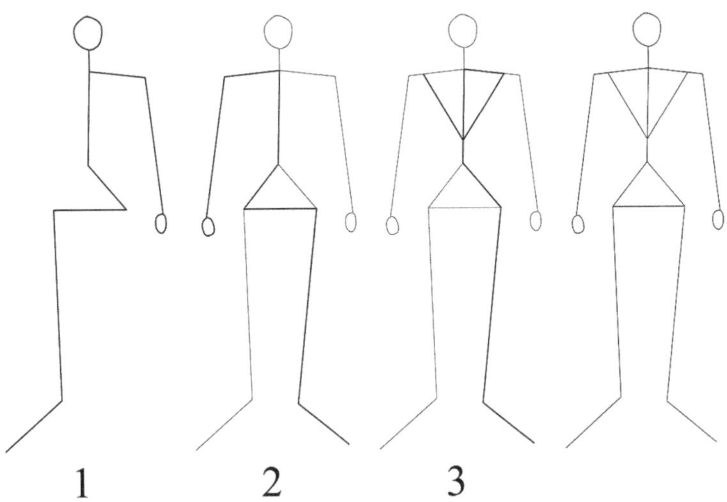

Figure 2.56. Wire figure template

***Tip**: Some useful online scaled theater furniture sources include:*

- *BK Scenics, https://bkscenics.com/*
- *Paul Pape Designs, Popout-People & Furniture, https://paulpapedesigns.com/*
- *Pretty Small Things, https://www.shapeways.com/designer/prettysmallthings*
- *Printamodel, https://printamodel.com/*

Related Modelmaking Disciplines

It is advantageous for the scenographic modelmaker to know about modelmaking in other disciplines such as architecture, model railroading, dollhouse and miniatures, dioramas, and role-play gaming (RPG). Companies specializing in such disciplines offer valuable materials, tools, techniques, and a wide variety of products one can use to build and accessorize the scenographic model. In addition, these modeling disciplines may offer employment opportunities for the theatrical modelmaker.

Architecture

Architectural scale models allow one to physically experiment with ideas, demonstrate options to clients, encourage investors, and provide a benchmark for draftspersons, civil engineers, and builders (figure 2.57). Architects build their own models, employ professional modelmakers, or subcontract this task to modelmaking studios. Architectural models are constructed from the traditional materials of clay, wood, cardboard, and foam, but rapid prototyping (3D printing), laser cutting tools, and computer numerical controlled routers (CNCs) have significantly advanced the craft of architectural modelmaking. Architects use both imperial and metric measurement systems to draft plans and build models. Architects also use a ratio, but with colons and semicolons indicating imperial inches and feet. For example: 1":24' or 1 inch equals 24 feet. Interior models are used to study internal spacing, traffic circulation patterns, color palettes, textures, finishes, and furniture arrangements. These models are often made in 1:48 and 1:24 scales, so materials, figures, and scenery elements for these models are appropriate for theatrical models in 1/4" and 1/2" scales.

Exterior models are built to display individual buildings or groups of buildings as well as civic areas such as parks and playgrounds (figure 2.58). Due to the large spaces represented, exterior models are built in scales from 1:500 to as small as 1:20,000.

Landscaping models represent outdoor public spaces displaying foliage plantings, walkways, streams, ponds, bridges, and ornamental features like pavilions, fountains, and statuary (figure 2.59). The scales for these models range from the larger scales for interior models to the smaller scales used in exterior models. Landscape modeling typically requires realistic and detailed miniature foliage, and terrain materials, which can add authenticity to theatrical models. Small-scale trees and bushes can even be used as houseplants on larger scales.

A quick online search for "architectural modelmaking supplies" reveals dozens of companies and stores that supply tools, materials, premade features, furniture, and figures for this profession.

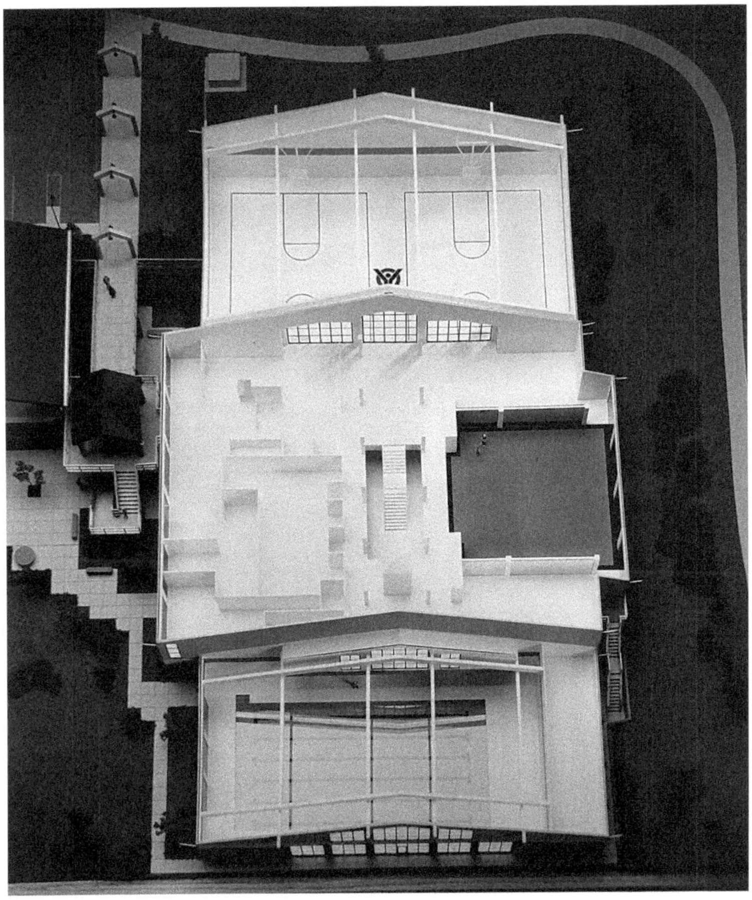

Figure 2.57. 1/8" Interior architectural model. *Courtesy of Jonathan E. Cagle, 3D Workshop, Inc.*

Figure 2.58. 1/8" Exterior architectural model. *Courtesy of Jonathan E. Cagle, 3D Workshop, Inc.*

Figure 2.59. 1/16" Landscape architectural model. *Courtesy of Jonathan E. Cagle, 3D Workshop, Inc.*

Some useful architectural model sources include:
Evergreen Scale Models, https://evergreenscalemodels.com/
Microform Models, https://www.microformmodels.com/
Plastruct, https://www.plastruct.com/
Preiser, https://www.preiserusa.com/

Film and Television

Models are used in television and film both as part of the design process and for miniature special effects. This section will only deal with models used as a design tool, as the subject of miniature effects is a vast subject requiring its own study. The production designer, like the scenographer, is responsible for conceptualizing the overall visual style, period, and concept of a film or television production, including all interior and exterior locations, properties, and set dressing. Working in collaboration with the director and cinematographer, the production designer is a significant contributor to the success of any production. The art director works under the production designer by managing the art department staff of set designer draftspersons, modelmakers, and properties artisans to develop the design. On smaller films and television programs the production designer may also serve as the art director. The standard scenographic model scales are most useful for shooting interiors on sound stages, but the smaller scales used in landscaping and exterior models are used when planning larger scenes such as streets, towns, battlefields, science fiction, and fantasy settings (see figures 2.60 and 2.61).

Figure 2.60. *The Happy Prince* by Oscar Wilde. 3/16" exterior project model by Andrew Chung. Dodge College of Film and Media Arts of Chapman University, 2023

Film and television models are usually white because their primary purpose is to study spacing and proportion, explore potential camera and lighting angles, reveal actor movement, and serve as a communication forum for the director, cinematographer, and production designer. The first models are typically white sketch or study models that are refined as the design progresses into detailed working models that incorporate information from the technical plates drawn to construct the setting. These models show stairs and levels; windows and ceilings; and impediments that affect camera placement

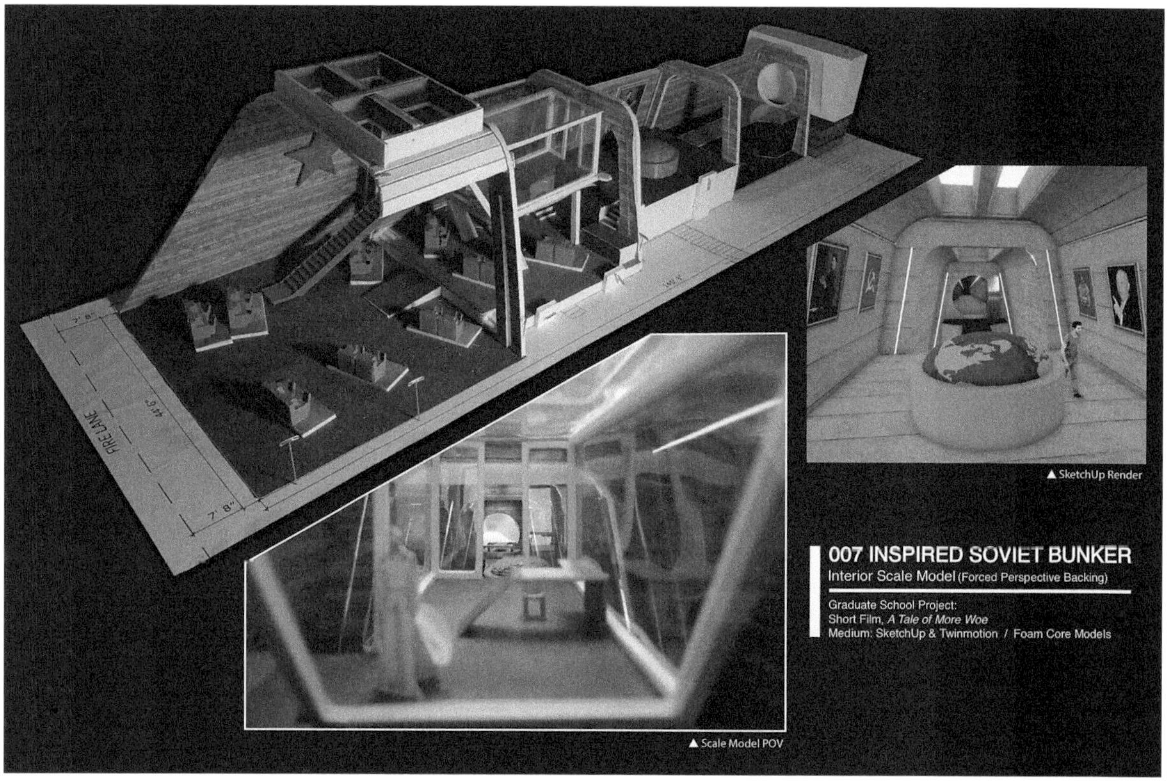

Figure 2.61. *007 Inspired Soviet Bunker.* 1/4" interior project model by Andrew Chung. Dodge College of Film and Media Arts of Chapman University, 2023

and lighting equipment, and serve as a dimensional guide for carpenters, painters, and set decorators. The model can also provide the producer with an early cost estimate.

Virtual modeling has gained wider acceptance in television and film than in theater because directors, cinematographers, and other production staff also use virtual modeling software to determine lighting positions, create storyboards, and establish camera angles.

Themed Entertainment

Themed entertainments are environments and events unified by a central theme of fairy tale, mythology, science fiction, geographic location, historical period, or holiday, especially Christmas and Halloween. These environments include theme parks, resorts, restaurants, shopping malls, casinos, museums, science centers, historic cultural parks, zoos, and aquariums. Theming also includes smaller venues like event design for receptions, parties, festivals, and product launches. Companies showcase their products and services at over 10,000 expositions, trade shows, and conventions each

Figure 2.62. 1/8" Model for Bavarian-themed entertainment experience. Project model by Nathan Naversen and Jim Tyckoson

year in the United States alone. Scale models are an effective means to display a company's products and projects when these are too large to exhibit. Themed entertainment design is a fusion of the arts employing theater designers, architects, landscape designers, production designers, art directors, cinematographers, painters, sculptors, and modelmakers. Like architects and landscape designers, themed entertainment modelers begin in small scale to develop an estimate of the entire site. Larger, more detailed models of individual units are then crafted to refine each element in the event site (see figures 2.62 and 2.63). A scenic unit may be built in progressively larger scales all the way to half-sized mockups by fine artists and sculptors who painstakingly refine proportions and textures prior to building the full-sized unit.

The above modeling practices are examples of designers previsualizing a scenographic environment prior to construction of the real setting. There is also the reverse process of building scale models that simulate existing objects and structures.

Figure 2.63. 1/8" Retail, Dining, and Entertainment (RDE) model of foamboard, Gatorfoam®, and paper by Nathan Naversen and Jim Tyckoson

Dollhouses and Miniatures

Dollhouses are key sources for scaled furniture and architectural building materials, including railings, balusters, stairs, molding, trim work, brickwork, fencing, siding, and roofing (see figure 2.64). Doll scales include one-inch scale (1:12 or 1" = 1'-0"), half scale (1:24 or 1/2" = 1'-0"), quarter scale (1:48 or 1/4" = 1'-0"), and eighth scale (1:96 or 1/8" = 1'-0") accessories. Scenic elements like balusters and newel posts in one scale may serve as columns in a smaller scale while the same elements may be used to construct furniture and ornaments in larger scales. Dollhouse supplies and furnishings are available in hobby stores, but a much greater selection is available in specialty dollhouse stores and their online counterparts. Antique malls frequently have stalls that specialize in vintage children's toys, dollhouse furnishings, and figures that can be obtained in various scales.

Dollhouse furniture often has exaggerated proportions and styling while miniaturists create detailed, balanced furniture and accessories that are usually too expensive for use in scenographic models. However, expensive accessories might be a justifiable investment if they correspond to available properties stock and will be reused for many productions.

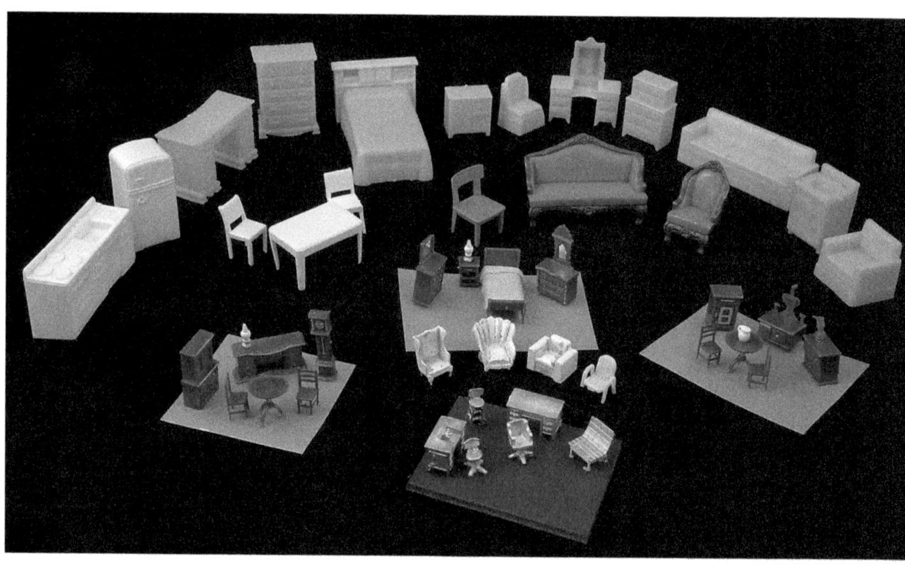

Figure 2.64. Dollhouse furniture in various scales

Kit Models

A *kit model* is a commercial replica made for hobbyists to assemble; these kits could feature simple "snap-together" plastic pieces, whereas others involve materials that require specialized tools for assembly. Popular kit models include civilian and military equipment, such as automobiles, trucks, watercraft, aircraft, spacecraft, as well as robots, aliens, and superheroes. Kit model scales are listed in numerical ratios with the model size relative to the size of the original. The scale may be listed as 1/24 or 1:24, which means the model is one twenty-fourth the size of the real object. Again, the scales of 1:96, 1:48, and 1:24 are equivalent to the 1/8", 1/4", and 1/2" scales used in scenographic modeling. Kit model cars and trucks are particularly useful for exterior scenes in scenographic models.

Dioramas

There are different definitions for *diorama*, but in reference to modelmaking it is a three-dimensional scene depicting a historic, military, nature, holiday, or fantasy setting built from miniature to larger-than-life scales (figure 2.65). Dioramas are usually viewed in museums, galleries, conventions, and private collections. The most popular scales for diorama kits are 1:35, 1:48, 1:72, and 1:87. Scenic elements like barrels, crates, rocks, and landscaping come in assorted sizes and may work in a variety of scenographic model scales. Fences, gates, and other thin profile objects are available in photo-etched, die, and laser-cut brass and aluminum sheets. Foliage, including trees, bushes, grasses, plants, and leaves, are also available in metal, paper, and plastic. There are many well-photographed books, websites, and online videos that teach how to build, paint, and accessorize dioramas.

Figure 2.65. *Capitulation.* 35 mm scale military diorama by Barbarossa Models

Diorama contains the Greek prefix "di," meaning "through," and the root "orama," meaning "which is seen."

Holiday tabletop dioramas are popular during Christmas, Halloween, Easter, and other celebrations. Possibly evolving from the Christmas creche or nativity scenes, these holiday dioramas draw inspiration from Victorian-era and European villages, rustic or rural farm settings, and fantasy locations like Santa's workshop (complete with miniature toy factory, elves, wrapped presents, reindeer, and Santa's sleigh). These dioramas offer a number of scenic accessories useful to the modelmaker including snow, picket fences, streetlights, fire hydrants, bandstands, sleds, foliage, and holiday decorations. The scales vary widely from 1:12, 1:24, 1:48, 1:60 to miniature HO, 1:87, scale. When purchasing holiday diorama accessories, it is helpful to use the human scale reference cards in figure 2.69 to determine the scale.

Role-Play Gaming

Role-play gaming (RPG) enthusiasts use soldiers, fantasy figures, and *scatter terrain* elements to enact historic, science fiction, and fantasy battles. Gamers use abstract figures and objects, but scaled figures help instill a stronger identification with their characters and also assist in telling the story of the game world by indicating areas of interest or providing clues about what happens in a particular location on the gameboard. These gaming accessories are available in paper, cardboard, plastic, and metal. Toy soldiers and their equipment were first made of tin and lead, but contemporary military models are now primarily injection-molded polystyrene, polyethylene, or plastic resin. Gaming supply manufacturers use the metric system, where the height of a figure in millimeters determines scales ranging from 2 mm to 54 mm high. The measurements that are most useful to scenographic models are 3.175 mm, 6.350 mm, 9.525 mm, and 12.70 mm, which roughly correspond to 1/8", 1/4", 3/8", and 1/2" scales, respectively. Scale is a complicated issue in gaming as some manufacturers measure from the foot to the top of the head, whereas others measure from foot to eye level. In addition, gaming characters often have distorted proportions with larger faces and hands, and fantasy figures depict elves, ogres, and giants that have no applicable human scale. Another issue of scale is the fact that the model figures and terrain must fit on a tabletop gameboard, so accessories may be compressed to fit the limited space. *Abstract scale* refers to gaming where there is no consistent scale across all gaming pieces.

Some useful role-playing and military diorama model sources include:
AK-Interactive, https://ak-interactive.com
American Diorama, https://americandiorama.com/
DioDump, https://www.diodump.com
Hobbylinc, https://www.hobbylinc.com

The broad range of gaming elements requires the modelmaker to visit the local RPG store or research online to discover what is available. Games are usually set on battlefields, so scenic elements like broken tree trunks, rocks, lampposts, fire hydrants, trash cans, fencing, walls, and tombstones are popular. Heavy metal foil is folded and draped to recreate fabric flags, banners, and tents. Highly detailed fencing, gates, barbed wire, mesh, trees, and bushes come in molded plastic and die-cut or photo-etched metal sheets, and laser-cut cardstock. 3D printing has also become extremely popular in gaming, and there are numerous companies that sell these items directly or sell downloadable files for the players to print themselves. This has the advantage of allowing the modelmaker to print objects in various scales (figure 2.66).

Figure 2.66. Role-play game pieces. *Courtesy of The Print Ever Goes On*

Model Railroading

Model trains were originally manufactured as children's toys, so expense, durability, and children's smaller hand sizes were the principal design factors. The first model trains were not built to any standard size, so trains from one company could not operate on tracks from another company until manufacturers standardized measurements. Toy trains eventually evolved into the adult hobby of model railroading, where scale and accuracy became essential. Model railroads are now categorized in scale and gauge. Scale is expressed as the numerical ratio of the model train in proportion to its full-size counterpart (1:48 or 1.48) or as a fraction (1/4). Gauge refers to the measurement between the rails of the full-size train track, and is expressed in letters (HO, O, G, etc.). The terms *gauge* and *scale* are confusing, owing to inconsistencies in the evolution of model trains, imperial versus metric measurement systems, and whether manufacturers are making toys or precise miniatures. Model railroading scenery elements in various scales and gauges are particularly useful in detailing exterior and industrial scenographic landscapes. Printed and embossed paperboard models of houses, buildings, and backdrops provide good examples when learning model assembly (see figure 2.67). Visiting local hobby stores or searching online for "model railroad supplies" will lead the modeler to a wealth of model railway figures, accessories, materials, tools, and instructional "how-to" videos. Again, the modelmaker should be aware that scenery elements in one scale may be useful in other scales. For example, a barrel in O scale could be a nail keg in G scale, or a bush in G scale could be a small tree in O scale.

Figure 2.67. Model railroading card models and embossed cards

Some useful online railroading sources include:

Arttista Accessories	https://arttista.com/
4D Model Shop	https://modelshop.co.uk/
Builders in Scale	http://www.builders-in-scale.com/
Evemodel	https://www.eve-modeler.com/
HobbyLinc	https://www.hobbylinc.com/model-trains
Micro-Mark	https://www.micromark.com/
Oakridge Stores	https://oakridgestores.com/trains/
Preiser	https://www.preiserusa.com/
Walthers	https://www.walthers.com/

Carte Maquettes

Carte maquettes (model cards) are useful examples for learning cardstock modelmaking. These scaled-down representations of famous houses, buildings, monuments, and villages are lightweight, colored, pre-cut, and pre-folded paper models that can be assembled often without glue or scissors (figure 2.68). Carte maquettes are perfect for children and adults alike who want to learn the basics of cardstock modeling. They provide a practical way to visualize and experiment with fresh design ideas before committing to more detailed and permanent materials. Carte maquettes are sold as kits and also as postcards in historic cities. "Carte" is French for paper and a "carterie" typically refers to a place where one can buy or create greeting cards.

Figure 2.68. Carte maquettes

Understanding the nuances of the various modeling scales requires extensive knowledge of the subject, so table 2.3 provides a comparative table that lists common scales for scenographic models with scales used in the disciplines described above.[6] Searching for "model scales" online will lead to numerous sites with comprehensive charts useful for matching various modeling scales. These charts often include sources and links to companies that supply figures, vehicles, and other scenic elements.

Tip: *The business-size cards in figure 2.69 may be photocopied, cut out, and kept in one's wallet for quick reference when buying modelmaking accessories in stores. The male figures are 5'-10", and female figures are 5'-6".*

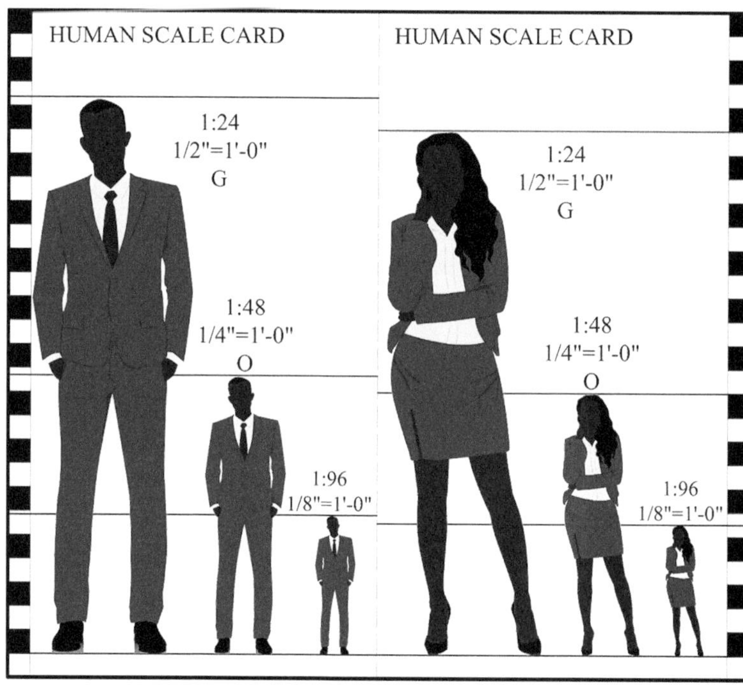

Figure 2.69. Human scale reference cards. Copy and cut to standard business card size 2" × 3 1/2"

Table 2.3. Comparative Chart of Modeling Scales

Imperial Scale	*Train Gauge*	*Metric Scale*	*Gaming*	*Kit Models*	*Description*
1/8"=1'-0" or 0.125"		1:96	3.175 mm	1/96 or 1:96	Standard scenographic and architectural model scale. Some doll furniture collections are available in this scale. Kit models of boats and spaceships.
	HO	1:87.1	3.5 mm	1/87 or 1:87.1	HO scenic elements can be used for 1/8" scale models but not human figures. HO stands for "Half O scale." HO is 9.27% larger than 1/8" scale.
1/6"=1'-0" or 0.167"			4.011 mm	1/72	Common scale for military dioramas and board gaming.
1/4"=1'-0" or 0.25"	O-American Originally 0 (zero) scale	1:48	6.35 mm	1/48 or 1:48	Standard scenographic and architectural model scale. Dollhouse quarter scale. Railroad accessories & architecture. Kit models of airplanes, automobiles, and boats.
	O-British	1:43	7.088 mm	1/43 or 1:43	Kit models of airplanes, automobiles, and boats. 10.42% larger than American O scale.
3/8"=1'-0" or 0.35"		1:32	9.525 mm	1/32 or 1:32	Useful scenographic model scale. Common scale for military dioramas and board gaming.
1/2"=1'-0" or 0.5"	G-American	1:24	12.70 mm	1/24 or 1:24	Standard scenographic and architectural model scale. Dollhouse half scale. G stands for "Garden" scale railroads. Kit model scale for cars, trucks, boats. Diecast cars. Toy farm animals.
	G-German	01:22.5	13.55 mm	1/22.5 or 1:22.5	From the German "groß" or "big" German model railroad manufacturers produce many scenic elements useful in 1/2" scale models. 6.25% larger than American G scale.

3. The Scenographic Model in Fashioning Stage Space, Mood, and Atmosphere

Stage Space

Communication between the director and the scenographer is accomplished largely through dialogue and sketching, but verbal descriptions of size, distance, depth, and height are subjective, while graphic plans, sketches, and renderings can be misread or misunderstood. Using models in early design meetings immediately introduces the concept of real space into the conversation and is a helpful first step in moving from the intangible world of the imagination into the real world of form, texture, materials, and stage space. As an example, compare the sketch to the model for the garret scene in *La Bohème* in figure 3.1 to see what each reveals. While it is easy to grasp the scenographer's basic idea for the scenic environment in both sketch and model, the spatial arrangements are more easily understood through the model. The model allows directors to examine the stage configuration, visualize blocking, and quickly adjust the ground plan as necessary.

Figure 3.1. *La Bohème* by Giacomo Puccini. Sketch by Darwin Payne. Southern Illinois University Carbondale, 1982. 1/2" white study model recreated by Ronald Naversen 2023

The ground plan is essential to the director and actors as it, more than anything else, determines their movements on stage, including direction, speed, and rhythm. As director Robert Benedetti notes:

> "Blocking" is really the spatial manifestation of the action within the configuration of the environment; if the configuration is correct the blocking will emerge naturally from the actors as they

experience the action. For this reason, I say that it is the ground plan—not the director—which truly blocks the show. I know that the ground plan is right when I need do no blocking at all.[1]

Benedetti recognizes that the space humans occupy plays a significant role in our psychological behavior. Arrangement, scale, proportion, color, texture, lighting, and acoustics all influence individual senses and generate a spectrum of emotion and behavior. Both the actor and the audience can immediately sense whether a space is safe, inviting, comfortable, dangerous, hard, or unpleasant.

Collaborating with models from the beginning compels the director and scenographer to concentrate on the spatial configuration and ground plan before they begin to consider the more decorative pictorial elements of a design. In some instances, concentrating on the spatial requirements of the production will help the designer and director see just how little scenery is truly needed to create the scenic environment. Working primarily from sketches can produce a great deal of scenery with little consideration of the essential spatial requirements of the play.

It is helpful for the scenographer to seek out images that evoke a powerful sense of a ground plan, especially in the preliminary stages of research. One such research image shown in figure 3.2 inspired the design for David Storey's *Home* shown in the rendering in figure 3.3 and the model in 3.4.

Figure 3.2. *The Mall, London*, 1962. *Estate of Evelyn Hofer*

Figure 3.3. *Home* by David Storey. 1/2" Color rendering by Darwin Payne. Southern Illinois University Carbondale, 1962

Figure 3.4. *Home* by David Storey. 1/2" presentation model by Darwin Payne. Southern Illinois University Carbondale, 1962

The theatrical ground plan's importance has increased as the theater has progressed from the pictorial wing and shutter stages of the nineteenth century into the thrust, arena, and found space stages of the twentieth. Some might argue that the ground plan is the most essential element in scenographic design today. The ground plan for some productions becomes not only the most obvious scenic element but virtually the only one.

Another important function of the model is that, by beginning in all three dimensions, it becomes quicker and easier to extend these ideas into the fourth. Live theater not only engages the two- and three-dimensional aspects of the painter's palette, and the sculptor's use of form, mass, and texture, but also must encompass the four-dimensional aspect of movement and transformation over time. The stage is a dynamic flow of performers moving in front of, behind, and between objects while also passing through light and shadow. The scenery itself is in a constant state of change either under the transformative power of light, during set changes, or when scenic units shift "avista" to enhance the dramatic action of the moment. This perpetual movement is what helps make the theater truly "live."

Scaled figures representing the actors can be positioned within the model to explore movement patterns and placement, but scenic units can also be experimentally moved to explore how they might shift during scene changes and throughout the production. This is especially important for plays written in a cinematic structure where scenes blend into each other with no discernable beginning or end. Models can incorporate turntables, swing stages, flying units, and elevators to demonstrate movement to pronounced effect. Extremely sophisticated models can even incorporate programmable automated scene shifts.

What is not apparent in a floor plan, sketch, or model is how the scenographer and director determine the specific configurations of objects and units that create the scenographic environment. How do they know what configuration is needed? As noted, the performers' actions are highly governed by the ground plan, but rehearsals often begin long after the stage space has been defined. How do scenographers ensure their choices will complement and enhance the work of the director and the performer? How does the designer decide what objects and configurations are intrinsic to or required by the text? The chart in figure 3.5 outlines one possible collaborative process by which the director and scenographer may interact in their design deliberations.

The scenographer should review the script carefully, making a list of requirements and inferences to help them understand the necessary spatial configuration. Sharing and discussing these items with the director will allow them to determine which elements are necessary for their production as described and labeled in the model for Ugo Betti's *Crime on Goat Island* shown in figure 3.6.

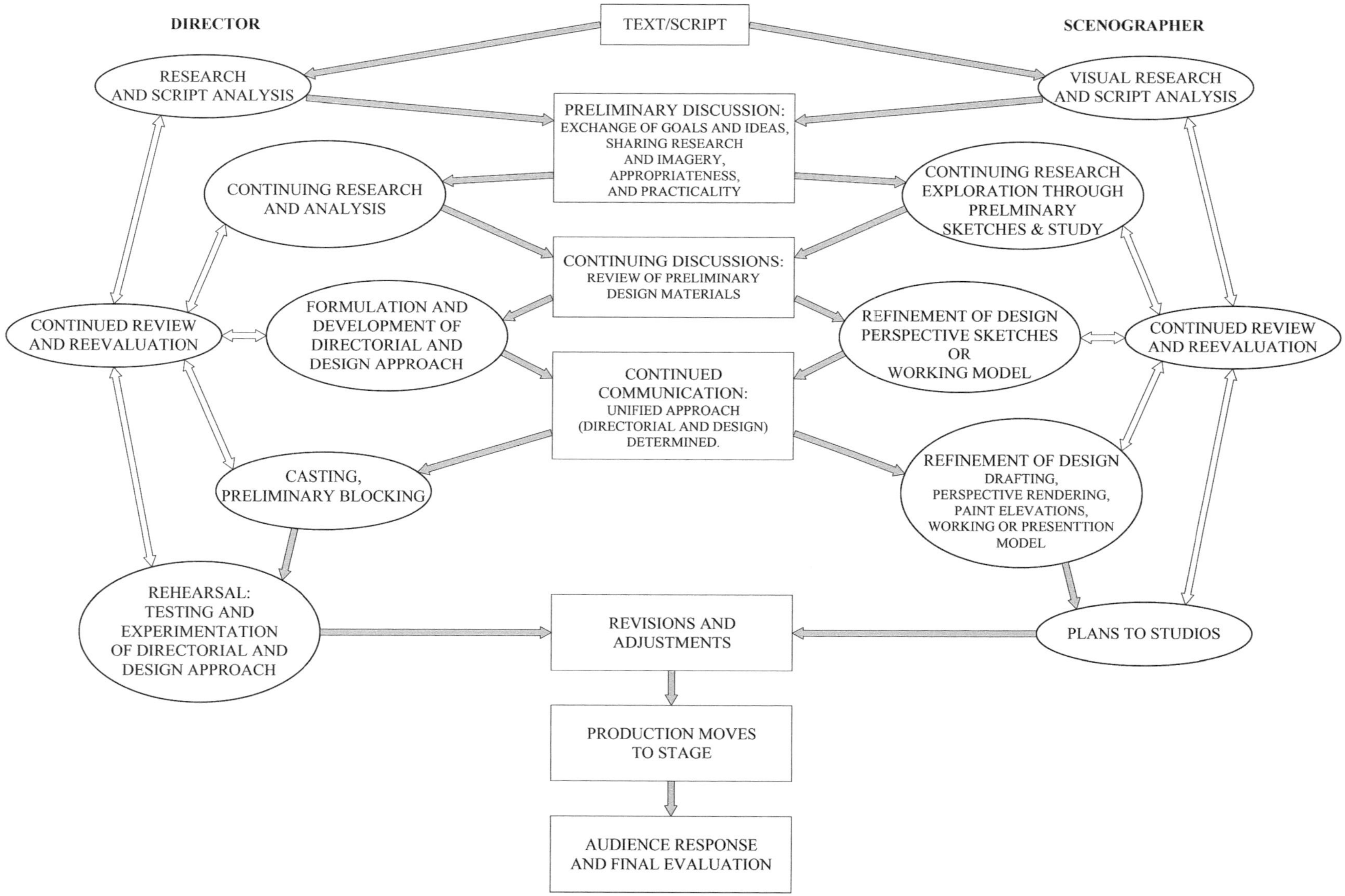

Figure 3.5. Chart showing potential director-scenographer collaboration

Figure 3.6. *Crime on Goat Island* by Ugo Betti. 1/2" model by Darwin Payne. Southern Illinois University Carbondale, 1975

A. Ground plan playing areas, including levels, steps, and ramps.
B. Objects directly described and used in the action of the production, including furniture, seating units, set business, and personal properties.
C. Barriers that dictate movement and the flow of the performer's actions, including entrances, exits, walls, doors, arches, windows, drapery, level changes, and so on. Barriers may not be actual physical obstacles. Painted tiles on the floor will imply where actors can move, or a line of window frames suspended in the air will suggest an exterior wall.
D. Scenic elements and objects that provide visual suggestions to the audience but are not direct influences on the performers' actions, including ceilings, moldings, and chandeliers flown above the actors' heads to define an interior room, tree branches to suggest a forest setting, or symbols like a cross to represent a spiritual setting.

Lighting, Mood, and Atmosphere

Lighting serves as an all-important fifth influence that enhances but does not physically alter all of the aforementioned categories. It reveals form by altering the perception of onstage shapes, particularly three-dimensional stage elements. By creating areas of emphasis, it directs the viewer's attention to specific parts of the stage and key moments in the scene. Through an infinite variety of visual transformations, lighting introduces movement to the stage space's physical form. Ultimately it sets the mood and atmosphere of a scene.

Lighting can be suggested in two-dimensional sketches and rendering, creating mood and atmosphere that is often lacking in theatrical modeling. However, the addition of lighting to the model combines spatial awareness with mood and atmosphere, creating a heightened sense of drama. This blending of space and atmosphere is foundationally the most important decision the director and scenographer must make when approaching the design for a production, and it must be reflected in the model.

Lighting effects are not as easily produced in a model as they are in sketches or virtual models as demonstrated in the scenic rendering for *Crime on Goat Island* in figure 3.7, but some approximations can be made using simple lighting fixtures. Even modest lighting efforts can spark creative ideas for the director and design team. More sophisticated lighting effects can be accomplished using lighting systems specially designed for modeling. Techniques for lighting models are discussed in greater detail in chapter 6, "Photographing and Archiving the Scenographic Model."

Figure 3.7. *Crime on Goat Island* by Ugo Betti. Rendering by Darwin Payne. Southern Illinois University Carbondale, 1975

Even without actual lighting, the scenographic model is still an efficient tool to bring space and atmosphere together into an integrated whole. Figure 3.8 shows the effect of adding atmospheric qualities to a simple white model for *La Bohème*. While the white model clearly shows the use of space, the addition of gray tones increases the sense of depth, dimensionality, mood, and atmosphere. These tones can be introduced into the model by drawing and shading with pencils, burnishing graphite powder onto the surfaces, or by using neutral gray markers and paints to create a tonal or grayscale model. Color can be later introduced by layering transparent or opaque watercolor over the shading on the model. These model studies can be effective in helping the designer develop an evocative combination of spatial and atmospheric qualities prior to introducing color. A tonal model is also easier for the viewer to see than a white model, especially when sharing models in printouts and on monitor screens.

Figure 3.8. *La Bohème*. Tonal sketch by Darwin Payne. Southern Illinois University Carbondale, 1982. 1/2" tonal model recreated by Ronald Naversen, 2023

4. Experimental Modelmaking

All work in the theater starts as an idea, a concept, an image without physical form. Scenographic design is no exception. Scenographers are often asked, "Where do your ideas come from?" The answer is quite simple: everywhere. But explaining this answer is complicated, and the entire process can never be fully articulated. Aspects of the design process may remain unknown even to the scenographer.

Through textual analysis and historical and cultural research, the scenographer begins to previsualize the design. Sketching and experimenting with three-dimensional forms and materials then allows the design to take physical form. Using models early in the design process allows the designer to experientially explore abstract three-dimensional themes, textures, masses, and spatial relationships rather than relying on two-dimensional sketches. Early experimental modeling relies on the scenographer's intuitive ability to see possibilities when juxtaposing shapes and forms. It is, in effect, creative play, but with the serious purpose of achieving a finished design. Experimental modeling helps spark the design via accidental and unplanned compositions that may fortuitously lead to practical solutions.

Experimental models are temporary compositions collaged and assembled with bits of paper, research images, and found objects. Initially, exploratory models might not be built to a specific scale, so it is beneficial to include proportional two- or three-dimensional figures to provide a benchmark and identify these environments as meant for human activity. Experimental models can be placed within a simple cardboard box or shoebox stage if a model box or model stage is not available.

Scenographers often show these experimental models to the director to solicit their thoughts prior to further development. Other times they may wish to solidify and refine their ideas before showing a more polished design to the director. This decision is based upon the personal dynamics of the designer and director's relationship. In either case, it is wise for the scenographer to photograph these conceptual models for documentation and to serve as a reference point in case the initial design idea becomes muddled or lost during further development.

Contemporary artists regularly use materials, techniques, and approaches unknown just a few decades ago. They view the world through devices that allow them to see almost anything and everything in a quick succession of still or moving images and then procure nearly limitless materials all at the stroke of a keyboard. Artists today spontaneously combine diverse elements and mediums into a single work, embracing fortuitous results. The resulting art is often one of collage, with the artist functioning as an expert composer of images, materials, and forms gathered from their tangible world.

Experimental modelmaking is a productive approach to resolving the complex problems in contemporary scenography while aiding in the discovery of novel and unimagined forms. As mentioned, it is creative play, but with a serious purpose. Random, accidental, and unanticipated compositions allow the designer to explore the interrelation of form, space, color, texture, and time with the performer.

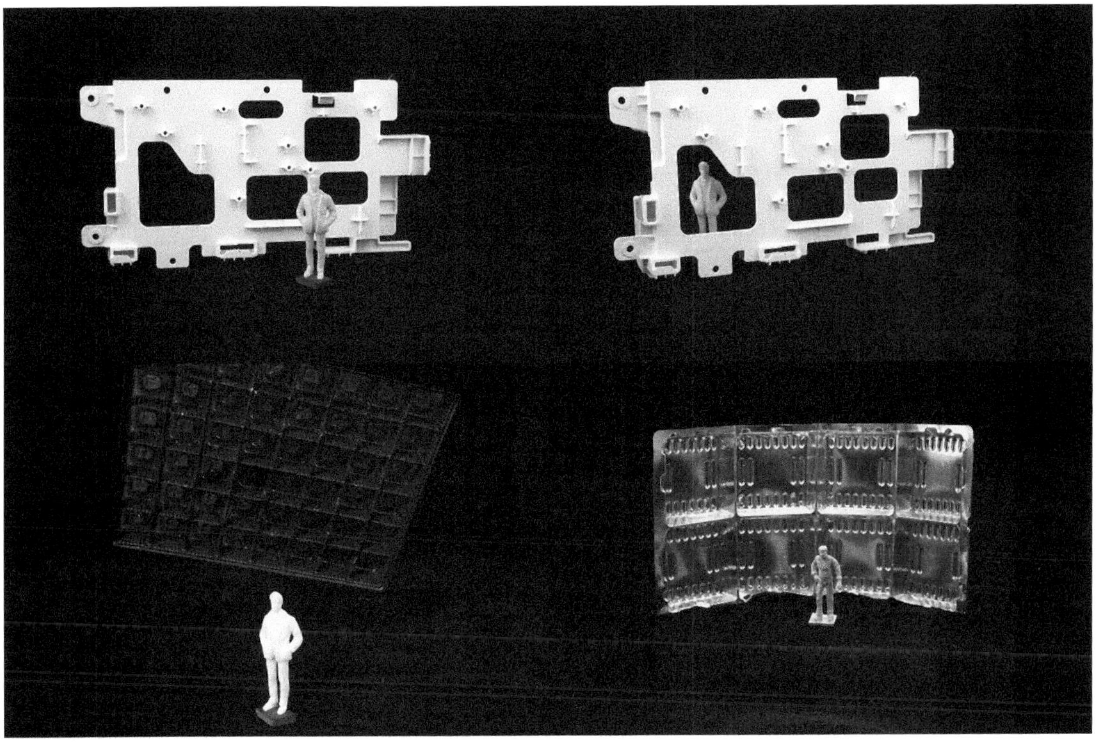

Figure 4.1. Experimental model variations

Experimental models can be assembled from traditional materials of cardstock, illustration board, foam board, and balsa. But modeling with wire mesh, metal foils, fabrics, string, plastic, foams, and found objects can spark richer inspiration. Found objects including photographs, beads, bottle caps, food packaging, toys, and holiday ornaments can instantly jumpstart the scenographic imagination (see figure 4.1). Designs are often inspired by miscellaneous found objects that trigger the imagination in unforeseen ways. For this reason, it is suggested that scenographers develop a collection of inspirational and evocative items into a design "morgue." A two-dimensional morgue consisting of print or digital images can be cataloged physically in file folders, digitally on a hard drive, or in an online storage service. A three-dimensional morgue, sometimes called the "designer's toybox," can be filled with interesting textures and dimensional objects, including pieces of past models (figure 4.2). Designers never know just when these random acquisitions will prove useful for experimentation or as a catalyst for a design. The scenographer should not worry when experimenting with unusual and interesting materials as almost any form or texture assembled in a scaled model can be simulated in full scale using various traditional scenic materials. Much of the raw material of the scenographer's art may be found in the collections of our numerous museums, but these are not their only sources. Scenographers should maintain an equal sensitivity to the broken, discarded refuse in our junkyards, recycling centers, and secondhand shops. Contemporary theater rarely focuses on the finest examples of art and architecture of our society but often explores the abandoned relics of our culture. The scenographer must consider all visual, tactile, and auditory phenomena as sources for their art.

Figure 4.2. Design morgue examples

An extraordinary example of using experimental modeling to unlock the creative imagination is evident in the work of the Spanish architect Antonio Gaudí (1852–1926). Gaudí chose not to base his design of the Church of the Sagrada Familia in Barcelona, Spain (figure 4.3), on traditional architectural principles. Through years of research, he experimented with unique upside-down models, allowing gravity to reveal novel and unique catenary arching forms, and, in the process, invented a new vocabulary of structures to build his cathedral (see figure 4.3). Without experimental modeling, his Sagrada Familia would not have been possible. Like Gaudí, scenographers can use experimental modeling to look beyond historic scenic forms to achieve a more expansive vision.

Figure 4.3. Upside-down experimental model by Antonio Gaudí for La Sagrada Familia Cathedral. *Photographer Manuel Cohen / Art Resource, NY*

The experimental work suggested in this text cannot be neatly outlined through step-by-step instructions. Experimenting is based on the idea that the scenographer should engage in sessions of creative play that are not directly goal oriented but geared toward exploring the random and chance possibilities that emerge through unintentional and undirected activity. This creative play, next to full-scale experimentation, is one of the most productive ways of engaging the scenographer's sensitivity and awareness of the potential design that exists within a playscript.

Collage: Found Images

An alternative to sketching as the first step in the design process is to experiment through collage. This can be particularly helpful for the novice designer who has yet to master drafting and sketching skills. When approaching a classical play such as *Antigone*, the scenographer often starts by researching ancient Greek art and architecture. Assembling these historic research images into a collage allows the scenographer to experimentally combine images into different arrangements until a design evolves.

Collage techniques actively utilize research imagery, allowing the scenographer to experiment with the relationship of the various images as a foundation for a scenographic model as shown in figure 4.4. When progressing from collage to the three-dimensional model, the scenographer and director must begin to consider the ground plan. The research image of the circular altar references the rounded orchestra of the Greek theater but also suggests levels with opportunities for movement and seating as revealed in the physical model in figure 4.5.

Figure 4.4. Statue of Archaic Kore figure (*Photographer G. Dagli Orti /© NPL - DeA Picture*) combined with the Altar of Chthonic Deities (*Photographer Manuel Cohen / Art Resource, NY*) to create a collage rendering for Sophocles's *Antigone* by Darwin Payne. Project design. Southern Illinois University Carbondale 1976

Tip: *When using collage techniques, it is helpful to select images with similar visual viewpoints and scale them relative to one another. The image size can be altered with a photocopier or through image-editing software. Once revised, these images can be physically cut and assembled into a collage or by layering the pictures in image-editing software.*

Figure 4.5. *Antigone* by *Sophocles*. 1/2" project model by Darwin Payne. Southern Illinois University Carbondale 1976

Found two-dimensional images often become the basis for three-dimensional scenic units. British scenographer Jocelyn Herbert (1917–2003) used Matthias Grünewald's 1525 painting *The Crucifixion* as inspiration for her design of John Osborne's play *Luther* as shown in figure 4.6.

This same research image can also be used as an example of experimental modeling by integrating its flat rectangular form into more dynamic arrangements as shown in figure 4.7.

Working with Projections in Experimental Modelmaking

Digital projection equipment and software have revolutionized theatrical design as a means of creating dynamic scenic environments, but they may also be used to assist the scenographer in the creative process of designing a production. Projecting images on basic model forms and textures is a stimulating experimental technique and a productive phase in the design process. These projections provide creative play for scenographers, even when they have no specific project in mind; the results of which might inspire solutions to future design projects.

Figure 4.6. *The Crucifixion* by Matthias Grünewald, 1525. *Courtesy of Staatliche Kunsthalle Karlsruhe (State Art Gallery in Karlsruhe).* *Luther* by John Osborne. Scenic design by Jocelyn Herbert, Theatre Royal, Nottingham, 1961. *Courtesy of the Mary Evans Picture Library*

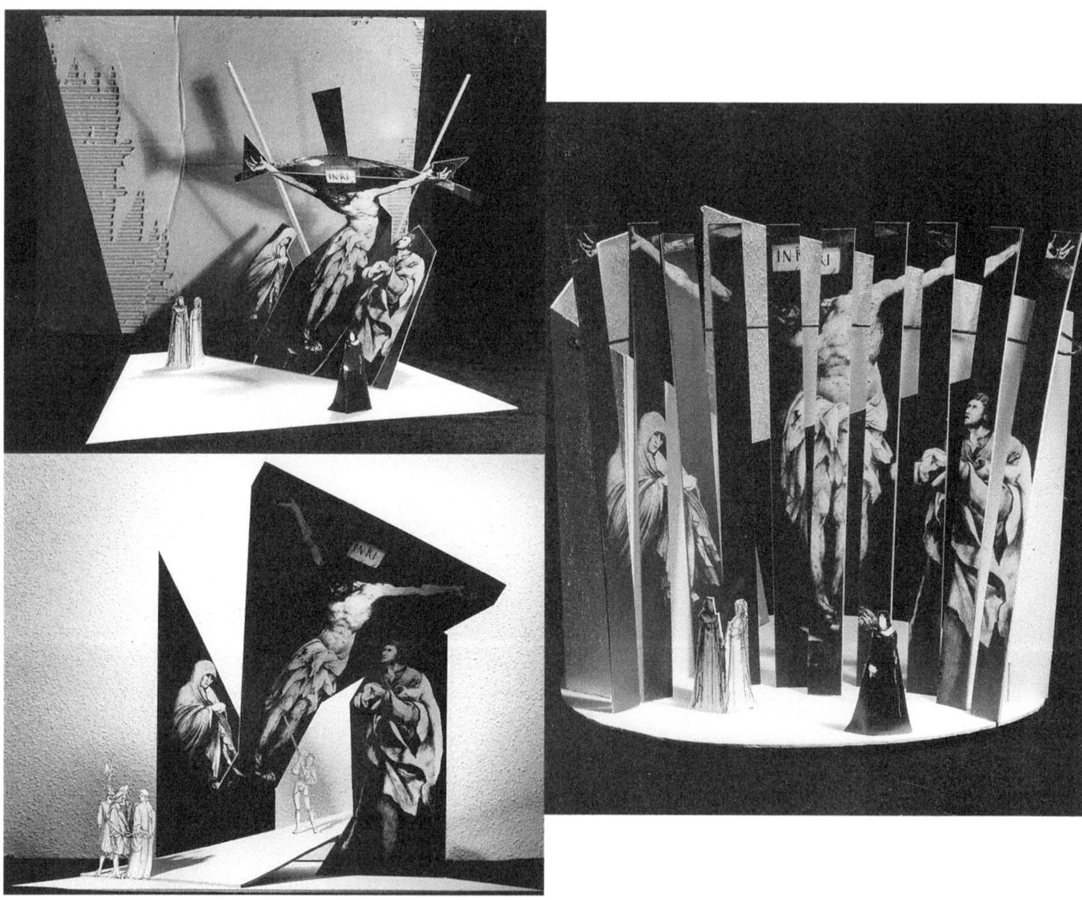

Figure 4.7. *The Crucifixion* used in experimental models by Darwin Payne

Tip: The use of found images either in scale or overscaled can be a valuable addition to the scenographer's toolbox. There are, however, some cautions that must be observed in their use. No performer can hope to compete for focus with an image ten times their size. When using overscaled images, their purpose must be thoroughly considered, and their effect carefully controlled.

Tip: When working with projections on models, the modelmaker does not necessarily need to use an exceptionally powerful projector. Mini video projection units (VPU) are relatively inexpensive and can be operated wirelessly using a laptop, tablet, or smartphone. When selecting a projector to use for model experimentation, the modelmaker should consider brightness, contrast ratio, and throw distance. Brightness will usually be measured in lumens; this unit relates to the overall brightness of the image created by the projector. In general, high brightness is desired. However, because of the small size of projections needed for model experimentation, clear bright images can be achieved with brightness as low as 300 lumens. The contrast ratio is almost as important as brightness. The contrast ratio measures the difference between the brightest and darkest points of a projected image. The higher the contrast ratio, the more vibrant an image will appear. A contrast ratio of 1,000:1 or higher is preferred. Perhaps the most important consideration for a model projector is the throw distance. The modelmaker should seek out a short or ultrashort throw projector. This will allow the projector to be placed close to the model while producing a small, focused image. Throw distance may be measured in a ratio such as 1:2—the smaller the ratio, the closer the projector can be placed to the model. There may also be a minimum distance listed at which the projector will remain in focus. A short minimum distance is preferred.

As in the previous collage project, the images are projected onto various shapes, for texture. These surface textures will affect the quality of the images. Fabrics, granular surfaces, fractured forms, and linear groupings all deliver markedly unique effects. Figure 4.8 shows an arrangement of forms without projections. Figure 4.9 demonstrates how this same arrangement is transformed when different images are projected onto it.

Figure 4.8. Model with basic arrangement of forms

Figure 4.9. Same forms with different projections

> ***Projection Mapping***
> Regardless of the projector used, there may need to be some image adjustment or projection mapping to place the image on the model. Most projectors will have a keystone adjustment that can correct image skew. When fitting images to models, the scenographer may find it necessary to use software to achieve more complex image mapping. With still images, basic image mapping can be achieved by manipulating images in image-editing software, using skew, distort, warp, and other editing tools. Using image-editing software may prove frustrating as it is difficult to edit the image while projecting it cleanly on the model. Programs such as QLab® or Isadora® are designed specifically to support projection mapping and are commonly used for projection design for live performance. Both QLab® and Isadora® can also accommodate video, including live camera feeds, which may be useful for visualizing projection designs.

While the resulting designs created by this method can often be replicated on stage with larger projectors, the images can also be painted rather than projected. Figure 4.10 shows a model for *Aida* with a projection on the left and a presentation model where the projected image has been traced onto the model and then painted. One of the most positive reasons to experiment with projections on models is that not even the most imaginative scenographer could predict the myriad results obtainable by simple alteration in the distance, direction, and surface form on which an image can be projected.

Figure 4.10. *Aida* by Giuseppe Verdi. 1/2" projected and painted project model using experimental projection by Darwin Payne

Assemblage: Found Objects and Materials

Scenographers constantly kit bash various objects into their designs. In interior settings especially, whether period or modern, modelmakers assemble appropriate items, including furniture, properties, and dressing. Since scenic designs often deal with specific characters in a distinctive environment, part of their modeling skill depends on the development of a sensitivity to the precise mood and atmosphere that this collection of objects can evoke. Even settings without furniture and dressing require understanding the visual language resulting from the juxtaposition of objects and performers. It is often part of the scenographer's function to convey complex and meaningful ideas to an audience using an object or a configuration of objects. These messages will not be perceived by the audience on a conscious level, but they can amplify a character's position or clarify a director's point of view in situations where words are insufficient. Carefully curated objects enrich the play's meaning and the author's intent.

Inspiration for the use of found objects can be seen in the work of artists such as Edward Kienholz (1927–94). His assemblages of commonplace and familiar objects convey powerful statements. His evocative and meaningful configurations are strikingly similar to those created by the scenographer as shown in figure 4.11.

Figure 4.11. *The Wait*, 1964-1965. Mixed media tableau by Edward Kienholz. *Whitney Museum of American Art, New York; Gift of the Howard and Jean Lipman Foundation, Inc. © Estate of Nancy Reddin Kienholz. Courtesy of L.A. Louver, Venice, CA. (Digital image © Whitney Museum of American Art / Licensed by Scala / Art Resource, NY)*

Scenographic modelmakers should also be familiar with the work of Kris Kuksi (1973–), who crafts intricate sculptures composed of thousands of individual found and created objects that he collects and reshapes to use in his theatrically baroque art (figure 4.12). Kuksi's work is strongly related to experimental modelmaking. Other notable collage and assemblage artists to study are Joseph Cornell, Tracey Emin, and Tomoko Takahashi.

Figure 4.12. *The Deadly Sins*. Assemblage. Mixed media, by Kris Kuksi. 2009

The scenographer's morgue of inspirational images and toy box of found objects are excellent source materials for collage and assemblage experiments. These collections should be continually renewed by fetching novel items back to the studio. It is impossible to suggest what the scenographer should collect or how they might go about using collected items. Aside from the infinite range of materials available, the scenographer's personal aesthetic will determine the selection of materials and their arrangement on the model stage. Some scenographers are partial to organic forms and emphasize them in their work; others are more painterly; still others will lean toward the architectural. Working scenographers often reuse, reconfigure, and repurpose these inspirations that have proved effective in the past. Undirected as an experimental model might be, it can have constructive effects on the scenographer's future creations. For example, discarded packaging materials or surplus computer parts can suggest completely different possibilities when put into a relationship with the human figure, as shown in figure 4.1. An integral part of the scenographer's aesthetic is a constantly evolving sensitivity to the entire visual world in which they live.

Composition Chess Exercise

Composition Chess, created by Michael J. Griffith and adapted by the authors for this text, is a game to help scenographers strengthen their visual imaginations and improve collaborative skills through experimental modelmaking. Composition Chess is an opportunity for creative play during a design class session or as a means for scenographers, directors, and members of a production team to devise scenic environments in a collaborative method. Each participant adds to the overall composition, making sure that it remains balanced.

Composition Chess

A Participatory Exercise for Students of Stage Design

by Michael J. Griffith, Miami University, Ohio.

A supervisor should be appointed to oversee the rules and moderate discussions. The supervisor may be the instructor of a class or appointed by the participants of the game.

The participants will be provided with:

1. A piece of music to set the tone and theme of the chess match. Instrumental music is preferable.
2. A scaled proscenium or thrust stage. This can simply be a cardboard box open at one end. If a proscenium frame is used, it should be easily removeable to facilitate the participants' moves.
3. A background unit (black on one side, white on the other) may be used as is, or as a surface on which two-dimensional or three-dimensional collage compositions may be attached.
4. Two- or three-dimensional scaled human figures that can be moved about the stage as each participant adds to the composition.
5. White paper, cardstock, poster, and foam board.
6. A variety of white materials and shapes such as blocks of wood, pieces of foam, dowels, fabric, string, etc.
7. Found objects including containers, bottle caps, straws, paper or foam coffee cups, lids, etc. Color should not be an issue, so any object not already white should be painted with flat white paint.
8. Tools including scissors, utility knives, steel-edged rulers, markers, pencils, tape, tacky glue, hot glue, etc.

See figure 4.13 for examples of materials and tools.

Figure 4.13. Composition Chess materials

Figure 4.14. Composition Chess models. *Photograph by H. D. Motyl, 2024*

Teams of three to four participants will come to an agreement regarding the sequence of turns and the background to be used for the session, either a "neutral" background (black or white) or participant-created background. If participants choose to create a background, it may be created by a collage of cutouts from black, white, and neutral materials. Each participant has 60 seconds to add to the composition of the background. Once the background is complete, it should be placed at the back of the model stage. Once the background is in place, the chess match begins.

Rules

1. Each participant has 60 seconds to place a unit into position in the space.
2. A unit may be made of no more than three shapes or objects available from the playing pieces or created by the player; for example, customized cutout shapes.
3. The scaled figure(s) should be (re)positioned by the player at the end of their turn.
4. All players should strive to create a new composition as the play progresses. As the composition develops, it should always provide viable acting areas within the space.
5. At the completion of each round, when each player has had their turn, there should be a brief discussion about the developed composition (3 minutes maximum). Issues such as balance, rhythm, harmony, direction, and mood should be addressed. Play continues at the end of the discussion.
6. Players may not begin making their piece until the last player has added their piece and finished their move.
7. If a player feels they cannot make an addition, they must pass and are then out of the "active" play the rest of the game. They will continue to participate in evaluative discussions of developing compositions.
8. The game ends when all players pass—that is, they all agree that they cannot add another element to the composition without altering the balance, rhythm, etc., and without encroaching on potential playing areas for the actors.
9. Participants may choose to photograph the developing composition at the end of each round and at the end of each play to record the results.
10. Accidental "knockdowns" of playing pieces must be restored. The focus of the play should be on visual composition, not on the engineering of literal balance.

Figure 4.14 (on the previous page) shows examples of completed compositions.

The Effect of Gamma Rays on Man-in-the-Moon Marigolds by Paul Zindel. 1/2" model by Darwin Payne. Southern Illinois University Carbondale, 1972

As You Like It by William Shakespeare. 1/2" model by Darwin Payne. Wake Forest University, 1992

Dracula by Steven Dietz. 1/2" model by Darwin Payne. Wake Forest University, 2001

La Bohème by Giacomo Puccini. 1/2" model by Darwin Payne. Southern Illinois University Carbondale, 1981

The Pirates of Penzance by Gilbert and Sullivan. 1/2" model by Darwin Payne. Wake Forest University. 1987

Man of La Mancha book by Dale Wasserman, music by Mitch Leigh, and lyrics by Joe Darion. 1/2" model by Darwin Payne. Southern Illinois University Carbondale, 1978

5. Emergent Technology

Since the last edition of this book, there have been numerous advancements in technology, materials, and processes that have introduced potential efficiencies in the modelmaking process. Advancements in computer-aided design, increased access to online resources, and the development of collaboration software and platforms have changed the way that scenographers work and communicate with the director and design team. Even though CAD and visualization software has given the scenographer the ability to create lifelike virtual 3D computer models, the physical model is still an incredibly valuable tool in the design and production process.

There are emergent technologies that can aid the modelmaker in the creation of the physical model. 3D printing and 3D scanning have expanded the complexity and speed with which model components may be crafted. Computerized cutting machines make producing intricate two-dimensional patterns much easier than manual methods. Vacuum forming, computer numerical control (CNC) routing, and advancements in molding and casting materials allow for the easy duplication of three-dimensional forms.

3D Printing

Originating in 1970s and 1980s manufacturing, 3D printing became more commercially viable to consumers in the early twenty-first century with the introduction of low-cost printers. While there are several technologies associated with 3D printing, the three most common technologies are fused deposition modeling (FDM), stereolithography (SLA), and selective laser sintering (SLS), but all printers work on the same basic principle of additive manufacturing. Through additive manufacturing, objects are built one layer at a time, each layer being placed on top of the previous layer to create the finished object.

The most common and the least expensive printing technology is fused deposition modeling (FDM). This type of printer makes use of a process where thermoplastic is melted and extruded through a small nozzle to be deposited on the object being printed. As the plastic is extruded, either the print head or the build plate is moved to create the outline of the object being printed. When the plastic cools, it becomes solid and produces a rigid object. Several types of thermoplastics can be used with this technology; the most common is polylactic acid (PLA). PLA is an inexpensive polyester-based plastic that has a relatively low melting point, which makes it easy to use in most 3D printers. PLA is considered an environmentally friendly material as it is made from organic compounds.[1] Another plastic that is commonly used is acrylonitrile butadiene styrene (ABS). ABS tends to be less rigid, lighter, and more durable than PLA plastic, but its higher melting temperature and tendency to warp during printing make it a more difficult material with which to work. There are numerous other types of thermoplastics available. Makers should consult the 3D printer manual to determine the thermoplastic compatibility.

Another relatively inexpensive printing technology is stereolithography (SLA). In SLA printing, objects are built layer by layer using an ultraviolet laser that reacts with a photoreactive polymer resin. The resin is cured by the laser to a hardened or semihardened state. Very thin layers are possible in SLA printing, which leads to a more detailed finished product. Once printed objects are completed, they must be cleaned with a solvent to remove excess resin from the surface of the object. Some SLA printers require extra curing after printing. There are special curing devices that incorporate a rotating platform and an ultraviolet chamber. Printed objects are placed in the curing machine, where they are bombarded with ultraviolet light that further hardens the object. Several types of photoreactive resins are available for SLA printers, including assorted colors as well as clear and flexible materials. Makers should consult the 3D printer manual to determine the selected resin compatibility.

Selective laser sintering (SLS) is a more expensive printing technology that uses a laser to fuse powdered polymer into solid objects. Powdered polymer is spread in successive thin layers while a laser is used to melt and fuse the powder together in each layer. The main advantage of this process is the ability to print hollow objects without any support structure as the layers of powder support the object during printing. SLS printers tend to be more expensive than FDM and SLA printers.

Selecting a 3D Printer

Perhaps the most significant factor in selecting a 3D printer is build volume. Build volume will determine the maximum size of a single printed object. Small footprint printers with a build volume of 125 × 125 × 125 mm (4.9" × 4.9" × 4.9") will be adequate for printing most furniture in 1/4" and 1/2" scales. Larger objects can be achieved on small-footprint 3D printers by splitting the object into smaller component pieces that can be printed separately and assembled after printing. If the maker is printing larger scenic elements, it may be worth investing in a printer with a larger build volume; printers with 250 mm^3, 500 mm^3, and larger print volumes are available.

As with any electronic device, it is not advisable to purchase the least expensive 3D printer available. There are numerous open-source 3D printers on the market, some of them of decent quality, but others may produce inferior-quality prints and may be difficult to operate. It is also advisable to purchase a printer that provides online technical support and tutorials. Established 3D printer manufacturers like Makerbot® and FormLabs® offer extensive community forums and individual support for their printer models.

All 3D printers will produce odors when operating, either through off-gassing of photoreactive resin when working with an SLA printer or from heating plastic in FDM and SLS printers. While PLA plastic tends to be less offensive than some other materials used, precautions should be taken to protect respiratory systems whenever using a 3D printer. Setting up a printer in a well-ventilated area is recommended. There are also fume extractor devices that remove the air near the printer and filter it before venting it back into the room. Some 3D printer companies also offer enclosures to help contain odors produced by printers. These enclosures offer exhaust ports that can be connected to fume extractors or exhaust fans that vent the air outside. If no ventilation is available, the modelmaker should avoid prolonged exposure to the printer while it is operating and consider wearing a respirator with appropriate organic vapor filter cartridges.

3D Modeling

Regardless of the printing technology used, all 3D-printed objects start out as 3D computer drawings. These drawings can be created from scratch in CAD programs such as Vectorworks® or AutoCAD®, downloaded from internet file warehouses such as turbosquid.com or thingiverse.com, or 3D-scanned as captures of physical objects. Creating 3D drawings using a CAD program has obvious advantages. The ability to create exactly what is needed for a design and to amend that object as the design evolves offers the modelmaker great flexibility. Creating 3D objects with any level of detail in CAD software does take a significant amount of experience, but simple objects can be made quickly using basic 3D drawing tools. Most CAD software can add or subtract solids, allowing the modelmaker to create complicated objects by combining basic 3D shapes such as cubes, spheres, and cones. When working with CAD software, it is best to draw objects in full scale and reduce the object to the desired scale before exporting. To print objects created in CAD software, the objects need to be converted to a format that the printer will recognize. Companies that sell 3D printers will typically package a slicing program with their printer. The slicing program will translate the CAD file into the code file that the printer can interpret. Slicing programs often provide tools to scale objects, print multiple objects on the same print, and set the print speed, among other printer settings.

3D scanning is another method used to create a model of a real-world object. There are two types of technology available for 3D scanning useful for the modelmaker, photogrammetry and laser scanning. Photogrammetry uses a series of photos taken from multiple angles and sides of an object. This process requires several photos, potentially hundreds, to create an accurate computer model of the object being captured. The advantage of photogrammetry is that it does not require special hardware. Digital cameras, including smartphone cameras, may be used to create the source photos. There are several different software packages available to compile the images into an editable computer model, including free software options.

Laser scanning uses infrared lasers to accurately measure the distance from the scanner to the surface of the object being scanned. Depending on the object, makers may choose a small desktop laser scanner with built-in turntable or a handheld scanner. Modelmakers who have access to a stock of model or real-sized furniture or scenic items may review their stock to create a digital collection of their inventory that can be printed as needed for use in their models.

Model Assembly

When working with relatively large objects, the modelmaker might consider splitting the object into separate printed pieces that can then be assembled into the completed object. There are different strategies employed for splitting objects into smaller segments. The modelmaker may choose to split objects by creating a seam or separating objects into component pieces. When creating a seam, it is advisable to split the object at the least complex part of the model. A straight seam, easily achieved in CAD software, is the simplest way to split objects. It may be difficult to align objects split with a straight seam, particularly if they are irregular shapes. The modelmaker may consider adding a registration key to seams to facilitate alignment during assembly. Registration keys serve as an alignment guide and can be created by changing a straight seam to interlocking geometric shapes, adding channels or holes for separate tabs or pins, or by adding mortice and tenon elements to seams. Figure 5.1 shows two examples of registration keys. When using registration keys, the printed objects must be accurate for the objects to fit together properly. If print accuracy is slightly off, pins or tenons may not fit into their respective holes or mortices.

Another method is to split objects into component pieces. This method is particularly helpful when printing substantial portions of a scenic model. Individual flats and platform structures can be printed separately and assembled in the finished scenic model (see figure 5.2 for examples of model pieces split by component). Makers should separate printed items into relatively flat components when printing to reduce printing time. Overhanging and

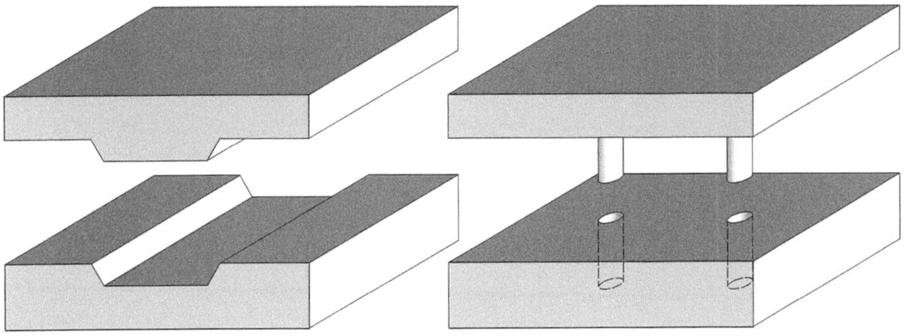

Figure 5.1. Illustration of registration keys

cantilevered elements tend to be difficult to print successfully. Individual components may be rotated to achieve the highest quality print possible; this is typically done in the printer's slicing program. Slicing programs can also be used to add support structures to complex shapes or overhanging elements. Support structures can easily be removed once the object is printed. Modelmakers should consider printing objects in an orientation that limits the amount of support structure needed; printing a table upside-down or a wall lying on its back with the finished surface up may produce a higher-quality print with little or no need for support structures.

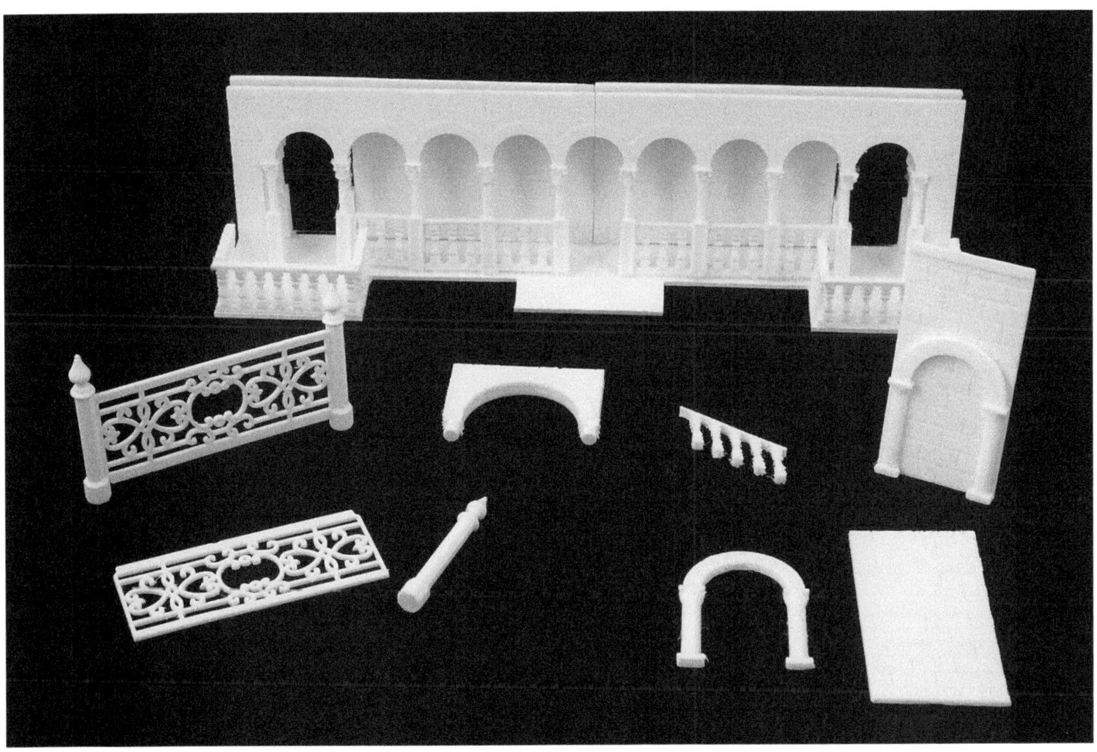

Figure 5.2. Examples of splitting by component

Whether working with printed objects that have been split into smaller components or printing larger items, the modelmaker will need to adhere 3D-printed objects to other printed objects or other materials. Not all adhesives are effective for use on 3D-printed objects. Cyanoacrylate (known generically as instant, power, crazy, or super glue) will bond to most plastics used in 3D printers. Cyanoacrylate will also make a strong bond between 3D-printed objects and other modelmaking materials. For objects printed on an SLA printer, the liquid resin used in the printing process can be an effective adhesive between components printed from the same resin, but it must be cured with an ultraviolet laser. Laser light pens that operate at the correct wavelength to cure liquid resin are available. A curing machine may also be used. Liquid resins are not effective adhesives for bonding printed objects to other modelmaking materials. When working with ABS plastic, acetone can be used to "cold-weld" printed objects together, but it is not effective at adhering ABS to other model materials. If the modelmaker is bonding PLA to PLA or ABS to ABS, they may consider the use of a 3D pen as a bonding tool. 3D pens are handheld thermal devices that heat and extrude thermoplastics like PLA and ABS. A 3D Pen may be used to extrude a thin layer of plastic that can bond two printed objects together. The modelmaker must work quickly using a 3D pen as a bonding tool, and it is recommended that this technique only be used on small 3D-printed objects. While it does not form a strong bond to plastic, traditional hot melt glue may be used to bond furniture, figures, and small objects to other modelmaking materials. PVA glues, such as Elmer's® Glue-All® are not effective on 3D-printed objects. When in doubt, it may be beneficial to evaluate the adhesive quality of a glue with sample pieces before using it for model assembly.

Postprocessing

Different printing technologies and materials have different postprocessing and finishing needs. When working with PLA and ABS plastics, printed model objects may need to be sanded with fine-grain sandpaper or emery board before they can be painted. Complex printed shapes may require the removal of support structures before finishing. Support structures are easily removed with a hobby knife, a rotary tool set at low speed, or a small hand file, then sanded smooth with fine-grain sandpaper or emery board. Any dust should be removed before priming and painting. ABS plastic can also be smoothed using acetone, which partially dissolves and softens the ABS plastic to produce a smooth glossy surface. Care should be taken when using acetone; follow all label warnings, and wear appropriate protective equipment. Acetone should not be used on PLA as it softens the surface, leaving it sticky. Other solvents that will smooth PLA, like tetrahydrofuran and dichloromethane, are available but tend to be difficult to purchase and are potentially hazardous to use. There are two-part epoxy coatings that will bond to PLA printed objects and leave a smooth glossy surface. Some acrylic paints may be painted directly onto printed objects. However, it is generally recommended that modelmakers prime printed objects before painting. Thin layers of spray primer formulated to bond to plastic will produce a smooth surface for finished painting. Spray primer designed for the hobby model industry works well for this application. Gesso may also be sprayed or brushed onto printed objects, which creates a good painting surface when using watercolor, gouache, or other water-based paints. Primed model objects may need to be lightly sanded before applying the finished paint treatment. The use of 400- to 600-grit wet or dry sandpaper or sanding sheets is recommended for a smooth finish. Figure 5.3 shows examples of 3D-printed objects pre and post processing. Objects printed with SLS printers have a porous surface that produces a matte finish and may require additional coating or finishing before painting.

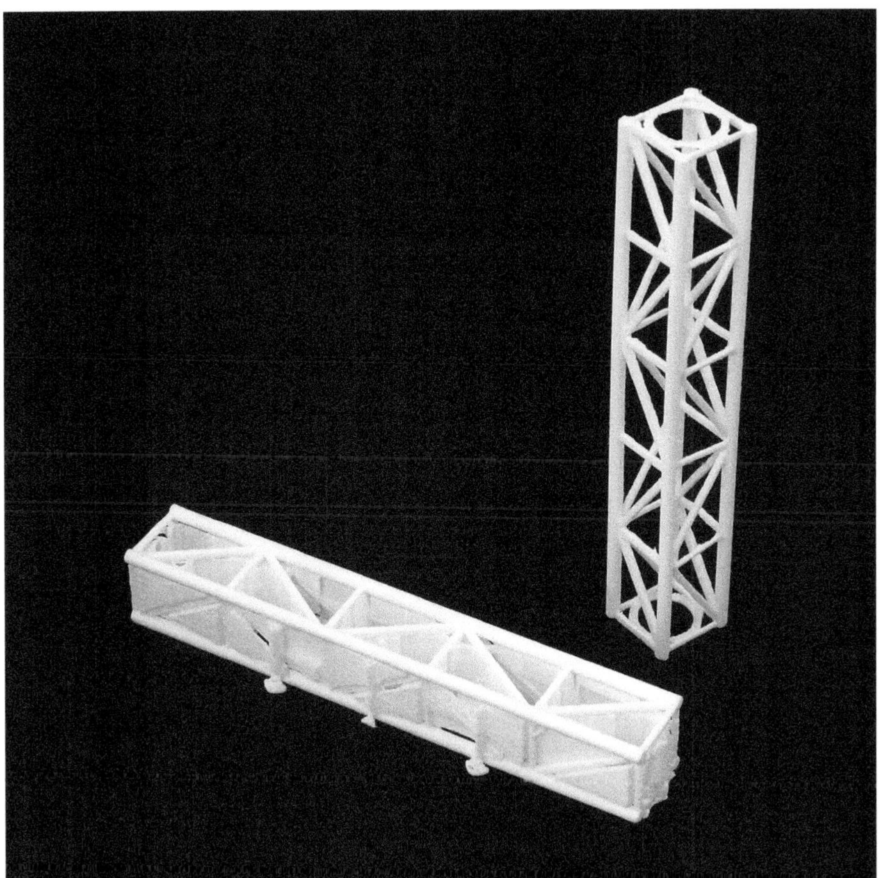

Figure 5.3. 3D-printed examples pre- and postprocessing

Automated and Laser Cutting

Electronic cutting machines from companies like Silhouette®, Cricut®, and Brother® offer an inexpensive option for intricate flat cutting projects. While these cutting machines were designed for the craft industry, they can be utilized by the modelmaker. Electronic cutters work similarly to a printer but use a small, agile blade to cut complex shapes. Capable of cutting smooth curves in addition to straight lines, most machines will cut various thicknesses of paper, including heavy card stock or Bristol board as well as vinyl and fabric. One advantage to using a computerized cutter is the ability to cut shapes derived from images or drawings. Images can be downloaded or scanned and converted for use in the cutter. Additionally, images can be printed on paper that is then cut to the image shape. Some machines like the Brother® ScanNCut 2 can scan the material to align the cutout shapes with the images printed on the material surface. Intricate designs can also be created in CAD software and cut into model pieces. Electronic cutting machine models come in various cutting widths, including wide formats capable of cutting up to 24" wide. When working in 1/4" scale, a medium

Figure 5.4. Laser cutout model foliage, audience seating, human figures, and doilies

footprint cutter is adequate, but the modelmaker may wish to consider a large cutter when working in larger scales.

Like blade-based electronic cutting machines, laser cutters can cut intricate shapes out of two-dimensional materials. Cardstock, Bristol board, plastics, fabric, wood, and even thin metal can be used with many laser cutters. As the name implies, laser cutters utilize a laser beam to burn through materials. Focused mirrors are used to move the beam across the surface being cut to create detailed shapes. Small-footprint desktop laser cutters, similarly sized to large home inkjet printers, are available. As with any laser cutter, makers should carefully consider ventilation in their workspace. Filtration units can be used to help mitigate strong odors and the potentially toxic fumes produced when the laser cutter is in operation. Appropriate exhaust ventilation is recommended. Some laser cutters utilize a liquid cooling system to keep the laser assembly from overheating, so access to a water source may also be a consideration when determining where to place the laser cutter in the model studio (see figures 5.4, and 5.5 for examples of automated and laser cut materials).

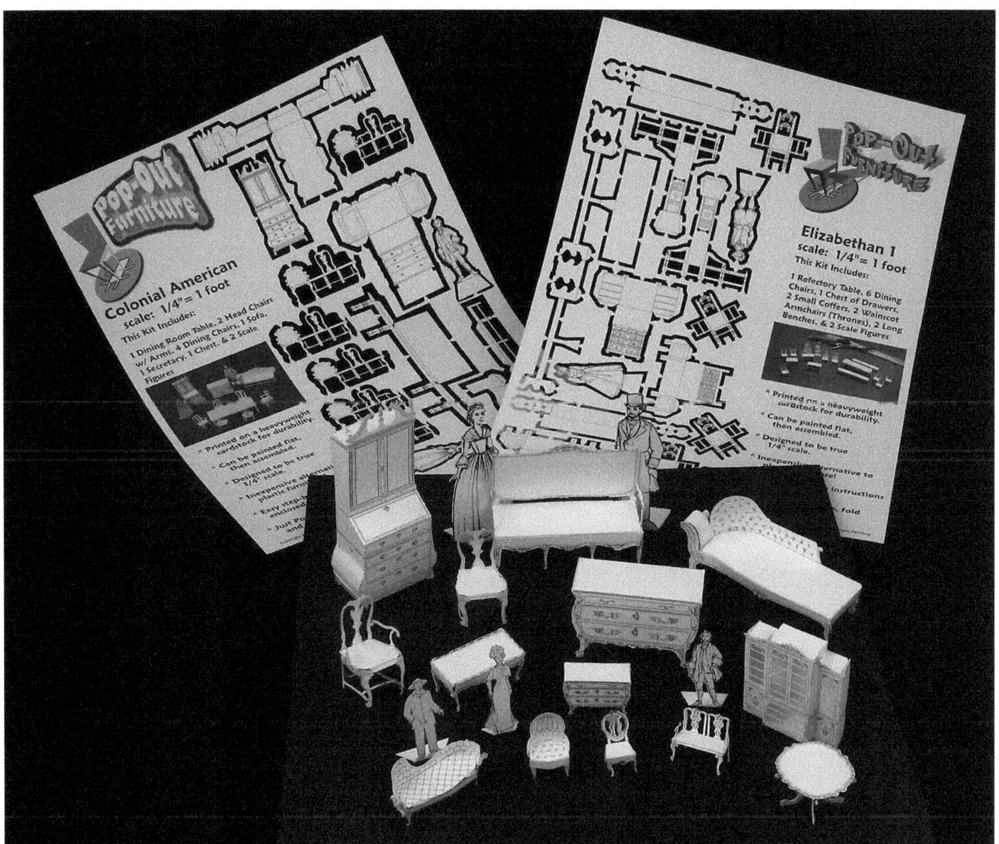

Figure 5.5. 1/4" and 1/2" scale laser-cut Pop-Out Furniture. *Courtesy of Paul Pape*

Tip: *Beowulf Boritt uses acrylic sheets for the show decks for his models. The acrylic is cut to shape with a laser cutter and then primed with white primer spray paint. The deck, as with illustration board, can then be primed and painted with acrylic paints or watercolors. This prevents the model show deck from warping during the painting process. If the floor design is textured with wood planking, parquet floors, or other patterns, these can be etched by the laser cutter prior to painting. If the deck requires a complicated pattern, Boritt instructs the laser cutter operator to peel the paper before cutting so he doesn't have to peel numerous individual pieces off the acrylic. Boritt can also etch a pattern in the protective paper that allows him to peel away specific cuts to create a frisket that masks portions of the exposed acrylic. He then peels away the remaining paper to reveal the base color in that pattern. On complicated decks he will build up the deck with several sheets of acrylic and use the laser to cut a bottom layer that can hold ball bearings to support a turntable in the top layer. The laser can also cut deck tracks into a top layer to guide moving scenic units. Broadway show decks are typically 9" to 12" thick, so Boritt uses the appropriate sheet thickness or a series of layers to approximate the thickness of the theater's show deck. If the floor needs to be super shiny, he will select an acrylic sheet in the appropriate color instead of priming and painting.*

Vacuum Forming

Vacuum forming uses thermoplastic and vacuum pressure to duplicate three-dimensional objects. Thermoplastic is heated to a pliable state then placed over the object to be duplicated; vacuum pressure pulls the plastic down tightly to the object. Once the plastic cools, it becomes rigid, and the original object can be removed. Vacuum-forming machines are available in both small desktop-size units as well as larger-footprint machines used for full-scale scenic units. Figure 5.6 shows a desktop vacuum-forming machine and examples of formed elements. Vacuum forming is particularly effective when creating textured and organic surfaces. A variety of thermoplastics are obtainable for use with vacuum-forming machines. ABS and polyethene sheeting are common materials that come in different thicknesses and colors, including clear and translucent. When using vacuum forming, the modelmaker must use heat-resistant materials for the object being duplicated. Careful consideration should also be given to ventilation when working with thermoplastics. In addition to manufactured vacuum-forming machines, there are several online DIY tutorials on how to build your own vacuum-forming machine from store-bought materials. Many of these do-it-yourself projects use a shop utility vacuum to generate the vacuum pressure needed and will work on normal household voltage.

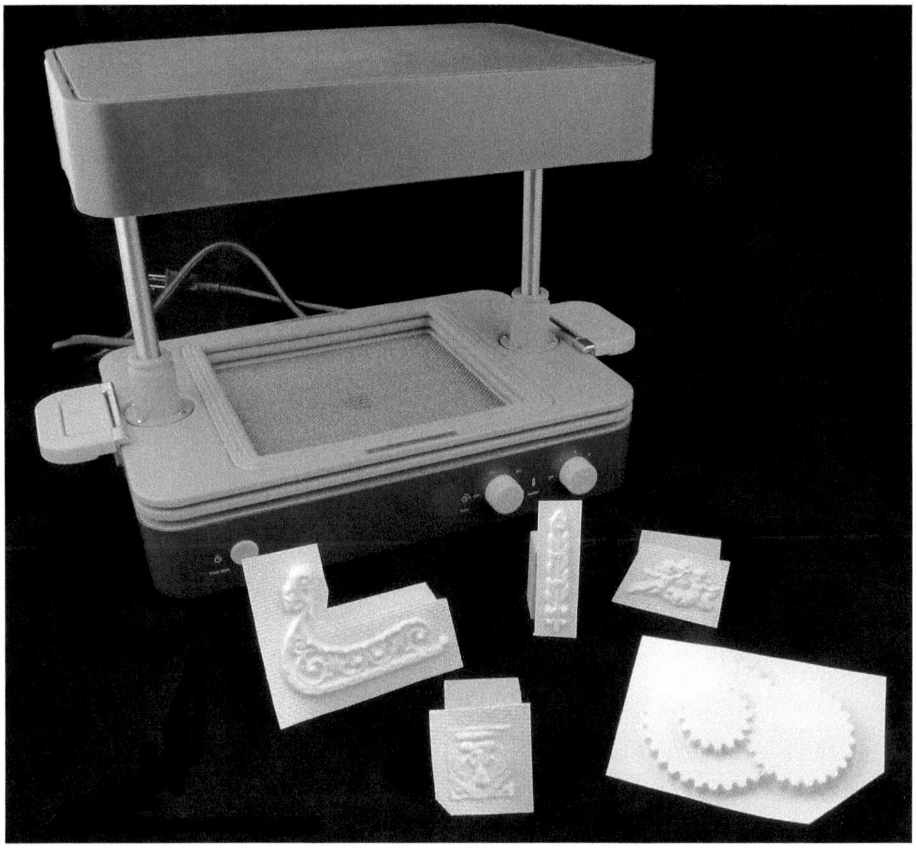

Figure 5.6. Vacuum-formed model pieces

CNC Routing

While 3D printers offer an additive process for the creation of model objects, CNC cutting is a subtractive process where material is removed from a solid block to create the finished object. While CNC cutting is more often used on full-scale scenic pieces, there are small-footprint CNC machines, like the one shown in figure 5.7, that can be useful to the modelmaker. CNC cutting employs a small rotary cutter that is guided by a computer program along the x-, y-, and z-axes to create intricately carved objects. This process works best on flat surfaces and can be used to make low-relief patterns. High relief is also possible on some machines provided there are no undercuts where elements are not supported by the substructure. For carved elements where strength is desired, medium-density fiberboard (MDF) is recommended. Foam, plastics, and other soft materials can also be carved with CNC cutting machines. It is advisable to check the documentation for the CNC cutting machine to determine recommended settings for the type of material used.

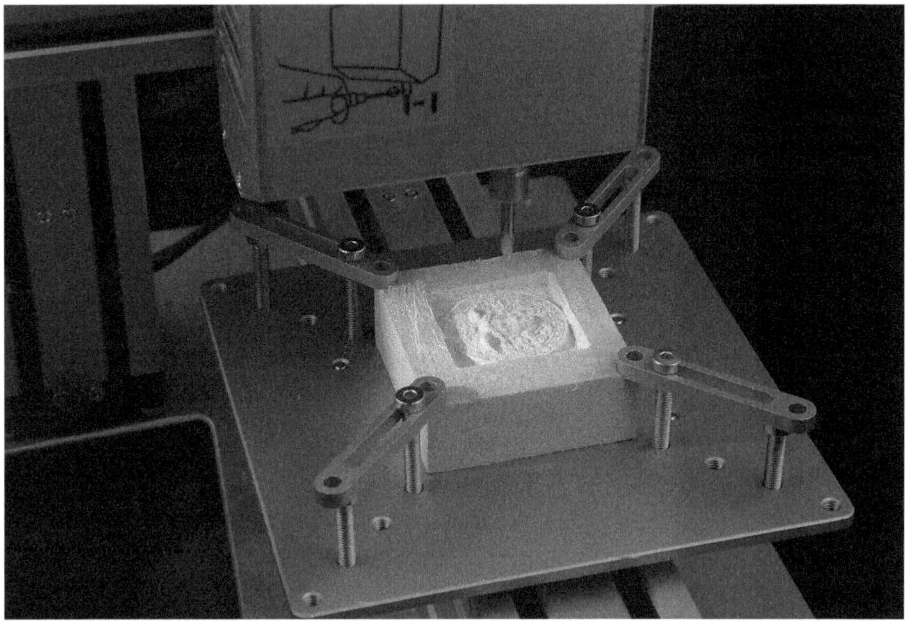

Figure 5.7. CNC-routed model pieces

Measurements

The technologies outlined in this chapter generally use metric units. As mentioned previously, if the modelmaker is working in imperial measurements (inches and feet) it may be necessary to convert from one measurement system to the other. One inch equals 25.4 millimeters. To convert millimeters to inches, divide the millimeter measurement by 25.4 to get a decimal equivalent in inches. To convert inches to millimeters, reverse the process and multiply the inch measurement by 25.4. There are several online metric conversion forms available, some of which will also display fractions of an inch instead of decimal measurements. Smartphone apps are also available for metric conversion.

Molding and Casting

The use of molding and casting techniques allows the modelmaker to quickly duplicate objects, which is particularly effective when working with organic shapes. While molding and casting technologies have been used by modelmakers for centuries, the introduction of new casting materials has opened new possibilities. Low-cost silicon molding materials are readily available online and at hobby stores. Liquid molding materials are particularly good for capturing intricate details. Silicone putties can simplify the process of creating a mold for small objects. Two-part silicone putties work similarly to two-part silicone liquids: a portion of each part of the two-part putty is mixed together, then formed around the object being duplicated. After a waiting period, the putty will become firm. Two-part liquid plastic casting resins come in assorted colors and densities, including clear, translucent, and flexible. Molding and casting materials can be expensive, but the small amount of material needed to cast model pieces and the ability to easily duplicate objects make them a useful tool for the modelmaker. Various molds and cast objects are shown in Figure 5.8. For a listing of best practices, the modelmaker should refer to the specific instructions for the molding or casting material being used. In *The Prop Building Guidebook for Theatre, Film, and TV*, author Eric Hart lists many molding and casting materials and guidelines for creating several types of molds.[2]

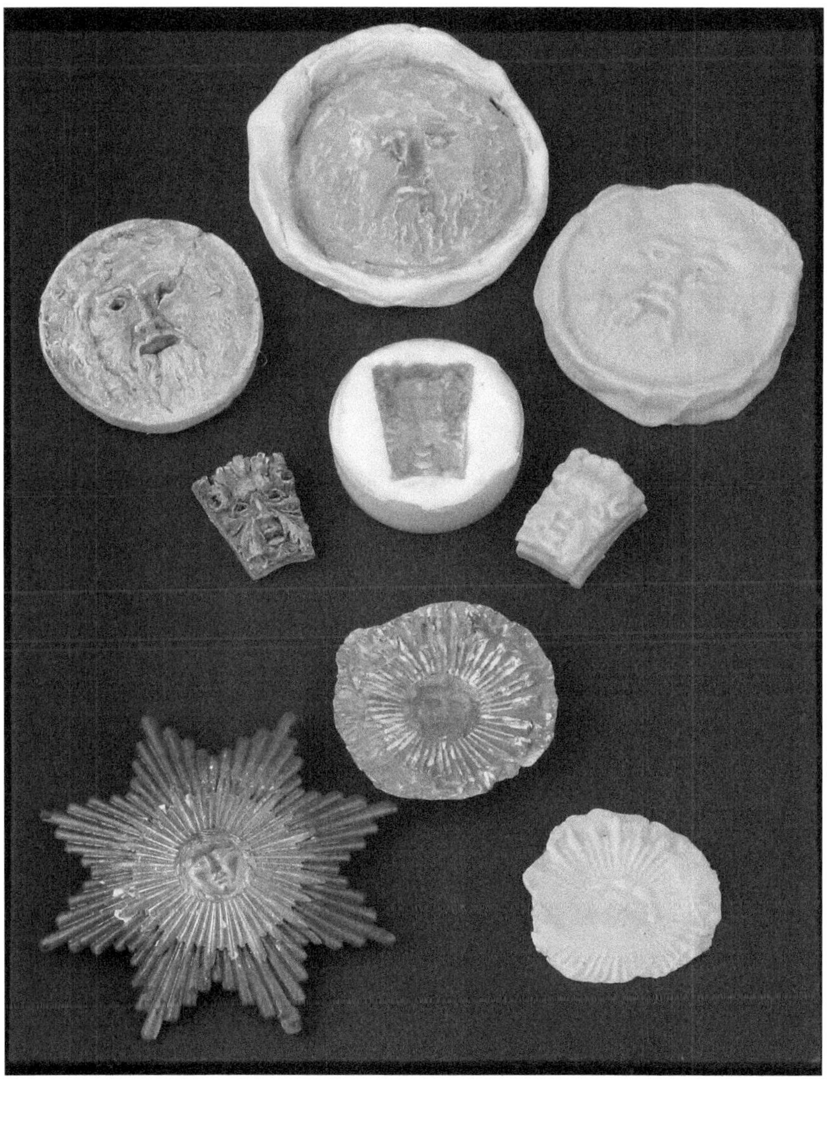

Figure 5.8. Molded model pieces

Using Technologies Together

Many of the technologies outlined in this chapter may be effectively used in combination to expedite the modelmaking process. Additionally, 3D-printer companies, like Snapmaker®, offer combination machines that are capable of 3D printing, laser cutting or engraving, and CNC cutting.[3] These combination units offer great flexibility for the modelmaker, particularly if model studio space is limited.

Objects produced on a CNC machine may be duplicated using a vacuum-forming machine, provided the material used with the CNC machine is heat resistant. Detailed smooth surfaces are possible with MDF because of its lack of grain, which makes it a desirable choice for creating a positive form to be vacuum molded. Careful attention should be paid to prevent melting 3D-printed forms, but 3D-printed objects may be used with vacuum-forming machines. PLA has a melting temperature close to many of the materials used in vacuum forming, so, provided that the 3D form being duplicated is not too close to the heating element, PLA should retain its shape in the vacuum-forming process. ABS has a higher melting temperature and may be a better option for use with vacuum forming.

Casting 3D-printed parts can provide the modelmaker with the ability to quickly create objects out of materials that are not available for traditional 3D printing techniques. Molds of 3D-printed objects may be made from liquid or putty silicon casting materials—clear, transparent, and flexible castings and those of assorted colors can then be made using the silicon mold. Objects created through CNC or vacuum forming may also be used with casting materials.

Future Design Technologies

Innovative design technologies are continually being created. Even as this book was being revised, a revolutionary new tool in the field of art and design emerged. Generative design is a computer-aided design technology that uses artificial intelligence (AI) to mimic human intelligence to enhance creative processes. AI generative design shows enormous potential to streamline the artist, designer, engineer, and scenographer's creative tasks by automating repetitive chores, including researching and assembling images from a variety of sources to create concept boards that align with the desired aesthetic and thematic direction, rapidly generating a multitude of design options based on initial inputs or themes, and analyzing literally millions of images according to pattern, shape, form, texture, color, period, technique, and genre to recombine these into bold new experimental designs.

AI is already being used to generate 3D models of sets and props that are then coordinated to 3D print select model pieces or entire working white models, saving time on manual modelmaking. The AI-generated models can then be sent to CNC routers to carve actual scenic pieces for production as is shown in Michael Hansmeyer's design for *Die Zauberflöte* in figure 5.9.

Figure 5.9. *Die Zauberflöte* (*The Magic Flute*) by W. A. Mozart. Directed by Romeo Castellucci. The Royal Theatre of La Monnaie, Brussels. 3D-printed model, computer rendering, and scenography by Michael Hansmeyer, 2018

AI is being used to create virtual environments that are projected onto screens or forms, allowing for more elaborate and immersive environments than is possible with physical scenery alone. AI is also used in conjunction with haptic sensors, infrared cameras, and other input devices to respond in real-time to the action on stage to manipulate projection, lighting, and sound to create psychologically powerful experiences.

Scenographers will someday be able to teach their AI generative software to include stage configuration, size, exits, entrances, heights of stairs and ramps, furniture placement, budget, genre of plays, styles of production, and even their aesthetic preferences or those of specific directors. This will allow generative design to offer rapid insights and recommendations to help scenographers make more informed and nuanced decisions. Through generative design, theater designers will be able to provide new opportunities in performance that would have been impossible to achieve using traditional tools and processes.

At present there are limitations to the use of generative design in theater and other performance-based entertainments. AI can assist in many individual tasks in scenic design, but, as of yet, it cannot replicate the human ability to perceive depth, form, texture, and color or duplicate the nuanced and subjective decisions that designers must make when creating a physical environment that actors interact with and within. Furthermore, scenographic design involves a wide range of skills such as script and character analysis, conceptualization, spatial awareness, technical knowledge, estimating budget, labor, and build schedules. Currently, artists and designers must offer effective prompt keywords, which requires an extensive knowledge of art, literature, music, media, performing arts, and world history—a level of interpretation and contextualization that is far beyond current AI capabilities. The theater's collaborative nature also requires flexibility and adaptability on the part of each team member. AI cannot effectively adapt to the changing requirements of a collaborative art, especially with our all-too-human preferences, passions, predilections, and idiosyncrasies.

The evolution of AI generative design is moving at such a rapid pace that any discussion of specific technology that this book can offer will be outdated by the time of publication. But in this preliminary stage it is prudent to review the ethical implications of AI generative design so that practitioners can leverage the benefits of AI while mitigating potential risks to ensure that personal creativity remains at the forefront of the design process. Generative design uses or appropriates the intellectual property of other artists and designers, requiring each to research the ways they share their work on social media and how to acknowledge the works of others. AI algorithms are trained on data, so personal or cultural biases inherent in the data, whether intentional or unintentional, can therefore be manifested in generated designs. The decision-making processes of AI systems are often opaque, making it difficult to know where the data is coming from and how decisions are being made, which can lead to misunderstanding and distrust. Designers must be vigilant for biases that may emerge in AI-generated content and strive for inclusivity and diversity. As AI technology continues to advance, it will replicate some of the more routine or mechanical aspects of scenographic design, which will likely lead to a decrease in demand for human designers and their assistants. This is a troubling issue when considering such a uniquely human art form as theater. Artistic expression and creativity are highly valued in the entertainment industry, and many producers may prefer to collaborate with human designers who can bring their personal vision to the task at hand. Others may not.

Additionally, developing AI generative design software for scenographic design will require significant investment in technology, resources, and training. The rapid advancement of this technology will make investing in quickly outdated AI tools a risky venture. This will limit opportunities for smaller theaters and production companies to utilize this technology. Designers themselves must also be prepared to adapt and continuously learn about this rapidly evolving technology.

Ultimately, AI, like previous technological advancements, will be adopted and accepted as an enhancement to the design process much like felt-tip markers, plastics, and computer-aided drafting expanded the designer's toolkit. AI-generated designs are not perfect, so, for the present, it will be necessary to envision it using human expertise and experience to ensure that scenographic design will meet the requirements of theatrical production.

6. Photographing and Archiving the Scenographic Model

Producing high-quality images of scenographic models is useful in communicating with the production team and for archiving the design. There are many factors the modelmaker should consider when evaluating their photography needs, including the type of equipment needed and how it can best be used, when images are needed, what type of lighting is most appropriate, and whether digital image editing is desired.

Equipment

Assuring high-quality images begins with selecting the right equipment. It is possible to capture high-quality images using relatively inexpensive equipment, such as smartphone or tablet cameras. Of the many camera varieties available, three stand out as options the modelmaker might consider for model photography: digital single-lens reflex (DSLR) cameras, point-and-shoot digital cameras, and smartphone cameras.

The most expensive category, DSLR cameras (professional models), offer the most customization with interchangeable lenses and accessories. The modelmaker should consider getting a DSLR not only for photographing the model but also for photographing realized productions. There are many factors to consider when purchasing a DSLR camera as many makes and models are available. Note the size of the optical sensor that may be listed as CCD (charged coupled device) or CMOS (complementary metal oxide semiconductor).[1] Large sensors generally mean higher-quality images and work better in low light conditions. The sensor will also determine the number of megapixels in an image. Megapixels are related to image quality: a high number of megapixels will mean a high-quality image and a larger file size. When purchased as a complete camera or kit, DSLRs typically come with an 18–55 mm lens. This lens is good for general photography, but the modelmaker will require other lens options. A 28–135 mm macro zoom lens provides good magnification without needing to position the camera too close or too far away from the model. A zoom lens will also aid in taking production photos. Macro lenses are designed specifically for close photography, allowing the photographer to focus on an object a short distance from the lens while also providing some magnification. If the modelmaker has available funds, a 50 mm prime lens would be a worthwhile investment. A prime lens will allow more light to enter the camera and work better in low light conditions, but it has a fixed focal length and will not zoom.

Point-and-shoot digital cameras have integrated lenses that are not typically interchangeable. The integrated lenses tend to be zoom lenses but will also work well for relatively close photography. Much like DSLR cameras, point-and-shoot cameras usually indicate the number of megapixels a camera can take. Although remarkably high megapixel cameras are available, the sensor in point-and-shoot cameras will generally be smaller than in DSLR cameras, offering slightly lower overall image quality and a diminished ability to take images in low light. Despite these differences, point-and-shoot cameras are a great option for model photography but are not as useful when taking production photographs.

Smartphone and tablet cameras are an increasingly viable option for model photography. While phone and tablet camera sensors tend to be small compared to standalone cameras, there are high-resolution cameras available in many phones and tablets. Some phones also come with multiple built-in lenses with different focal lengths and may provide a macro lens for higher-quality images of close objects. External wide-angle and macro lenses designed to fit over some smartphone camera lenses are available. Generally, phone and tablet cameras function similarly to point-and-shoot digital cameras, offering the ability to adjust zoom, focus, and exposure settings. Ease of use and availability make phone and tablet cameras valuable tools for capturing model images, particularly when collaborating remotely.

Tripods and Accessories

Regardless of the type of camera used, it is recommended that the modelmaker employ a tripod, like those featured in figure 6.1, to help ensure that images are in sharp focus. The type of camera used will affect the choice of tripod. A DSLR camera will require a more substantial tripod than a smartphone. If the modelmaker is also taking production images, it is advisable to invest in a high-quality adjustable tripod with a three-way pan tilt head. When using a phone or tablet for model photography, a small desktop tripod with a phone or tablet mount can be employed. A desktop tripod may also be adequate for point-and-shoot cameras. The modelmaker should note the maximum camera weight recommended by the tripod manufacturer to ensure that it will support the camera being used.

Another accessory that can help maintain a sharp focus is a shutter-release cable or remote control. Primarily available for DSLR cameras, shutter releases attach to the camera and allow the modelmaker to take images without directly touching the camera. This prevents jostling the camera while photographing. Some DSLRs and point-and-shoot cameras will work with infrared remote controls. A remote control can be used to distantly trigger the shutter in a similar fashion to a shutter release. Some remote controls may adjust other camera settings. Increasingly, cameras include Wi-Fi or Bluetooth controls that are activated remotely with a phone, tablet, or computer. Shutter releases and remote controls are specific to camera models, so the modelmaker will need to check compatibility before purchasing any of these accessories.

Figure 6.1. Tripod options

Camera Settings

While DSLRs have more options, virtually all digital cameras will have multiple automated shooting modes as well as some manually adjustable settings. There are numerous online tutorials and videos that describe camera settings in detail. This book will focus on the most common settings. The modelmaker should experiment with automated and manual camera settings to find the settings that work best for their camera and setup.

Automated modes help make the process of photographing the model much easier. Shooting in fully automatic mode, often indicated by a green camera icon or a green rectangle, the camera will manage most settings on its own—adjusting the aperture, shutter, flash, and potentially the International Organization for Standardization (ISO) number to produce the best balance. ISO originally referred to film sensitivity or speed. High-speed films reacted more quickly to light striking the film surface, allowing for a quicker shutter speed. The ISO setting on a digital camera works in a similar fashion to changing film speed. A higher ISO setting allows for a faster shutter speed, while a lower ISO setting reduces the amount of noise inherent in the image.[2] The static nature of model photography allows for a relatively low ISO setting that will reduce image noise. Great images can be achieved on most cameras using fully automated settings, but the special conditions of model photography may require the modelmaker to adjust some camera settings to achieve better images.

DSLRs and some point-and-shoot cameras have additional partially automated modes, aperture priority and shutter priority. Some cameras indicate the partially automated mode with a P for "program mode." Indicated by an A or Av on most cameras, aperture priority mode will allow the operator to adjust the aperture manually while the camera automatically adjusts the shutter speed. Experienced photographers may recognize the aperture setting as f/stop. A wider aperture opening means a lower f/stop, which increases the amount of light entering the camera. In aperture priority mode the camera will compensate by increasing the shutter speed. Aperture is also associated with depth of field. A wide aperture will reduce the area of an image that is in focus and blur the background (a narrow depth of field). Whereas a narrow aperture will increase the area of an image that is in focus (a large depth of field). The modelmaker can experiment with different aperture settings to find the depth of field that best captures the model. Figure 6.2 shows the same model photographed with narrow and large depth-of-field settings. A model image that is fully in focus may be desirable for archival model images, but an image where some of the more distant elements of the model are slightly out of focus may feel more natural and may better communicate dimensionality to the production team.

Shutter priority mode, often indicated by an S or Tv, allows the operator to adjust the shutter manually while the camera automatically adjusts the aperture. A fast shutter speed is good for capturing quickly moving people or objects. Because there is typically no movement associated with photographing models, it is possible to use slow shutter speeds. If the modelmaker is working with a handheld camera without access to a tripod, or other means of stabilizing the camera, then a fast shutter speed will help reduce blurred images.

Many cameras have additional special modes, such as sports or portrait modes. These special modes are typically not useful for the modelmaker. One possible exception is the macro mode available on most point-and-shoot digital cameras. Typically indicated by a flower symbol, the macro mode is intended for close-up photography. Depending on the camera, the macro mode may either mean that the aperture is opened fully to narrow the depth of field, or it is at its minimum setting. Using the macro mode on a camera can produce exceptionally good model images, so the modelmaker should experiment with this mode.

When photographing the model, the modelmaker should also consider where to set camera focus within the model space. It may be beneficial to have portions of the model slightly out of focus to accentuate the sense of depth. Most DSLRs and some point-and-shoot cameras allow selecting a single-point or area focus mode. In area focus mode the camera will automatically balance the focus between multiple points, usually indicated by small squares in the camera view. Area focus mode is useful for general photography and production images. When photographing the model in area focus mode, the camera may have difficulty identifying the appropriate focus for the model. The modelmaker can use the single-point focus mode to have more control over which areas of the model are in focus. On most cameras the point used in single-point focus mode is in the center of the frame, but many cameras allow the operator to identify different points. Most cameras also have a manual focus mode. Figure 6.3 compares the same model with focus set downstage versus upstage.

Setup and Types of Photographs

Prior to taking photos of the model, the modelmaker should consider lighting, masking, and the purpose of the image being taken. There are several points in the production process when it is desirable to take images of the model. Images of sketch models, white models, and color models are helpful during design discussions with the director and design team. Reference images for the scenic studio, scenic artists, and use in rehearsals are also recommended. The modelmaker should also take high-quality archival images. There are different approaches to setup and lighting depending on the type of model and function of the images.

Careful consideration should be paid to lighting the model. It is helpful to consult research materials or preliminary renderings provided by the lighting designer when determining an approach to lighting the model. Regardless of the lighting setup used, it is recommended that any built-in camera flash be disabled. If the modelmaker does not have access to a lighting lab or miniature theater, effective lighting can be achieved with inexpensive utility clip

Figure 6.2. *The Trojan Women* by Euripides. Example of narrow and wide depth of field. 1/4" presentation model by Brad M. Carlson, 2007

Figure 6.3. *The Trojan Women* by Euripides. 1/4" Presentation model by Brad M. Carlson, 2007. Figure with focus set on foreground and background

lights available at hardware stores. Warm white bulbs (3,000°K) are recommended as their color temperature closely resembles stage lighting. A light source with a high color rendering index (CRI) is also recommended. The color of the clip lights can be modified by taping or clipping gels to the front of the fixture. When using a clip-light setup, at least two lighting fixtures should be employed: one placed in front of the model and to one side, and the other placed in front of and to the other side of the model and focused on a reflective surface—the reflected light is focused on the model (see figure 6.4). When lighting is set up in this way, a strong key light provides primary illumination, while the reflected light provides a diffused fill light that softens shadows and provides a sense of depth. Professional photography reflectors and reflective umbrellas are available, but white cardstock or poster board are good inexpensive reflectors. A slight concave curve to

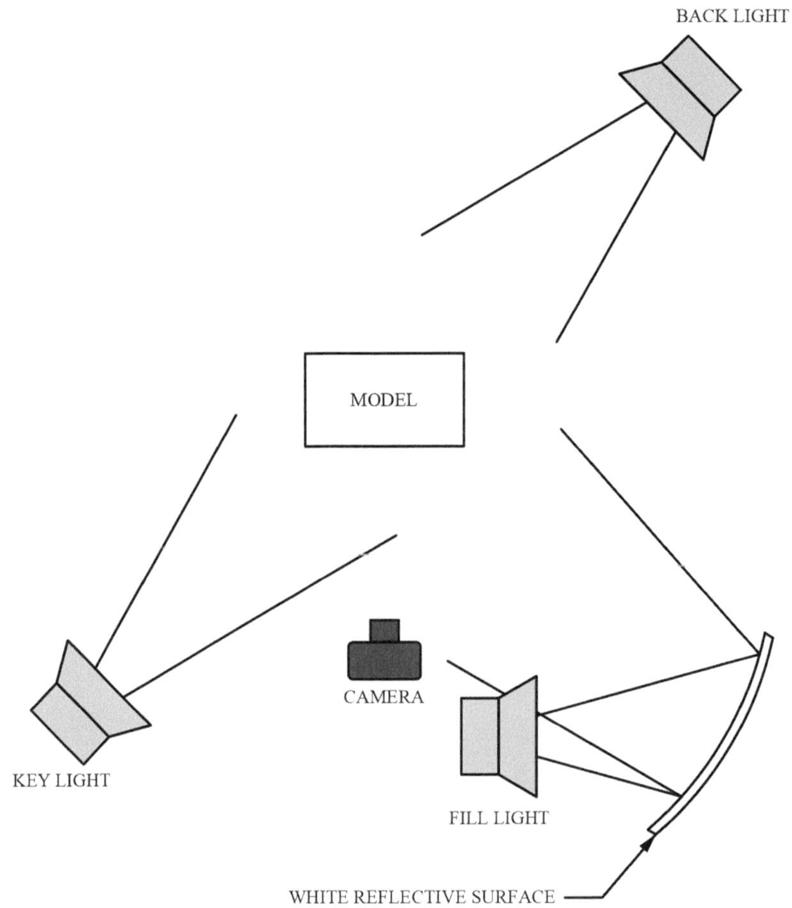

Figure 6.4. Diagram of key and fill lighting

the reflective surface can help focus the reflected light on the model. The addition of a third light source behind the model can help further fill in the shadows and soften the overall lighting on the model. If the modelmaker has access to a lighting lab, it is good practice to place lighting instruments in positions that will emulate the direction, intensity, and color of the final lighting design. A lighting lab can employ either full-sized lighting fixtures or miniature fixtures. When using lighting fixtures that are not to model scale, a single lighting fixture can replicate the light that would be created by several individual scaled lighting fixtures. Color filters, or gels, may be used to adjust the color of light hitting the model to help provide dimensionality. Placing one lighting fixture with a warm gel in front of and to the left of the model and one lighting fixture with a cool gel in front and to the right of the model will produce effective theatrical lighting. While scaled lighting fixtures are expensive, model theaters that utilize them allow the designer to model the design in greater precision. Scaled lighting fixtures typically use fiber-optic or LED light sources, which can be focused and used much like their full-scale counterparts. Some miniature lighting fixtures are capable of projecting patterns, and even miniature moving lights are available. When using any of the lighting methods mentioned above, the modelmaker should consider contrast ratio and dimensionality of the model. Lighting fixtures may be placed to provide contrast between the model and the background. The choice of color of the lighting will also help provide contrast. The position and angle of lighting fixtures can be adjusted to alter the dimensionality of the model. Lighting positioned directly in front of the model will reduce the perceived dimensionality of the model, where lighting placed at an angle will increase dimensionality.

The modelmaker may wish to add lighting specials to emphasize portions of the model or model figures. Adding special spotlights can produce lighting effects simulating the realized design and help to visualize how the scenic design will be seen on stage. If the modelmaker has access to a lighting lab or model theater (mentioned above), small lighting fixtures can be focused on specific areas of the stage as lighting specials. Flashlights with focusable beams can be secured to tripods for lighting specials. Small mirrors can also be used to reflect light from a key or fill lighting position to highlight a specific area of the model.

Careful consideration should be given to lighting when photographing the white model. The modelmaker should use pale color-corrective lighting filters and avoid saturated colors. Saturated color filters will produce undesirably strong hues on white surfaces. It is also good practice to save white model images in grayscale format, so images are true black and white. A true black and white photo may also be useful to other members of the design team. For instance, the lighting designer may request a high-resolution image of the white model in order to experiment with visualizing lighting effects with specific software.

The modelmaker should also pay close attention to the background visible in model images. If the design makes use of a cyclorama or other backdrop it should be included in the model. If a black background is desired, matboard or fabric may be used. Additional black masking materials may be needed outside of the model box or model stage depending on the camera position.

When photographing the model for communication with the production team, it is effective to take images from several different perspectives. A straight-on front view, dynamic side views, and a top view should be included. When taking front and dynamic side view images it is important to position the camera to show an accurate audience perspective. Placing the model on a stand or elevated surface will help with camera positioning. To adjust the height of the model relative to the camera position, a simple stand can be constructed using a stack of books. For the front view, the camera is placed in a position that approximates the center of the audience seating. The dynamic side views are also taken from the audience perspective by placing the camera in an off-center position 0–45 degrees from center. Dynamic side views help show the depth of the playing space and provide a better sense of the overall scenic design. If the theater has a balcony, an image approximating the balcony view should also be taken. The top view is useful for ground plan discussions. If it is difficult to move the camera position, the model itself may be reoriented to capture images of the side and top view. If the model is reoriented, the lighting positions will need to be similarly repositioned to create an even wash of light.

If the modelmaker intends to print photos to share with the production team, high-resolution images are recommended. When sharing images through email, websites, or cloud file-sharing applications, it is best to reduce the resolution to one suited for viewing on a computer or device screen. Reducing the resolution will also reduce the file size, making it easier to post or share images. Images of 1 MB or less are easy to send or upload. An easily viewable file format (JPG, PDF, PNG) should be used. Presentation software, like Microsoft® PowerPoint® or Google Slides™, can also be used to share images.

Archival Images of Models

While the modelmaker may archive images used in production communication, the modelmaker should take additional photos of their model. Process images taken on a phone or tablet work well, and these may serve archival purposes in lieu of more sophisticated photography setups if no other camera is available. The objective of archival images is the scenographic model itself and not necessarily how the design is actualized in production. Archival images may require a different background and lighting setup from those used for production communication. If possible, it is recommended that the model be removed from the model box or model stage and placed against a neutral background. One option for a neutral background is to use a large piece of white paper or fabric placed flat under the scenic model, then gently curved vertically behind the model. This gentle curve helps diminish hard shadow lines in the background that may distract from the model. This background should be lit with a diffused light to soften shadows. A black background can be used in a comparable manner.

When lighting the model for archival images, the modelmaker should use at least two lighting sources. Place one light source at a 45-degree angle to the side of the camera and inclined 45 degrees above the camera. The second light source should be placed opposite of the first lighting source, 45 degrees to the opposite side of the camera and inclined 45 degrees above the camera. When the lighting sources are placed in this configuration, shadows on the model will be minimized without losing too much dimensionality. If there are too many shadows with this lighting arrangement, experiment by placing additional light sources above the model. Inexpensive clip lights with soft white light bulbs provide diffuse lighting for archival photography. Diffusion lighting gels can also help soften the light. Photo light tents with diffusion surfaces, when lit from the outside, provide a soft, even light on the surface of the model (see figure 6.5). Photo light tents are available with interchangeable backgrounds in white, black, or gray. The modelmaker may also experiment with natural sunlight as a diffuse lighting source by placing the model near a window with indirect sunlight.

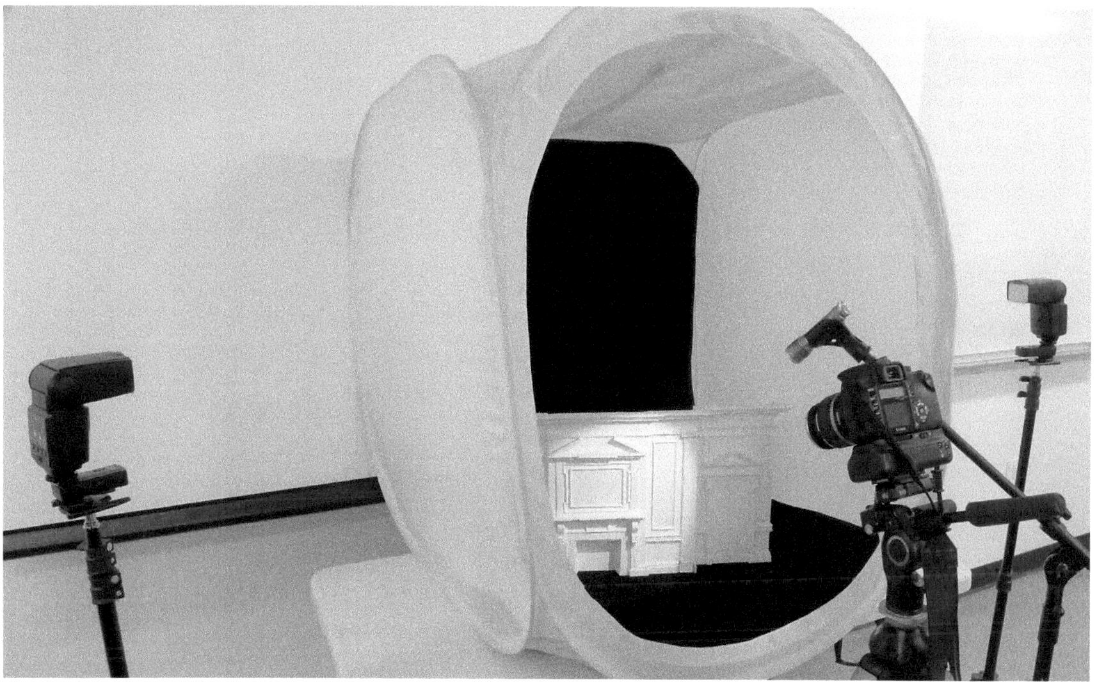

Figure 6.5. Archival photograph setup

Digital Image Editing

Digital image editing is an essential tool for the modelmaker. An image-editing program like Adobe® Photoshop®, Corel® Photo-Paint®, or the freeware GIMP can correct color aberrations, add digital figures and backgrounds, and suggest lighting effects. While careful use of lighting and camera settings can produce color-accurate images, the modelmaker may find it necessary to further adjust the color of digital images so they more closely match the model. It is worth noting that not all devices and computer monitors are the same. Color and intensity may vary greatly from the system used to edit images. Most image-editing programs have an automated or semiautomated process for adjusting color and exposure in images. The modelmaker can try the automated tools first before manually adjusting color or exposure. If the modelmaker is new to image editing, they are strongly encouraged to review the numerous online tutorials that demonstrate image-editing software.

This section will explore some of the adjustment options in Adobe® Photoshop®. Many of the tools and settings discussed have corresponding options in Corel® Photo-Paint®, GIMP, or other image-editing programs. Adjustment layers in Photoshop® offer a quick way to experiment with adjusting images. In the Adjustments window there are several different options available. Some of the most useful for the modelmaker are Brightness/Contrast, Levels, Exposure, Vibrance, Hue/Saturation, and Color Balance (see table 6.1 for

Table 6.1 Photoshop© Adjustments

• **Brightness/Contrast** provides two sliding scales that may be used to adjust the overall brightness and contrast of an image. Both scales adjust all the colors simultaneously and should be used for broad adjustments to the whole image.
• **Levels** adjust the lightness or darkness of shadows, midtones, and highlights separately. Several presets are available to lighten, darken, or increase contrast in an image.
• **Exposure** adjusts the brightness of an image in steps labeled the same manner as a camera light meter. This adjustment is good for correcting images with minor under- or overexposure.
• **Vibrance** provides a sliding scale that adjusts the saturation of midtone colors in an image. There is also an overall saturation sliding scale with this adjustment tool.
• **Hue/Saturation** can change the color of an image. There are also sliding scales for adjusting the saturation and lightness of an image. Presets are available that duplicate the look of historic photography methods like sepia and cyanotype. Additional presets are available to boost specific colors. A specific color range can be selected from the drop-down menu for manipulation by hue, saturation, and lightness scales without affecting other colors in the image. The Hue/Saturation adjustment also features a Colorize option. With this option selected, the original color of an image is removed, and the hue, saturation, and lightness are applied to the now colorized image. The Hue/Saturation tool is particularly useful for adjusting color to match the real-world model.
• The **Color Balance** option adjusts three sliding scales: cyan/red, magenta/green, and yellow/blue. This tool is also good for modifying color to match the real-world model.

a description of each adjustment). Many of the adjustments have an "Auto" button that will adjust the settings based on the software's best guess for a good balance. It is efficient to select the Auto button first to see how the software adjusts these settings and then make additional corrections as needed.

Image-editing programs are also valuable for adding backgrounds in models. A background image may be gathered from print or internet sources or created in a drawing or illustration program. Once an image is selected, it can be added as a layer in Photoshop, placed underneath the model image. Sections of the model image may be carefully selected using one of the available selection tools (the marquee tool, lasso tool and its submodes [polygonal, and magnetic], object selection tool, quick select tool, or wand tool) and removed to reveal the background behind the model. These selection tools work in different ways. For a model with straight edges, the polygonal lasso tool works best. When working with curvilinear forms, the quick selection tool is a better option.

Image-editing software allows the modelmaker to add additional elements to the model. One option may be to add a figure, potentially an image of the costume renderings for the production. If the production calls for projections, the modelmaker may add images representing the projection design to the model image. Images from the projection designer can be manipulated using the transform tools (scale, rotate, skew, distort, and perspective) and placed in the model image to represent the planned projection surfaces.

This chapter has focused on digital photography, while many of the concepts and recommendations presented also apply to film photography. If the modelmaker wishes to take photos with film, additional research into film speed and camera settings will be necessary.

Notes

Bibliography

Index

Notes

Introduction

1. *Merriam-Webster Dictionary*, "verisimilitude," accessed February 2, 2023, www.merriam-webster.com/dictionary/verisimilitude.

2. *Merriam-Webster Dictionary*, "model," accessed February 2, 2023, www.merriam-webster.com/dictionary/model.

3. Vitruvius, *The Ten Books of Architecture*, trans. Morris Hicky Morgan (Harvard University Press, 1914), book 10, chap. 16, p. 316. "There are some things which, when enlarged in imitation of small models, are effective, others cannot have models, but are constructed independently of them, while there are some which appear feasible in models, but when they have begun to increase in size are impracticable."

4. Sebastian Serlio, "A Treatise of Scenes, or Places to Play In," *The Five Books of Architecture*, trans. Robert Peake (English Edition, 1611; New York: Dover Books, 1982), book 2, chap. 3, fol. 24. "Therefore I have always made a small modell of wood and paper, just of the same bignes, and by the same modell set it downe in gross, from piece to piece. But this may will fall out hard for some men to understand, nevertheless, it will be necessary to work by models and experiments, and by studie a man shall find the way: and for that a man can hardly finde any Halls how great soever, wherein he can place a Theater without imperfection and impediment."

5. Jérôme de La Gorce, "Twenty Set Models for the Paris Opéra in the Time of Rameau," trans. Neal Zaslaw, *Early Music* 11, no. 4 (October 1983): 429–40. Also see: "The Illusion Factory at the Château De Maisons-Laffitte," *La Croix*, accessed May 24, 2024, www.la-croix.com/Culture/Expositions/fabrique-dillusions-Chateau-Maisons-Laffitte-2020-02-04-1201076172.

6. *Merriam-Webster Dictionary*, "maquette," www.merriam-webster.com/dictionary/maquette, accessed February 2, 2023. A maquette is "a small preliminary model derived from the Italian noun macchietta, meaning 'sketch,' and ultimately from Latin macula, meaning 'spot.'"

7. The "stage manager" was the title for the person who functioned as the director of the production prior to the twentieth century.

8. Gorce, "Twenty Set Models for the Paris Opéra," 429–40. Also see: "Illusion Factory."

9. *TheaterEncyclopedia.*, "Slingelandt Toneel," accessed February 2, 2023, www.theaterencyclopedie.nl//wiki/Slingelandt_Toneel. The Toneel website provides images of the model stage and videos showing scene changes.

10. Erna Auerbach, *Tudor Artists* (Athlone Press, 1954), 176. Feuillerat, Albart. *Documents Relating to the Office of the Revels in the Time of Queen Elizabeth* (Louvain: A., 1908), 81, 18–21; 247, 22–24; 277, 15–20; 340, 5–6. Exchequer: Treasury of the Receipt, Wolsey's Patents Miscellaneous Books 36, 227 folio 2, 16, 24ff., 52 etc., quoted in *The Builder* 8, no. 362 (January 12, 1830): 13.

11. Garrick Correspondence, Christopher Baugh, trans., "Stage Design from Loutherbourg to Poel," in Joseph W. Donohue, *The Cambridge History of British Theatre*, vol. 2: *1660 to 1895* (Cambridge University Press, 2008), 310. Loutherbourg also claimed his models created a new "harmony between the scene decoration, the costumes and the subject of the play"; Joppien Rudiger, *Philippe Jacques de Loutherbourg, RA 1740–1812* (Greater Council of London, 1973), n.p. In Restoration England the public theaters emphasized the playwrights and actors and developed an economical repertory system of stock scenery that was a hodgepodge of styles and periods usually created by multiple designers. The painter's duties consisted primarily of retouching worn scenery and adding any necessary drops for new scenes with no need for a model. The painter-decorator was rarely noted in programs or advertisements for their scenic achievements. Sybil Rosenfeld, *A Short History of Scene Design in Great Britain* (Basil Blackwell, 1973), 60–86. A catalog of Loutherbourg's possessions upon his death included a "collection of small, expertly painted models of stage scenery; and the entire equipment of his art studio" (380 models and drawings). Sadly only five models survive in the Victoria and Albert Museum; Thomas Faulkner, *The History and Antiquities of Brentford, Ealing, and Chiswick* (Simpkin, Marshall and Co., 1812), 33.

12. *Hibernian Journal* 13, no. 34, Wednesday, January 29, 1783, 1.

13. W. J. Lawrence, "A Century of Scene-Painting," *The Gentlemen's Magazine* (1888): 282–94.

14. Frederic Villiers, "The Property, Painting and Dressmakers' Rooms," *The Illustrated Sporting and Dramatic News*, December 19, 1874, 275.

15. Frederick Wentworth, "Mr. Beverly's Painting Room," *The Illustrated Sporting and Dramatic News*, December 19, 1874, 276. See Robin Thurlow Lacey, *The Bibliographic Dictionary of Scenographers 500 BC to 1900 AD* (Greenwood Press, 1990), for more information on William Roxby Beverly.

16. Arthur Pougin, *Dictionary of Theatre and Related Arts* (Firmin-Didot Co. Paris, 1885), 495.

17. Christopher Baugh, trans., *Backstage in the Theatre, Scenes, and Machines* (Smith Settle Ltd., 1998).

18. Charles Robert Paul, "An Annotated Translation: Theatrical Machinery Stage Machinery and Devices by George Moynet" (PhD diss., University of Southern California, 1970), 447. "The scene painter, who has familiarized himself with the manuscript, sets up his rough model while consulting with the stage carpenter. The model is presented to the authors who make their comments. The director, who is the producer or a production stage manager, is worried about proper egress for the entrances and exits of his characters. He already has the play in his mind's eye; he visualizes the leading roles being acted, his choruses and his extras moving. Finally, the model is definitely agreed upon; the carpenter makes his measurements; he has the curtains sewn [backdrops and flat fabric for shutters], the frameworks nailed; the painter prepares his colors."

19. Georges Moynet, *La Machinerie Théâtrale: Trucs et Décors* (La Librairie Illustrée, 1893), 381. Moynet also included engravings of a model sailing ship, foundering during a storm, for Giacomo Meyerbeer's *l'Africaine* (*The African Woman*). These illustrations of the ship, shown in its model stage, demonstrate how scenographic models "served for the building of the structure" and helped to devise the engineering of the opera's complex stage machinery.

20. John R. Wolcott, "A Case Study of American Production, English Source and American Practice," *The Ohio State University Theatre Collection Bulletin*, no. 15 (April 1968): 11. In 1816, scene painter John Worroll (fl. 1794–1822) sent models, possibly based upon toy theater models, to Henry Warren, manager of the Chestnut Street Theatre in Philadelphia, with descriptions of the London production of *Aladdin*. "The models I have sent you will be pleased with. You can copy them if you choose. When you return them I will let you have more . . ." When the theater burned down in 1820. the insurance claim listed an irreplaceable loss of "models of scenery and machinery, imported at a large cost."

21. Lacey *Bibliographic Dictionary of Scenographers*, 124–25, 394–95.

22. Jeffrey Collom, "The Role of Contemporary Scene Building Houses for Broadway Theatre" (PhD diss., Michigan State University, 1975), 30, 36. Lynn Pecktal, *Designing and Painting for Theatre* (Holt, Rinehart, and Winston, 1975), 167 and 170. *New York Times Illustrated Magazine*, August 21, 1989, 6–7.

23. Wendy Waszut-Barrett, "Behind the Curtain, Lies and Misrepresentation," *Tales from a Scenic Artist and Scholar*, accessed March 10, 2024, www.drypigment.net.

24. Richard Marsten, "The Art of the Theatre: The Decline of Scenic Art in America," *Magazine of Art* (April 1894): 163–68. "If a scene painter's function is to show the natural circumstances of time and place of the play with as much accuracy and beauty as will explain and adorn the action [then] a model of the setting should be made before the actual construction begins. The scene, when modeled in true perspective proportion, shows the

effect of full natural scale. However, the preparation of a model may take a full week of the artist's time to complete and only a few American managers like Augustin Daly and A. M. Palmer are willing to incur this extra expense.

25. *The World*, March 6, 1898, 43. Stanhope Sams, "How a Play Is Staged," *New York Times Illustrated Magazine*, August 21, 1989, 6–7.

26. Alfred Gradenwitz, "A Glimpse of a Scenic Painter's Studio: A Profession That Calls for an Intimate Acquaintance with Historic Conditions," *Scientific American* (October 26, 1912): 348–49.

"After reading the manuscript, the scene painter first draws a rough sketch, fixing the 'principles' of the scenery, with the pencil, pen, carbon, or crayon, but preferably with water colors and brush, thus allowing his imagination a wider scope. Much skill is required to produce even this first sketch, so that the painter may effectually defend his plans in discussion with the director and the author, both of whom have, of course, their own ways of looking at the matter. This sketch, which often is completed in an hour or so, will be used in producing a small sized model or 'maquette,' a miniature stage-similar to those put together by children with cut-out paper and wood-which is so designed as to give an adequate idea of the scenery to be produced. Any details are shown in the form of small pieces of cardboard cut out and fixed on a horizontal cardboard reproducing the floor of the stage. This is how any trees, houses, rocks, in fact, the whole of the scenery, are reproduced in a diminutive compass, inside a box opened in front and on the top, so as to insure adequate lighting effects. On this miniature stage the artist arranges his scenery. Here he sees on a reduced scale where the various parts of his work should be placed. He is in a position adequately to judge of effects, adding and cutting down, and altering any inconvenient arrangement. A 'maquette,' like a painting, should be the artist's personal work. Its successful design reveals the capacities of its author, and a poor 'maquette' often foretells failure of the whole of scenery. A good stage model of this kind, which may be a master-piece in itself, is most useful in arranging with the author and director any minor alterations that the case may require; the scales generally chosen are 3, 4, and sometimes 5 in 100. It is a welcome means for the painter to test his light effects, to ascertain the height. of the ceilings and to check the perspective. In order to prevent any disagreement between the dimensions of the scenery and those of the actors, the foreground should always be painted in real dimensions." The metric system was instituted in France in 1875, so the units used for the ratio would have been centimeters; 3 in 100 or 1:33 is a little smaller than 3/8" scale, 4 in 100 or 1:25 is a little smaller than 1/2" scale, 5 in 100 or 1:20 would be a little smaller than 5/8" scale.

27. *Carnegie Institute of Technology General Catalogue*, 1915–1916, 214–16. *Yale University School of Fine Arts Catalogue*, 1926–27, 58.

28. Dixon M. Morton, "The Theatre Goes to Yale," *Theatre Arts Monthly* 10 no. 4 (1926): 255.

29. Walter Rene Fuerst and Samuel J. Hume, *XXth Century Stage Decoration*, vol. 2 (Alfred A. Knopf, 1928), plate 201.

30. David Bisaha, "'Robert Edmond Jones' Scenic Rendering as Design Artifact and Professional Tool," *Theatre Performance and Design* 1, no. 3 (2015), 221–35.

31. Bisaha, "'Robert Edmond Jones' Scenic Rendering," 221–35.

32. There were numerous descriptions and advertisements for miniature lighting systems for stage models in magazines, including *Tabs, Theatre Arts Monthly, Theatre Arts,* directed toward Little Theater companies and college drama programs.

33. Mary C. Henderson, *Mielziner, Master of Modern Stage Design* (Back Stage Books, 2001), 121.

34. "Scene Designers Make a Must of Authentic Replica Models," *Variety* 115, no. 6 (July 17, 1934), 46.; David Bisaha, "Developing the Modern Scene Design Process: Cognition and Process" (PhD diss., University of Pittsburgh, 2015), 177–82.

35. *United Scenic Artists Almanac 1940–1941* (United Scenic Artists, 1941), 37.

36. Christopher Innes, *Designing Modern America* (Yale University Press, 2005), 177; Anne Fletcher, *Rediscovering Mordecai Gorelik* (Southern Illinois University Press, 2009), 23 and 212.

37. Mordecai Gorelik, *Personal Diary,* November 14, 1921, 47.

38. Sofia Pantouvaki, "(Re)performing Scenography: Josef Svoboda as a Tutor." *Theatre and Performance Design* 6, no. 3 (2020), 211.

39. A photograph of the model for the ballet *The Great American Goof* in 1940 shows a lighting box with switches and rheostats for adjusting lighting levels. Boris Aronson Collection of the New York Public Library for the Performing Arts, box 82.

40. Several Polaroid photographs and photostats show experimentation with coloring and texturing. Boris Aronson Collection of the New York Public Library for the Performing Arts, box 82.

41. Kris Stone, phone interview, January 6, 2021.

42. Alan E. Schwanke, e-mail, December 12, 2023.

1. Model Preparation

1. CRI is not the same as color temperature. Several light sources with the same color temperature can have different CRIs. Color temperature is often listed on product packaging and advertising, but CRI is often omitted. Artists should research the CRI of any light source they purchase for their studio. Incandescent, halogen, and full-spectrum fluorescent light sources have high CRI ratings, but light-emitting diode (LED) lamps are rapidly replacing these sources due to their energy efficiency, longevity, low heat, and versatility. LEDs tend to be more expensive, but their flexibility makes them very practical for studios. LED fixtures are available in a wide variety

of sizes and shapes, and offer directional and diffuse spreads. Some also have dimming capabilities and adjustable color temperatures. Small LED lights can be incorporated within the model itself. Any LED light source should be researched for the appropriate CRI.

2. Nancy Clark, Thomas Cutter, and Jean-Anne McGrane, *Ventilation, A Practical Guide* (Center for Occupational Health, 1984).

3. The SDS online library, accessed January 20, 2021. www.msdsonline.com/sds-search.

4. Giorgio Vasari, *Lives of the Most Eminent Painters Sculptors and Architects*, vol. 1: *Cimabue to Agnolo Gaddi*, trans. Gaston du C. de Vere (Macmillan, 1912), 10.

5. Early European paper mills sent their best papers to Bristol, England, to be pasted together.

6. Mike Chilson, "All about Balsa," RCSCALEBUILDER.COM, accessed January 20, 2021, www.rcscalebuilder.com/tutorials/Balsa/balsa_1.htm.

7. *Merriam-Webster Dictionary*, "plastic," accessed February 2, 2023. https://www.merriam-webster.com/dictionary/plastic. From *plastikos* meaning "capable of being molded or modeled" and *polymer* a conjunction of *poly* and *meros* "having many parts."

2. The Scenographic Modeling Process

1. J. Michael Gillette defined a design process in his book *Theatrical Design and Production* as being composed of seven steps or phases: (1) commitment, (2) analysis, (3) research, (4) incubation, (5) selection, (6) implementation, and (7) evaluation. This can be remembered as the acronym CARISIE.

2. Richard Southern, *Proscenium and Sightlines* (Faber and Faber, 1939), 216–25. Southern provides an illustration and description of how to build a model stage.

3. Horace Freeland Judson, *The Search for Solutions* (Henry Holt and Company, 1980), 112–15. Judson's full quote is worth reading. "A model is a rehearsal for reality, a way of making a trial that minimizes the penalties for error. Playing with a model, a child can practice being in the world. Building a model, a scientist can reduce an object, a system, or a theory to a manageable form. He can watch the behavior of the model, tinker with it—then make predictions about how the plane will fly, how the economy will move, or how a protein chain is constructed." Judson goes on to observe that "modeling, however serious, enshrines an element of play. Watching a child, one turns that observation the other way around: for the child, absorbed in play, modeling has an essential aspect of seriousness—it's a way of grasping the way things are. For the scientist or engineer, conversely, the seriousness of modeling retains something of the youthful delight. Scientists are incessantly saying to each other 'let's play around with that'—and modeling is

the quintessential way of playing with the way things might work and might be. . . . Curiously, model-building can also be a way to create a theory. . . . The performance of objects. The behavior of elaborate systems. A kind of theory-making. Modeling performs at these three levels."
4. The modelmaker should seek out materials that are labeled nontoxic, which tend to be safer to use, but they should also be wary of that container label. Being labeled nontoxic does not mean a material is completely safe, there may still be a hazard posed by use or misuse of nontoxic materials. Toxicity is a measure of acute, or short-term, reactions to a product and does not cover any allergic reactions or any potential long-term effects such as cancer or reproductive harm. The modelmaker should pay careful attention to all container hazard warnings, wear appropriate personal protective equipment, and follow proper use guidelines for all products used in the model studio.
5. Airbrushes produce a fine airborne mist. The modelmaker should take precautions when using airbrushes. Respiratory protection, such as a respirator fitted to the modelmaker, and a well-ventilated workspace are recommended.
6. Randall Wilkin, "Understanding Model Scales—A Comparison Study," The Designer's Assistant, accessed May 5, 2024, www.thedesignersassistant.com/2012/11/25/understanding-model-scales-a-comparison-study/. This chart is based on various scale model comparison charts available online.

3. *Fashioning Stage Space, Mood, and Atmosphere*

1. Robert Benedetti,. *The Director at Work* (Prentice-Hall, 1985), 68.

5. *Emergent Technology*

1. "Thermoplastics: The Strongest Choice for 3D Printing," White Paper, Stratasys, 2019.
2. Eric Hart, *The Prop Building Guidebook for Theatre, Film, and TV*, (Routledge, 2017).
3. "The 3-in-1 3D Printer—Snapmaker," Snapmaker, Accessed November 10, 2020, www.snapmaker.com.

6. *Photographing and Archiving*

1. "Cannon Science Lab: CMOS Sensors," Canon, Canon Inc., accessed August, 29, 2021, www.global.canon/en/technology/s_labo/light/003/05.html.
2. "DSLR Camera Basics," Nikon, Nikon Corporation, accessed August 29. 2021, www.imaging.nikon.com/lineup/dslr/basics/13/index.htm.

Bibliography

Auerbach, Erna. *Tudor Artists*. Athlone Press, 1954.

Baugh, Christopher trans. "Stage Design from Loutherbourg to Poel." In *The Cambridge History of British Theatre*. Vol. 2 : *1660 to 1895*, edited by Joseph W. Donohue. Cambridge University Press, 2008.

Benedetti, Robert. *The Director at Work*. Prentice-Hall, 1985.

Bisaha, David. "'Robert Edmond Jones' Scenic Rendering as Design Artifact and Professional Tool." *Theatre Performance and Design* 1, no. 3 (2015).

Bisaha, David. "Developing the Modern Scene Design Process: Cognition and Process." 2015. University of Pittsburgh, Ph.D. Dissertation.

Bisaha, David. *American Scenic Design and Freelance Professionalism*. Southern Illinois University Press, 2022.

Boritt, Beowulf. *Transforming Space over Time*. Applause Theatre and Cinema Books, 2023.

Burian, Jarka. *The Scenography of Josef Svoboda*. Wesleyan University Press, 1971.

Burgess, Robert. *Theatre Models in Paper and Card*. Guild of Master Craftsman Publications, 1999.

Canon. "Cannon Science Lab: CMOS Sensors." Canon Inc. Accessed August 29, 2021. www.global.canon/en/technology/s_labo/light/003/05.

Carnegie Institute of Technology General Catalogue. 1915 16.

Chilson, Mike. "All about Balsa." RC SCALEBUILDER.COM. Accessed January 10, 2023. www.rcscalebuilder.com/tutorials/Balsa/balsa_1.

Clark, Nancy, Thomas Cutter, Jean-Anne McGrane. *Ventilation, A Practical Guide*. Center for Occupational Health, 1984.

Collom, Jeffrey. "The Role of Contemporary Scene Building Houses for Broadway Theatre." PhD diss, Michigan State University, 1975.

"Joseph A. Physioc's Miniature Stage." *The World*, March 6, 1898.

Feuillerat, Albart. *Documents Relating to the Office of the Revels in the Time of Queen Elizabeth*. A. Uystpruyst, 1908.

Fletcher, Anne. *Rediscovering Mordecai Gorelik*. Southern Illinois University Press, 2009.

Fuerst, Walter René, and Samuel J. Hume. *XXth Century Stage Decoration*. Vol. 1. Alfred A. Knopf, 1928.

Fuerst, Walter René, and Samuel J. Hume. *XXth Century Stage Decoration.* Vol. 2. Alfred A. Knopf, 1928..

Gillette, J. Michael. *Theatrical Design and Production: An Introduction to Scene Design and Construction, Lighting, Sound, Costume, and Makeup.* 8th ed. McGraw-Hill, 2019.

Gradenwitz, Alfred. "A Glimpse of a Scenic Painter's Studio: A Profession That Calls for an Intimate Acquaintance with Historic Conditions." *Scientific American,* October 26, 1912.

Gorce, Jérôme de La. "Twenty Set Models for the Paris Opéra in the Time of Rameau." Translated by Neal Zaslaw. *Early Music* 11, no. 4 (October 1983).

Gorelik, Mordecai. Personal Diary, November 14, 1921.

Hart, Eric. *The Prop Building Guidebook: For Theatre, Film, and TV.* Focal Press/Taylor, 2013.

Henderson, Mary C. *Mielziner: Master of Modern Stage Design.* Back Stage Books, 2001.

Helveston, Harold. *Scenery: A Manual of Scene Design.* Stanford University Press, 1931.

Hibernian Journal. Vol. 13, no. 34 (Wednesday, January 29, 1783). Classified advertisements for provincial theaters announce the designs were based on models provided by the Drury Lane Theatre.

Hohauser, Sanford. *Architectural and Interior Models: Design and Construction.* Van Nostrand Reinhold, 1970.

Innes, Christopher. *Designing Modern America.* Yale University Press, 2005.

"The Illusion Factory at the Château de Maisons-Laffitte." *La Croix.* Accessed May 24, 2024. www.la-croix.com/Culture/Expositions/fabrique-dillusions-Chateau-Maisons-Laffitte-2020-02-04-1201076172.

James, Thurston. *The Prop Builder's Molding and Casting Handbook.* Penguin Publishing Group, 1989.

Jones, Leslie Allen. *Scenic Design and Model Building: A "Handybook" for Amateur Producers.* Walter H. Baker Company, 1939.

Judson, Horace Freeland. *The Search for Solutions.* Henry Holt and Company, 1980.

Kuh, Katharine. *Break-Up.* New York Graphic Society, 1965.

Kuksi, Kris. *Conquest: Kris Kuksi.* Rizzoli, 2017.

Lacey, Robin Thurlow. *The Bibliographic Dictionary of Scenographers 500 BC to 1900 AD.* Greenwood Press, 1990.

Lawrence, W. J. "A Century of Scene-Painting." *The Gentlemen's Magazine,* 1888.

Marsten, Richard. "The Art of the Theatre: The Decline of Scenic Art in America." *Magazine of Art.* April 1894.

McCann, Michael. *Artist Beware: The Hazards in Working with All Art and Craft Materials and the Precautions Every Artist and Craftsperson Should Take.* Updated and revised. Lyons Press, 2005.

McMills, Anne E. *3D Printing Basics for Entertainment Design*. Focal Press, Routledge, 2018.

Morris, Sylvia. "William Roxby Beverley, a Forgotten Theatre Artist at Stratford-upon-Avon." *The Shakespeare Blog*. Accessed June 2, 2024. www.theshakespeareblog.com/2017/03/william-roxby-beverley-stratfords-forgotten-theatre-artist.

Morton, Dixon M. "The Theatre Goes to Yale," *Theatre Arts Monthly* 10. no. 4, 1926.

Moynet, Georges. *La Machinerie Théâtrale: Trucs et Décors* [The Machines of the theatre: Scenes and décor]. La Librairie Illustrée, 1893.

Moynet, Jean-Pierre. *L'envers du Théâtre: Machines et* Décorations [Backstage in the theatre: Machines and decorations]. La Librairie Hachette, 1888.

Neat, David. *Model-Making: Materials and Methods*. Crowood Press, 2008.

Neat, David. *David Neat: A Maker, a Teacher of Making*. Accessed January 10, 2023. https://davidneat.wordpress.com/.

Nikon. "DSLR Camera Basics." Nikon Corporation. Accessed August 29, 2021. www.imaging.nikon.com/lineup/dslr/basics/13/index.htm.

Orton, Keith. *Model Making for the Stage*. Crowood Press, 2004.

Pantouvaki, Sofia. "(Re)performing Scenography: Josef Svoboda as a Tutor." *Theatre and Performance Design* 6, no. 3 (2020).

Parker, Oren, and Harvey K. Smith. *Scene Design and Stage Lighting*. Holt, Rinehart, and Winston, 1963.

Paul, Charles Robert. "An Annotated Translation: Theatrical Machinery Stage Machinery and Devices by George Moynet." PhD diss., University of Southern California, 1970.

Payne, Christopher. *The Encyclopedia of Model Making Techniques*. Chartwell Books, 1996.

Payne, Darwin Reid. *Design for the Stage: First Steps*. Southern Illinois University Press, 1974.

Payne, Darwin Reid. *Materials and Craft of the Scenic Model*. Southern Illinois University Press, 1976.

Payne, Darwin Reid. *Theory and Craft of the Scenographic Model*. Southern Illinois University Press, 1985.

Payne, Darwin Reid. *Scenographic Imagination*. Southern Illinois University Press, 1993.

Pecktal, Lynn. *Designing and Painting for the Theatre*. Holt, Rinehart, and Winston, 1975.

Pecktal, Lynn. *Designing and Drawing for the Theatre*. New York: McGraw-Hill, 1995.

Pougin, Arthur. *Dictionary of Theatre and Related Arts*. Paris: Firmin-Didot Co., 1885.

Ridge, Cecil Harold. *Stage-Lighting for "Little" Theatres*. W. Heffer and Sons, Limited, 1925.

Rossol, Monona. *The Health and Safety Guide for Film, TV, and Theater.* 2nd ed. Allworth Press, 2011.

Rossol, Monona. *The Artist's Complete Health and Safety Guide*. Allworth Press, 2001.

Safety Data Sheet online library. Accessed January 10, 2023. www.msdsonline.com/sds-search/.

Sams, Stanhope. "How a Play Is Staged." *The World*, March 6, 1898.

Seitz, William C. *The Art of Assemblage*. Museum of Modern Art. Doubleday, 1961.

Serlio, Sebastian. "A Treatise of Scenes, or Places to Play In." *The Five Books of Architecture*. Book 2, chap. 3, fol. 24. English ed., 1611. Dover Books, 1982.

Smith, André J. *The Scenewright: The Making of Stage Models and Settings.* Macmillan, 1926.

Snapmaker. "The 3-in-1 3D Printer—Snapmaker." Accessed November 10, 2020. www.snapmaker.com.

Southern, Richard. *Proscenium and Sightlines*. Faber and Faber, 1939.

Svoboda, Josef. *The Secret of Theatrical Space*. Applause Theatre and Cinema Books, 2000.

"Thermoplastics: The Strongest Choice for 3D Printing." White Paper. Stratasys, 2019.

United Scenic Artists Almanac 1940–1941.

Variety "Scene Designers Make a Must of Authentic Replica Models." Vol. 115, no. 6. July 17, 1934.

Vasari, Giorgio. *Lives of the Most Eminent Painters Sculptors and Architects.* Vol. 1: *Cimabue to Agnolo Gaddi.* Translated by Gaston du C. de Vere. Macmillan, 1912.

Villiers, Frederic. "The Property, Painting and Dressmakers' Rooms." *The Illustrated Sporting and Dramatic News*, December 19, 1874.

Vitruvius, Marcus Pollio. *The Architecture of Marcus Vitruvius Pollio: In Ten Books*. Translated by Joseph Gwilt. Priestley, and Weale, 1826.

Waszut-Barrett, Wendy. "Behind the Curtain, Lies and Misrepresentation." *Tales from a Scenic Artist and Scholar*. Accessed March 10, 2024. www.drypigment.net.

Wentworth, Frederick "Mr. Beverly's Painting Room." *The Illustrated Sporting and Dramatic News*, December 19, 1874.

Wescher, Herta. *Collage*. Translated by Robert E. Wolf. Harry N. Abrams, 1968.

Wilkins, Randall. "Scales-a-comparison-study." *The Designer's Assistant: An Information Site for Film and Television Set Designers*. Accessed November 10, 2020, https://thedesignersassistant.com/2012/11/25/understanding-model-scales-a-comparison-study/.

Winslow, Colin. *The Handbook of Model-Making for Set Designers.* Crowood Press, 2008.

Wolcott, John R. "A Case Study of American Production, English Source and American Practice." *The Ohio State University Theatre Collection Bulletin,* no. 15 (April 1968).
Wolf, R. Craig, and Dick Block. *Scene Design and Stage Lighting.* 10th ed. Wadsworth Cengage, 2013.
Yale University School of Fine Arts Catalogue. 1926.
Zinkeisen, Doris. *Designing for the Stage. A Studio "How to Do It" Book.* The Studio, 1949.

Index

Italicized page numbers indicate figures.

Darwin Reid Payne, professor emeritus of theater design at Southern Illinois University Carbondale, designed and directed in regional theaters throughout the United States and Canada. During his career Darwin designed and directed over four hundred productions. He published three books with SIU Press: *Theory and Craft of the Scenographic Model*, *The Scenographic Imagination*, and *Materials and Craft of the Scenic Model*. He passed away on July 30, 2016.

Ronald Naversen, professor emeritus of theater design at Southern Illinois University Carbondale, has worked as a freelance designer for the Westport Country Playhouse, Cincinnati Playhouse Summerfest, Le Petit Theatre du Vieux Carre, Corning Summer Theatre, New Harmony Theatre, Pennsylvania Shakespeare Festival, Vitalist Theatre of Chicago, and Retro Theatre in New York.

Brad M. Carlson, associate professor of design and chair of the Department of Communication and Theatre Arts at Truman State University, has worked as a freelance designer at the Omaha Theater Company, the Human Race Theatre Company, the Larry Clark Summer Repertory Theatre, and the New London Barn Playhouse.